The Heart of Man's Destiny

Can Luther's writings inform us on the fundamental questions of Freudian psychoanalysis? Does an intellectual filiation between early Reformation thought and psychoanalysis exist? Does Lacanian psychoanalysis offer an instrument for analysing theological writings?

In *The Heart of Man's Destiny*, Herman Westerink offers a new reading of Lacan's seventh seminar, *The Ethics of Psychoanalysis*. Working from an innovative perspective, this book explores the close relationship between Freudian psychoanalysis and the ideas of the early Reformation.

Lacan claimed that to be unaware of the connection between Freud and early Reformation thought constituted a fundamental misunderstanding of the kind of problems psychoanalysis addresses. Westerink carefully explores these problems and shows that Lacanian psychoanalysis, with its emphasis on desire and law, transgression, and symbolization, draws on fundamental ideas first formulated in the writings of Luther and Calvin. By relating psychoanalysis to early Reformation thought, Westerink not only shows Lacan's writings in a completely new light, but also makes possible an innovative reading of early modern theology itself.

The Heart of Man's Destiny breaks new ground by providing both a controversial and a fresh perspective on both Luther and Calvin, and on Freudo–Lacanian psychoanalysis. This valuable contribution to the complex character of psychoanalysis will be of interest to analysts and psychotherapists, as well as academics and postgraduates with an interest in theology, philosophy and ethics.

Herman Westerink is Assistant Professor of Psychology of Religion at the Protestant Theological Faculty of the University of Vienna, Austria.

Psychoanalytic Explorations Series

Books in this series:

The Heart of Man's Destiny
Lacanian Psychoanalysis and Early Reformation Thought
Herman Westerink

The Heart of Man's Destiny

Lacanian psychoanalysis and early Reformation thought

Herman Westerink

Routledge
Taylor & Francis Group
LONDON AND NEW YORK

First published 2012
byRoutledge
2 Park Square, Milton Park, Abingdon, Oxfordshire OX14 4RN

Simultaneously published in the USA and Canada
byRoutledge
711 Third Avenue, New York, NY 10017

First issued in paperback 2016

Routledge is an imprint of the Taylor & Francis Group, an informa business

British Library Cataloguing in Publication Data
A catalogue record for this book is available from the British Library

Library of Congress Cataloging-in-Publication Data
Westerink, Herman, 1968-
The heart of man's desire : Lacanian psychoanalysis and early Reformation thought / by Herman Westerink.
p. cm. – (Psychoanalytic explorations)
Includes bibliographical references and index.
1. Psychoanalysis and religion. 2. Psychoanalysis–Moral and ethical aspects. 3. Psychoanalysis–Philosophy. 4. Reformation. 5. Lacan, Jacques, 1901-1981. I. Title.
BF175.4.R44W445 2012
150.19′5–dc23 2012005537

ISBN 13: 978-1-138-63181-6 (pbk)
ISBN 13: 978-0-415-69392-9 (hbk)

Typeset in Garamond
by Cenveo Publisher Services

Contents

Acknowledgements

I would like to thank all those who contributed to a marvellous intellectual and social research environment: my students and colleagues at the Protestant Theological Faculty of the University of Vienna, particularly my colleagues at the Department of Practical Theology and Psychology of Religion – Susanne Heine, Wilfried Engemann, Marianne Pratl, Katja Bachl, Stefan Janits, Melanie Dormann, Nadine Mund and Jeanine Lefèvre. I thank Lukas Kaelin and Patrick Vandermeersch for reading and commenting (parts of) the first draft of the manuscript. I am indebted to, and grateful for, the inspiring conversation on double conscience and on the idea of reading Lacan as if he were a Protestant with Paul Moyaert in Boston (Fall 2009) that has turned out to be the initial moment of this study. I am also grateful for the conversations on Freud, Lacan, psychoanalysis and religion with the members of the Freud Research Group (International Society for Psychoanalysis and Philosophy). The meetings of this group, organized by Philippe van Haute, have been a profound stimulation for my research. I am indebted to Rockwell Clancy, who did an excellent proof reading of the manuscript – his comments and questions helped me to improve the text. I thank the Routledge publisher Kate Hawes and her colleagues for their efforts. Finally, I would like to thank my wife Marise Boon and my son Reijer for their loving support, confidence and patience.

Introduction

This book is not a "psychoanalytic interpretation" of religion in the classical Freudian sense of the phrase. It does not follow the tradition of studies in applied psychoanalysis that intend to explain cultural phenomena, works of literature, myths, or religion by working through their analogies with pathologies. The intention of this study is not to treat ways of thinking as the effect – at the level of symptom formation or reaction formations – of an author's personal experiences or development, digging through biographical layers underlying intellectual thought, thereby losing track of the historical development of ideas. And yet in this book I do follow Freud's archaeological method, as I understand its proper function: to recognize the meaning of the past in the present. Freud's method consists not so much in knowing the historical truth that Moses was murdered or establishing that the little Rat Man, while biting the maid, was forbidden to do so by his father. It consists much more in the Rat Man recognizing that his childhood memories of rage and feelings of hate are the vital part of his obsessional thoughts, or the apostle Paul recognizing the burden of history and tradition in the excessive Jewish sense of guilt. What is acknowledged as meaningful in the past is thus not the importance of the historical event as the cause of an effect, but recognition of the fundamental problem staged in the event and repeated in different forms, thereby safeguarding the importance of the problem in the present.

Hence, in psychoanalysis' view of history it is not the repressed as such that is at stake but the return of the repressed or, as Freud describes it, the insistence of a "prehistoric tragedy on being recognized" (Freud, 1939, p. 84). In *Moses and Monotheism* Saint Paul's works are presented as a moment of such recognition after a period of intellectual advancement and growing sense of guilt in Judaism. Luther, as depicted by Lacan, also identifies a "fundamental problem" disregarded and repressed in scholastic theology and medieval Aristotelian ethics, as well as the meaning and consequences of this repressed problem for theological thought.

Freudian psychoanalysis then, is a theory of recognition of the past in the present regarding those issues Enlightenment thought repressed from its official agenda: the body, the unconscious, the irrational, desire – in short – all those phenomena and their meaning that return from repression on Freud's sofa. A Lacanian perspective on the relation between Freudian psychoanalysis and early Reformation thought links up with this method, recognizing the meaning of the past in the present. In this study early Reformation thought is treated not simply as the historical event of which psychoanalysis is in some sense the secular aftermath. The focus will be on what Lacan describes as the "fundamental problem" conceptualized by Luther and other Reformers that constitutes the heart of psychoanalytic theory as well, "the kind of problems Freud's intellectual project addresses" (Lacan, 1992, p. 97). An assessment of this type, one invoking a cultural filiation between psychoanalysis and Reformation thought, is far from evident, and yet this claim lies at the heart of the present study.

> Not to recognize the filiation or cultural paternity that exists between Freud and a new direction of thought – one that is apparent at the break which occurred toward the beginning of the sixteenth century, but whose repercussions are felt up to the end of the seventeenth century – constitutes a fundamental misunderstanding of the kind of problems Freud's intellectual project addresses (Idem).

Lacan makes this remark in a passage where he refers to Martin Luther (1483-1546) and central ideas expressed in *De servo arbitrio* [*The Bondage of the Will*, 1525], the latter's furious response to Erasmus' *De libero arbitrio* (1524). His remark concerns "the cause, the *causa pathomenon*, of the most fundamental human passion", i.e. of an absolute passion or desire that reveals man's desolation and exile from the good. Luther is supposedly writing of "God's eternal hatred of man", a hatred not evoked because human beings freely fail to do the good. Rather, this hatred is eternal, one that "existed even before the world was created". It is God's hatred of man that initiates the fundamental human passion of a hatred against God, which takes the form of committing a crime against God as evidenced in the story of the Fall. According to Lacan it is this thematic dealing with the father, hatred, and prehistory that Freud addresses in the myth of parricide as humanity's primal scene. This Freudian myth expresses the fact that fundamental human needs, inclinations, and motives have nothing to do with a natural tendency towards the good or the maintenance of amicable relations with one's fellows. Quite to the contrary, taboos and laws are founded on "the problem of evil", on the tyranny of the primal father and the aggressive reaction evoked by his presence (Idem).

The filiation suggested by Lacan concerns, first of all, Freud and Luther. The latter is thought of here as the author of a text on the bondage of the will radically expressing what is elsewhere conceptualized more moderately. He is both a representative of the "authoritative Christian tradition, from the words of Christ to Saint Paul, Saint Augustine and the Church Fathers", and of a new direction in thought starting in the early sixteenth century and continuing its influence until the late seventeenth century. It is a way of thinking in which God's eternal hatred is articulated, albeit not always as radically as in Luther's response to Desiderius Erasmus (?1465-1536). Jacques Lacan, Roman Catholic in his upbringing, thus proposes the existence of a filiation between Protestant thought and the psychoanalytic thought of Freud, the "godless Jew", who lived in a predominantly Catholic environment in Vienna, Austria. Although this connection is admittedly far from self-evident, in the present study I explore the ways in which this claim allows for a better understanding of Reformation thought as well as Freudian and Lacanian psychoanalysis.

A focus on the relation between Lacan and Reformation thought means that no attempt is made to consider in detail either Lacan's relationship with Catholicism or his influence on, and the implications of, his ideas for theology.[1] This is certainly an interesting research field with important landmarks, some of which connect with different views from within both the Catholic and Protestant traditions. This is the case, for example, in the furious reaction of Lacan and his students to the publication of Paul Ricoeur's *De l'interprétation* in 1965, a large monograph on Freud that they considered a competing work with the potential to endanger Lacan's psychoanalytic project in France. One of the authors involved in the Lacanian attacks on Ricoeur was the Dominican, Jacques Pohier, who assessed Ricoeur's reading of Freud as too Protestant and, notably, criticized his view of the father function; Pohier defended the fundamental structures of paternity in Christianity (Vandermeersch, 2000). Focus on the father function and the primordial signifier of desire, i.e. on the law of the father as entrance into the symbolic order, seems to be a touchstone for engagements with Lacan in Catholic theology.[2] In the present study I leave research in this field aside, and only consider certain aspects when they are relevant for the topic at hand. By focusing on the filiation between psychoanalysis and Reformation thought I call into question an observation noted by various scholars, most clearly formulated by Elisabeth Roudinesco, "Lacan translated Freudian discourse into a language familiar to Catholic tradition" (Roudinesco, 1990, p. 262).

A study on the filiation of Freudian psychoanalysis and Reformation thought encounters some problems, of which the supposed inner consistency of both psychoanalysis and Reformation thought is the main problem. Lacan seems to suggest that the psychoanalytic thought presented in his originally unpublished seminars is nothing but a *retour à Freud*. In the meantime literature on Lacan has convincingly shown that his thought is certainly not just a repetition of Freud's theories supplemented with fitting philosophical ideas and various surrealist twists of the mind. Lacan rethinks and redefines Freud's insights considerably, and one of the points in which differences between Freud and Lacan become visible is linked to the subject of our investigation: Freud's thought is connected to a Jewish intellectual tradition whereas Lacan's thought is, as Michel de Certeau has argued, linked "to an entire current of Christian thinking which substitutes the *logos* for the lost body", i.e. substitutes the theological symbolic order for the ultimately lost object of desire, namely, the corporeal presence of Jesus Christ. In short, Lacan's discourse is "Christian" as evidenced by the many references to, and quotations from, biblical, theological, and mystical texts (De Certeau, 1986, p. 14, 56). The differing backgrounds of Freud and Lacan that resound in their psychoanalytic thought also colour their differing views on religion. For Freud religion is predominantly cultural morality in its civilizing and repressive function. *Totem and Taboo* (1912–1913) is a good example of this: the search for the origins of Kant's categorical imperative shows that it is merely a secular variant of moral taboos and commandments that, according to Freud, lie at the heart of religious thought and institutions. Religion has safeguarded the subjugation of amoral drives and thus contributed to the development of civilization. Freud's equation of religion and morality need not completely surprise us. Such an assessment makes sense in view of not only his observations regarding the moralizing and disciplining discourse and techniques of the Roman Catholic Church, but also the theological literature Freud was acquainted with. Liberal nineteenth century Protestant (often Kantian) theology, for example, was characterized by the deployment of religiosity in the service of an Enlightenment-inspired moral ideal of civil conduct. In this way *Totem and Taboo* reflects the theology of its time: religion acted in the service of the categorical imperative. For Lacan, religion is much more than a safeguard of cultural morality or a means through which one adapts to imposed duties and norms. To the contrary, the religious authorities he is primarily interested in do not simply impose a law of outer behaviour, thus veiling the repressed realm of desires, but recognize and articulate the fact that "at the heart of man's destiny" is something – some Thing – that resists and undermines socialization. These authors thus implicitly question attempts to harmonize man's nature with the social ideal of a life in the service of a common good. In Lacan's view this something points towards the "fundamental problem" that both Luther and John Calvin (1509–1564) were able to radically express before it was once again covered over in an enlightened discourse on self-consciousness, reason, autonomy, freedom, and humanity's progress. Lacan calls on Luther not as a defender of cultural morality, but as a critic of what he calls the traditional Aristotelian morality of merit, virtue, and duty in service of the common welfare.

We should not overlook the context in which Lacan presents his seminar on the ethics of psychoanalysis, one in which he calls on religious figures such as Luther as critics of certain forms of moralism. Lacan himself later speaks of "calculation" when he explains the reason he resisted publication of this seminar: "I'm not going to try to convince people who want nothing to do with me" (Lacan, 1999, pp. 52–53). Here he is referring to his being forced out of the *International Psychoanalytical Association* (IPA), which occurred three years after he gave his seminar on the ethics of psychoanalysis. His quarrels with the IPA started in the 1950s and primarily concerned his resistance to the dominance of ego psychology, which not only defined strict rules for psychoanalytic therapy but also aimed at the development of a strong self-conscious ego capable of adjusting to social norms.[3] It was against these rules and this aim that he formulated the subject of his seminar on the ethics of psychoanalysis.

Lacan identified with religious figures such as the apostle Paul and Luther because of their conflicts with established organizations and their subsequent role as founders of a new movement. However, there is also a deeper line of continuity between Lacan's thought and certain aspects of the Judaeo–Christian tradition, one that makes it possible to discern a few key themes that appear throughout his seminars and published works, upon which I elaborate in the following chapters. On the one hand is ego psychology's new moralism that Lacan associates with Aristotelian morality and Thomas Aquinas' scholastic ethics. On the other is Lacan's critique of ego psychology, his return to Freud, and search for historical figures that prelude psychoanalytic insights: Saint Paul's response to the Romans; Saint Augustine's resistance to Pelagianism; the Reformation critique of Scholasticism as well as Aristotelianism. Intertwined with this is Lacan's review of ego psychology as continuation of the Cartesian and Enlightenment focus on self-consciousness and autonomy versus his own Spinozistic interpretation of Cartesianism, which reconnects conscious thought with unconscious desire. The Freudian intellectual project then can also be understood as rediscovering and revitalizing fundamental insights first put forward by a number of seemingly unrelated philosophies and theologies such as, for example, those of Luther and Spinoza.

What I call here Reformation thought is actually described by Lacan in somewhat vague terms, namely, as "a new direction of thought" that starts with Luther and remains influential during the sixteenth century and the first half of the seventeenth century, radically reconceptualizing human nature: denying the good, calling into question the efficacy of merit and virtue, the relation between law and sin, and the cause of humanity's fundamental passion, i.e. God's eternal hatred (Lacan, 1992, pp. 96–97). Thus the direction Lacan's thought takes here cannot be simply reduced to that of Luther's or that of the later, often far more "Erasmian" Lutherans. His focus is on the radical aspects of this so called "new direction in thought". It is by no means my intention to reconstruct a history of theology or to provide a detailed account of doctrinal developments regarding sin, free will, or predestination. I merely focus on the radical variant of this new direction in thought, which necessitates an elaboration of Luther and Calvin, two Reformers that – in my opinion – have a relation comparable to that of Freud and Lacan. When necessary for providing a clearer picture of what is at stake, I will discuss aspects of Puritanism and Reformed orthodoxy. As I show in the course of this study, considering Calvin and Calvinism is fruitful because it establishes a link between aspects of Reformation thought and those of philosophies that influenced both Freud and Lacan, notably those of Thomas Hobbes and Spinoza.[4]

Chapter 1 provides a foundation for the rest of the book. In the first chapter I outline Freud's engagements with religion and Protestantism, the main aspects of Lacan's thought and his psychoanalytic project, as well as the historic roots, authoritative traditions, and inaugural moments in the history to which Lacan's claims of cultural paternity relate. In short, I map the terrain of Freud and Protestantism, cultural paternity and Lacanian psychoanalysis. In Chapter 2 the focus is on the main aspects of the filiation suggested by Lacan, including Reformation thought's views on predestination, God's hidden will and hatred of man, denial of free will, man's inclination towards evil, and its disavowal of good works. In Chapter 3 I further consider this claim of filiation, reflecting on man's disposition and "evil" nature, the value of self-knowledge, and the Freudian as well as Lacanian ethics of psychoanalysis. Chapter 4 deals with the formation and internalization of conscience and its dual role in the organization of inner and outer government, as well as Lacan's view on the superego's imperatives.

Chapter 1

Cultural paternity

Mapping the terrain

Jacques Lacan's interest in religion stems not only from Freud's writings on applied psychoanalysis and views concerning the relation between religion and morality, but also reflects the main traits of Lacan's own psychoanalytic thought. Throughout his writings he refers to central figures in Christian theology and mysticism, who often not only intuitively express psychological insights to which Freud gave his official approval, but who also inaugurate new ways of thinking, defining problems, and developing theories with which psychoanalysis could connect from its own unique point of view, its talking-cure-based insights into the structures and mechanisms of the human psyche that constitute subjectivity. According to Lacan, Luther's thought in particular and Reformation thought in general is such a way of thinking, anticipating certain fundamental problems psychoanalysis addresses.

In this chapter the following three interconnected lines of investigation are taken up. First, there is a survey of Freud's engagements with Protestantism, an exploration that leads to the heart of the psychoanalytic method and his core ideas on religion. Second, I present a sketch of the historic roots, authoritative traditions, and inaugural moments in history to which Lacan's claim of cultural paternity relate. My focus is on concepts that are investigated further in the proceeding chapters: predestination and free will, hatred, original sin, natural and divine law, and conscience. Third, I outline certain key aspects of Lacanian thought in general and of his seminar on the ethics of psychoanalysis in particular, focusing on facets relevant for our study.

Freud's scepticism towards liberal Protestantism

At first sight the suggestion of a filiation between Protestant thought and Freudian psychoanalysis seems strange, especially since Freud was largely unacquainted with Protestant traditions and denominations. Surely he was unfamiliar with both the more orthodox or radical variants and protagonists of Protestantism, apart from Oskar Pfister's study of Count Zinzendorf's excessive pietism. Yet Freud gained some insights into liberal Protestantism via

Carl Gustav Jung, son of a minister, and Pfister, friendly Swiss Reformed pastor. Although he generally criticizes religion for its excessive morality and overzealous repression of the drives, contributing to a culture in which the psychoneuroses could flourish, Freud agrees with Pfister that some forms of religion might also support a sublimation of the drives (Freud & Pfister, 1963, p. 16). It is in this context that he writes that he could call himself a "Protestant" because of his pleas for a less strict cultural and religious sexual morality. But this was in 1909, before his conflict with Jung, before Freud realizes that Jung's psycho-religious monism implies a criticism of Judaism – an anti-Semitic trait so to speak – and a higher praise of Christianity as a religion of love and freedom. He dismisses this "message of salvation", one in which the libido is presented as having a natural inclination towards a progressive unfolding of potentials. It is from this period onward that Freud becomes more sceptical regarding the "theological prehistory" of some of his Swiss followers, their "abstract trains of thought of ethics and religious mysticism", in short, of liberal Protestantism (Freud, 1914b, pp. 60–61).

Freud's correspondence with Pfister bears evidence of this. Whereas Pfister, for example, views Saint Paul as a neurotic Jew capable of sublimation through faith in Christ, Freud strongly defends the apostle's truly Jewish character. For Freud Paul's liberating analytical insights are essentially the outcome of a Jewish tradition in which sublimation of the drives is a core feature. Christianity begins when the evangelist John brings the cult of Mary to the Ephesians, a regression to primitive forms of religion compared to the high moral and intellectual standards of Judaism (Westerink, 2007). This is the context in which we should situate Freud's remark to Pfister that he is a godless Jew; Pfister argues that Freud is neither godless nor a Jew, but a good Christian because of his struggle to liberate love (Freud & Pfister, 1963, p. 63).

Pfister attempts to reconcile psychoanalysis and liberal – true, healthy, and non-illusionary – Protestantism. He argues that because psychoanalysis is 1) a theory of the human psyche and its interactions with reality and 2) a therapy that aims at sublimating libido for higher-level, socially acceptable goals, psychoanalysis necessarily leads to a philosophy of life, since it has something to say about the nature of what is (metaphysics) and ought to be (ethics) (Westerink, 2009a, pp. 54–71). At the very least this philosophy of life gives privilege to the ideas Pfister favours, ideas characterized by a moralizing pedagogy and – what his admired friend Albert Schweizer would have called – a "life-affirming" ethics of "active love" (Dawes, 2001; Nase, 1993). It is Pfister's project that Freud opposes in *The Future of an Illusion* (1927) when he writes that religion is neither the precipitate of experience nor the end result of thinking; what Freud opposes is a type of religion associated with either truth or moral and intellectual progress rather than doctrine and illusion. He interprets religion in terms of the acceptance of authority and the continuation of narcissistic wishes and needs.

Freud explicitly says that the illusionary and doctrinal character of religion is applicable to all forms of religion, including ones that "give the name of 'God' to some vague abstraction which they have created for themselves" boasting that "they have recognized a higher, purer concept of God, notwithstanding that their God is now nothing more than an insubstantial shadow and no longer the mighty personality of religious doctrines" (Freud, 1927, p. 32). Pfister represents precisely this form of religion, one that aims at a higher, purer conception of God.

According to Freud there is no such thing as an authentic individual religious experience because religion is always ultimately rooted in the acceptance of an authoritative doctrinal tradition, "teachings and assertions about facts and conditions" one "has not discovered for oneself" (Idem, p. 25). Against both Jung and Pfister he argues against the existence of a natural inclination towards the moral or religious good. In a passage that sounds almost Spinozistic he writes:

> We may reject the existence of an original, as it were natural, capacity to distinguish good from bad. What is bad (...) may be something which is desirable and enjoyable to the ego. Here, therefore, there is an extraneous influence at work, and it is this that decides what is to be called good and bad. (...) what is bad is whatever causes one to be threatened with loss of love.
>
> (Freud, 1930, p. 124)

Hence, accepting a certain distinction between good and bad is motivated by a fear of losing love in the situation of helplessness. The pleasure principle organizes the psychic apparatus' inner structure; good and bad are simply correlates of pleasure and pain. Nor is there anything like a natural religious intuition or spiritual feeling. Freud makes this particularly clear in his correspondence with Romain Rolland (Vermorel & Vermorel, 1993) and again in Chapter 1 of *Civilization and Its Discontents* where he discusses the claim that the oceanic feeling is a natural religious sensation: "I could not convince myself of the primary nature of such a feeling" (Freud, 1930, p.65). He recognizes that both Jung and Pfister – beyond their criticisms of outdated and repressive religious doctrines and institutions – have nothing to say about religion other than its role as an ethics *par excellence*, as something that contributes to moral progress and helps to realize social cohesion (Lilla, 2007, ch. 5). Yet neither does psychoanalysis make a distinction between true and illusionary moral-religious ideals, nor healthy and unhealthy religious experiences; psychoanalysis analyses religion by means of its archaeological method alone. It is precisely this method and aim that undermine the possibility of a religious ethics capable of safeguarding the Enlightenment ideals of self-consciousness and autonomy, as well as the illusionary faith that at the heart of man's destiny lies something good.

Historical-critical methods

Another engagement by Freud with Protestantism comes to light with regard to his methods. In all his major, as well as some of his minor, studies on religion, Freud is in debt to Protestant biblical scholars and theologians who provide the material on which he builds his arguments and analyses. Let us take, for example, *The Future of an Illusion*. Its central idea – that Christian religion is a doctrine, that it consists of dogmas developed in an authoritative tradition forcing itself on the masses, which can be analogously compared with neurotic thought constructs – is derived from Theodor Reik's studies on Christian dogmas (Reik, 1923, 1927). In these studies Reik mainly follows a train of thought first developed by the famous theologian Adolf von Harnack who argues that dogmas are thought constructs or even church-political compromises formed over time by religious authorities. These constructs obscure the true core of Christian religion, namely, the figure of Jesus Christ, his life as a rabbi, and his moral-religious message. As in the case of Pfister, here again we meet a liberal Protestant for whom religion is synonymous with morality, that is to say, the essence of religion is the individual development of a moral attitude. In short, Harnack regards the study of the history of dogmas as a historical-critical study: describing the origins and developments of dogmas in order to dig up the buried essence of Christianity (Basse, 2001).

It is precisely the historical-critical study of biblical and religious texts explored by Protestant theologians that coincides with Freud's archaeological method. Freud never questions the self-evidence of his turn to such exegetical studies as providing evidence of what he is looking for in religion: the meaning of the real fact or great historical figure, traumatic incident, primal scene. The reconstruction of the origins of culture, religion, morality, and social institutions would have been impossible without Freud's turn to William Robertson-Smith's *Lectures on the Semites*, a study firmly rooted in the exegetical works of J. Wellhausen and A. Kuenen; Freud's thesis regarding Moses' murder was only possible because of Viennese Protestant biblical scholar Ernst Sellin's study on Moses. Does this turn to historical-critical studies either naturally or conveniently follow from Freud's analytical methods, digging up the past and remembering hidden events? The exegetical material was of course there, and central aspects of these historical-critical studies coincide with Freud's convictions – they proceed according to an objective scientific method, presenting an approach in which the Scriptures are regarded as historical human products. Yet the parallel runs deeper than just this. The aim of the psychoanalytic therapeutic process is not the rediscovery of a primal scene definitively explaining who and why I am. The aim is much more the analytic process itself, following traces of an ancient guilt – as Freud calls it – a process that undermines the patient's tendency to relate identity to one decisive moment, fact, or attribute.[1] The analytic process indicates that one's own identity must be articulated time and again by working through and representing the past. It is precisely this point that matches a central feature of the historical-critical method in biblical studies, a method animated by a very Protestant idea: only the ongoing interpretation of the Scriptures, for example, "the quest for the historical Jesus" (A. Schweizer), can anchor Christian identity (Van Ruiten & Vandermeersch, 1994).

Religion as the aftermath of culpability

The call upon authorities such as esteemed biblical scholars to provide evidence for psychoanalytic claims and theories is omnipresent in Freud's studies on culture and religion – as well as art and literature. An engagement with scientific disciplines such as folk psychology, theology, religious studies, and cultural anthropology is logical given the programme of applied psychoanalysis. In 1912 Otto Rank and Hans Sachs outline this programme in the first edition of *Imago*, the journal for applied psychoanalysis in the human sciences. Psychoanalysis had left the laboratory, they argue, since it had established a clear theoretical framework to analyse psycho-neurotics as well as "normal" individuals. Cultural phenomena understood as the result of cooperation between individuals could, consequently, also be studied using this theoretical framework (Rank & Sachs, 1912). Freud's followers had already explored the terrain, which resulted in a series of publications in which the central theoretical concepts were projection, sublimation, and the Oedipus complex. The possibilities seemed endless – everything could be analysed – but Freud realized that the theoretical framework was still unclear. This became a pressing matter when Jung published his *Transformations and Symbolisms of the Libido*, a text that took as its starting point an analysis of psychosis and then develops into a critique of Freud. Jung puts forward the idea of a monistic, voluntaristic drive (the primal libido), visible throughout history in its emanations, transformations, and differentiations, and mirrored and realized in the life of every individual. In the course of presenting his theory Jung refers to all kind of scientific and mythological sources. Freud reacted using Jung's tools, sources and references, thereby claiming to stand in an authoritative, scientific tradition.[2]

But Freud's call upon James Frazer and Robertson-Smith is not just a tactical matter, one of strategy in the context of quarrels within the psychoanalytic movement. The most profound claim of Freud and his followers is that psychopathology shows aspects or mechanisms of the human psyche that constitute normal subjectivity in an excessive way. In fact, the distinction between pathology and normality "in spite of its practical importance, possesses only a conventional value" (Freud, 1940, p. 195). An important consequence of this can be seen in Freud's failure to provide a theory of sublimation: normality – supposedly the outcome of the drives' sublimation as a route between the pathological extremes of perversion and neurosis – is an unattainable ideal. How should we imagine successful sublimation given the fact that socially acceptable goals are defined in a cultural context that is always itself a neurotic construct? Culture, Freud argues, demands "normality" and the repression of the drives, and demands in turn sublimation as reaction formation controlling the sexual drives. But this demand unavoidably generates pathological symptom formations.

It is in terms of this perspective that we can conceive the leap from laboratory to culture. Culture or civilization (moral conventions, cultural and religious identities, and their histories, "the achievements and regulations" that "protect against nature" and "adjust mutual relations" between people (Freud, 1930, p. 89)) reflect neither an objective status of normality nor the completion of that which is lacking in pathology. Culture is the playground of the same psychological aspects and mechanisms that can be observed in pathology, yet to a different degree and within the bounds of conventional norms. This helps to make clear Freud's interest in not only comparative studies[3] but also group psychology[4] and the history of mental development, conscience, and morality.[5] These studies show the sources, the prehistoric dispositions from which cultural conventions and regulations emanate. They depict the common traits in various traditions and throughout history, and describe the cultural, moral, and religious formations that protect against archaic human nature and organize mutually beneficial interpersonal relations. They map the terrain of overt as well as repressed, disruptive psychic forces in various cultural settings. They provide insight into the psychic, cultural, and religious conflicts that exist between human nature and morality. They sketch various forms of "normality" that can be interpreted via various pathologies.

What then is the core of Freud's writings on culture and religion? Apart from *The Future of an Illusion* in which religion is interpreted as the product of desires and needs, his other studies dealing with religion understand it in terms of morality and as the aftermath of a primordial guilt (Vergote, 1998, pp. 17–37; Westerink, 2009b). The theoretical background of such an interpretation can be traced back as early as Freud's pre-psychoanalytic intuitions of the 1880s. Yet the question concerning the origin of morality and guilt gains momentum in the 1890s when Freud discovers that obsessional neurosis can be traced back to a sexually aggressive act that is experienced as pleasurable in childhood – he later refers to this as the libido' sadistic component. Somehow this act evokes a sense of guilt, a self-reproach that cannot be explained by the internalization of morality. In fact, later-internalized morality receives its strength from an already present guilt complex. It is in this context – a shift of attention from hysteria to obsessional neurosis – that a sense of guilt becomes the key to understanding basic psychic structures and conflicts. Freud's first and later descriptions of the Oedipus complex can be viewed from this perspective. It is not simply a model describing a boy that wants to have sex with his mother and kill his father. According to Freud *Oedipus Rex* is actually about Oedipus' search for the source of guilt that causes Thebes so much misery. Guilt is not then a secondary topic in his writings, only to appear in the context of an increasing focus on the Oedipus complex. The relation is exactly the reverse. The question concerning the origin of guilt is the context in which the complex is introduced. In short, the Oedipus complex less about sex than a sense of guilt triggered by dispositional and object-relational conflicts between love and hate. The complex is important because a sense of guilt is the key to understanding the compulsive neurotic's excessive morality.[6]

The application of obsessional neurosis' theoretical model to cultural phenomena amounts to Freud's scientific myth of primal parricide – the sons identify with and kill their father who is both loved and hated, resulting in remorse and a sense of guilt. It is from this complex that cultural institutions emanate, that is to say, the first social formations (totemism), and the first prohibitions and laws (taboos). It is this sense of guilt that is manifested and worked through in various religions throughout history. This sense of guilt is the real context of what Freud tries to capture in his idea of inherited psychic dispositions – Freud's psycho-Lamarckism. He repeats this in *Moses and Monotheism* – a sense of guilt is the main underlying force in the period of cultural latency and the Jewish tradition, ultimately resulting in Judaism's characteristic features and a Jewish identity. This historic development finds its zenith in Paul's analytic insight into the historic truth of Judaism, and his attempts to liberate Judaism from its pressing sense of guilt. It is no wonder then that Freud identifies a sense of guilt with sin. To be more precise, what Christianity calls original sin is actually a sense of guilt resulting from a primal crime.

Freud's equation of original sin with a sense of guilt has caused later scholars to reverse the picture – when Freud makes a sense of guilt the mainspring of both culture and religion he basically repeats in secular terms what theologians already made clear much earlier. In the 1950s the sociologist of religion Jacob Taubes remarked that nobody had defended original sin more radically since the times of Paul and Augustine than had Freud (Taubes, 1957). It is hardly a surprise then that we find Protestant theologians pointing out precisely this familiarity. Eduard Thurneysen, for example, argues that psychoanalysis could be an important auxiliary science in pastoral care, given that Freud's view on man as torn and guilt-ridden, ripped by conflicts between drives and morality is analogous to Paul's view on man as torn between desire and spirit (Thurneysen, 1946). Paul Tillich explicitly calls Freud's theory dealing with the libido and death drive a "rediscovery of the Christian view on man's predicament", that is to say, the libido as concupiscence and the death drive as a primal hostility against both God and man that results in guilt (Tillich, 1967, pp. 44ff). Theodor Reik expresses what seems like an obvious preliminary conclusion: "Christianity and psychoanalysis, in their attempts at elucidation, take off from the same premise, that is, that a prehistoric event is the cause of the feeling of collective guilt" (Delumeau, 1990, p. 251). The senses of guilt one finds in both Christianity and neurosis are both so firmly rooted in this event that they are unavoidable – this sense of guilt appears in people of the highest virtue, as well as those who do not actually sin or succeed in conquering temptations.

This brings us closer to a Protestant rather than Catholic view on sin. Catholicism's focus is much more on a casuistry of actual sins that can either be avoided (through virtue), forgiven (in confession), or compensated for (through penance, good merits). Luther certainly does not promote a detailed examination of conscience nor does he insist on the recollection of past sins. Instead he prescribes a general avowal of sinfulness in confession. Calvin goes a step further, asserting that confession is intolerable not only because it is embedded in the authority and hierarchy of church structures, but also because a complete confession of sins is simply impossible: the list of sins is too long, creating a tormenting and compulsive need for penance and compensation through merits. More importantly, such confession is undesirable because it veils the true abyss of evil present in every – virtuous or non-virtuous – human being (Calvin, 1559a, 3.4.16–18); Tentler, 1977).

In the following chapters I show that it is precisely this positive conception of evil (as opposed to the negative Catholic conception as lack of good) that points at a deeper filiation between Protestantism and psychoanalysis.

The roots of filiation: the church fathers

Tillich suggests a connection between the elements of the Oedipus complex (love, hate, a sense of guilt) and Christian thought, regarding the Fall and original sin. We should notice, however, that Freud never explicitly writes of libido in terms of sin; but by employing this concept and relating it to the drives' polymorphous perversity, immorality (and amorality), and sadism and aggression in *Three Essays* (1905), Freud's conception of the libido never completely loses its Christian connotations. It is Augustine of Hippo (354–430) who explains *libido* in terms of *concupiscentia*, which usually denotes sexual desire, although both libido and concupiscence can also indicate a desire for power (*libido dominandi*), i.e. a desire for mastery and not to be submissive to others (including God). *Libido* thus indicates in this way all the sinful desires that fundamentally distort the natural inclination to the good. Avoidance of evil through free choice and self-control, as Augustine's opponent Pelagius proposes, is impossible as slips of tongue and the unwilled erection of the male genital prove (Augustine, 1998, ch. 23–24; Brown, 1969, pp. 259ff; De Kesel, 2009, pp. 15–16). Here we see how certain unconscious desires rooted in the body are postulated next to a conscious will that tries in vain to control and repress them. It is a distinction between the *libido* and will that seems analogous to Freud's distinction between the Id and superego. However, Augustine also argues that in the future man's original goodness will be restored. Freud thought otherwise: man's constitution must always be thought in terms of the drives' polymorphous perversity and their vicissitudes in the context of cultural demands. It is for this reason that he strongly doubts whether the further development of culture could ever bring about a satisfying mastery of the drives. Thus the main difference between Augustine and Freud lies not in their respective models of libido versus will, but the fact that for Augustine a God exists with the moral authority to bring about the will's mastery over the libido. The absence of transcendence in Freud's work prevents such a conclusion.

Augustine is not the only church father who foregrounds control of the *libido* as a problem. John Cassian (?360–435), Augustine's contemporary, describes *libido* as a form of impurity (sin) to be distinguished from other sinful inclinations or habits, such as *fornicatio* or *immunditia*. Libido denotes feelings and passions that develop in the dark corners of the mind that give pleasure without bodily passions (Cassian, 1958, conf. XII.2). The reason for Cassian's careful classifications and analyses of the mind and body's various passions, feelings, memories, images, and movements is because these are all part of the monk's ongoing struggle to gain control over them and, thereby, advance towards chastity and sanctified life. As to free will and self-control, he holds a position between those of Pelagius and Augustine, reasoning that limited self-control is possible but that the absence of nocturnal erections and erotic dreams, for example, are signs of grace, since these are vices that cannot be consciously controlled. As Michel Foucault shows, Cassian is one of the first to systematically develop a technique for analysing and diagnosing various psychic and bodily manifestations, a process of subjectivization linked to self-knowledge as the self's objectivization through obedience to spiritual leaders (Foucault, 1985). He thus became the founding father of confessional practices in the West – "the machinery of the confession, within which in fact psychoanalysis and Freud figure as episodes" (Foucault, 1980, p. 211, 1976). Cassian's *libido* as a sexual passion without bodily sensation – hence, a mental sexuality – returns in Freud's use of the same concept while analysing the psychic representations of his patients or theorizing on it as a concept in the *Three Essays*. Foucault's archaeology of Western subjectivity is certainly inspired by Lacan's thoughts on filiations between psychoanalysis and aspects of the West's long tradition of thought concerning human subjectivity, the emergence of structures of thought, discourses, and practices that Freudian psychoanalysis addresses or repeats in a novel form and context (Roudinesco, 1997, p. 332).

Despite the filiation between Augustine and Cassian's conception of *libido* as sexual desire and psychoanalytic theory and practice, it is not this conception Lacan has in mind when he suggests a cultural paternity between Freud and Luther, the "mad man from Wittenberg" who confronts Erasmus with the authoritative tradition of Paul and Augustine. The filiation concerns not sexuality but the *libido*, insofar as it denotes sinful desires that distort one's natural inclination to the good. Lacan thus refers to what lies behind sexuality, which in Augustine's view is, after all, only the locus of corruption after the fall;

uncontrollable sexual passions are merely a penalty. However, original sin is Adam's freely willed disobedience (distortion of the will) to God's commands, a crime from which the human race suffers, a collective guilt that is inherited. When Lacan suggests the existence of a filiation or cultural paternity between Freud and Luther, this includes aspects of the doctrine of predestination. In (the former Augustinian monk) Luther's thought, as well as most Reformation thought, this is ultimately based on Augustine's ideas on predestination.

It is only in the final years of his life that Augustine's doctrine of predestination (Brown, 1969, pp. 398–407; Creswell, 1997) comes to occupy a central place in his thought, especially since it caused upheaval in some monasteries. Whereas monks like Cassian in Marseille preferred to see salvation as the outcome of both human and divine efforts (Chadwick, 1968, pp. 110–136), i.e. an interaction between human control of sin and acts of grace, Augustine consistently stresses the fact that salvation is to be thought of as an act of grace. Only grace can make man free again, that is to say, God can undo man's enslavement to sinful desires by binding the human will to his own.[7] On this point Augustine claims to be strictly following Saint Paul, although some resolute conclusions are added: salvation is a gift because man is sinful, unable to achieve salvation through good merits. According to Augustine, the relation between grace and merit is the reverse of what most monks hitherto thought: merit should be thought of as the effect of grace. He then goes a step further: God has foreknowledge and willingly permits man to sin, God foresaw man's disobedience. The Fall is then just punishment. Since God is good some were elected, effectually called and, hence, saved for eternal life. Others were not and, as such, damned – original sin is simply the just, sufficient ground of reprobation.

It is notable that, from Cassian's point of view, the final versions of predestination in Augustine's latest writings such as *De praedestinatione sanctorum* and *De dono perseverantiae* are in a sense revolutionary, since the semi-Pelagian monks always considered themselves saved necessarily, because of their decision to enter the monastery and freely-chosen life devoted to God. Run-of-the-mill Christians might be either saved or damned depending on their moral endeavours and merits. In his last writings Augustine proposes a conception of the human will in which one does either good or evil because of the presence or absence of a predestining gift of grace. Only through God is it thus possible for humans to will the good. Election is no longer based on a decree following foreknowledge and the fall, but preceding these – foreknowledge is based on an eternal decree before the world's foundation, in which some are elected for belief and salvation while others are not. Hence, in his last writings Augustine proposes for the first time a doctrine of double predestination. There is a development in his thought on this issue, which means that theologians in the Middle Ages and Reformation called on Augustine as an authority, providing arguments for various theological positions. Luther is one of them.

Augustine's scepticism regarding free will makes sense from a theological as well as psychological perspective. As Peter Brown argues, predestination originated as a doctrine of perseverance and survival, one that provided the church community of Hippo with an identity, an "irreducible inner core" during a time in which the Vandals swept through North Africa and its very existence was threatened (Brown, 1969, p. 407). The idea that God might permit evil or use the ungodly for good purpose – namely, the perseverance of the faithful – shows that, at bottom, God is good and can be trusted even in the worst of circumstances. Predestination can thus be seen as the ultimate doctrine that avoids a confrontation with a dark, evil-willing God. The semi-Pelagian opposition in Marseille offered the monks an elitist, somewhat eccentric model, one that could neither provide consolation to Augustine's community nor support its faith. According to Cassian, man has a sick will (Chadwick, 1968, pp. 123–124) that needs constant analysis, diagnosis, mortification, and – of course – God's healing grace. There is a natural capacity to be virtuous and, hence, advance in faith and sanctity, but the intense, complex practices involved are only possible in the context of a monastery. This constant, never-ending spiritual struggle is a sign of spiritual growth and salvation, and although Augustine is certainly not opposed to the importance of such deep self-examination, this is not what his community in Hippo needed in their profoundly uncertain, strife-ridden times.

Whether the doctrine of predestination includes biographical resonances, that is to say, its relation to Augustine's much discussed relationship with his mother, Monica, is not something that need concern us. The problem with psychoanalytic interpretations of historical persons is precisely their personalization of ideas, which frequently neglect historical debates and discussions, traditions and filiations, in short, which reduce complex matrices in which ideas come to fruition to that of personal motive or genius. This is what we want to avoid here.

The key issue: the problem of evil

What Augustine establishes in his doctrines of original sin and double predestination is the relation between a radical denial of free will as an individual's capacity to advance in moral and religious life, on the one hand, and predetermined motives that situate the individual in a history determined by the decisions made by others or the Other (God), on the other hand. Moreover, both man's will and inclinations are led by drives and sinful desires. Thus, good merits are to be viewed sceptically. At this point the question of whether God foresees, wills, or even creates evil is also introduced. Rejecting the heretic Manichean solution of a distinction between an evil and good god, Augustine denies that God could create evil and locates the source of evil in

Adam's libido. Nevertheless, the problem of evil in relation to predestination and free will is now on the agenda, and is dealt with by various theologians at a variety of councils and synods over the centuries. The mainstream of the Roman Catholic tradition seems to be a compromise between the two positions already mentioned, semi-Pelagianism and Augustine's. The importance of early controversies regarding predestination and free will should not be overlooked – the history of theology is full of references to it. Important theologians defending an Augustinian-inspired doctrine of double predestination such as Gregory of Rimini (?1300–1358) and Francis Gomarus (1563–1641) commonly call their opponents "Pelagians". In general these theologians were conscious of the terms into which theological debates were translated, namely, those of ancient landmark heresies.

The mainstream of the Roman Catholic position consists in the following. First, God wills the salvation of all men – Christ died so that all men could be saved. Second, sin occurs with God's permission since man is created with free will and God foresaw all possible human choices and their effects. Third, by willing evil Adam was justly punished, and those who willingly tend towards evil perish by their own fault. Fourth, even though man contracted original sin he is free to do good with the necessary aid of God's grace, hence, either man resists or cooperates with God. Fifth, God is the cause of neither evil nor sin. The main points of this position – which I sketch only very roughly here – is the defence of a certain degree of free will (since it certainly acknowledges the fact that sin distorts man's inner life, yet that man is also capable of leading of a virtuous life and can rationally decide contrary to his sinful inclinations) and a strong denial that God might have created evil. Thomas Aquinas (?1225–1274), for example, thought that God is the Supreme Good who, for this reason, could never be the source of evil; evil is thought of as the absence of good and thus has no positive content – it is defined as a lacking. In a sense the same goes for the damned: they are the non-elect who willingly choose evil and persist in it – they thereby lack membership in the elect. The *massa damnata* exclude themselves from salvation. The elect are those that accept God's grace, although this decision does not make election a human decision, since its acceptance is only possible through an act of grace (Aquinas, 1984, I.I.23).

In the fifth and sixth sessions (1546–1547) of the Council of Trent, where predestination is defined in contradistinction to Reformation thought, the council proclaims a Thomistic point of view: God does not will evil he merely permits it. Man is free to do good with the aid of grace, or resist grace and persist in sin (Denzinger, 1991). What is rejected here is clear. First, the idea that God wills and produces evil – hence a rejection of a negative motive on God's part (hatred); second, denial of free will and the importance of good merits and virtues; and third, denial of the natural human capacity to be and do good for the benefit of oneself and others.

In *The Bondage of the Will* Luther connects to Augustine's doctrine of predestination: the fundamental human passions and inclinations are created and predetermined by the decisions of, and struggles between, others. Hatred exists between two figures that are both fundamentally similar (Adam is created in God's image) yet estranged. Luther writes, for example: "God works in us good things and bad" and, consequently, he "rewards his own good works in us and punishes his evil works in us" (Luther, 1525, III-58). In other words, as the foundational nucleus of culture and moral law, "the problem of evil" as Lacan calls it, now has its locus in the relation between creator (father) and created (Adam/son). Neither is evil (sin) a choice nor an effect of something else, for example, a lack of goodness or moral failure. It has content, namely hatred, i.e. an innate passion or inclination towards pursuing evil. Its solution lies beyond human moral capacity and freedom, and can only therefore be resolved by an act of divine salvation. Luther makes this perfectly clear in his response to Erasmus, describing the function of law after the "flood-gate of iniquity is thrown open unto man": "The words of the law are no evidence for the power of free choice, but show what we ought to do and cannot do" (Idem, III-134). A person ought to rule over his sin, renounce the evil in him. Yet, he cannot accomplish this through his own strength and merits.

Neither does Lacan claim that this supposed filiation or cultural paternity implies Freud's thought regarding hatred is the same as Luther's nor does he say that their conceptions of hatred have the same meaning. In fact, he has to recognize that in Freud's thought hate is primarily understood in terms of sexual aggression – it is primarily the sadistic component of the libido – and that in Luther's thought hatred is not sexualized. The filiation is to be thought of as both structural (analogical) and historical. There is a convergence between psychoanalysis and Luther when Freud addresses a conglomeration of thematics – hatred, primal parricide, law, and a sense of guilt – that is first coherently established and expressed in a radical fashion by Luther: hatred, fall, law, and sin. This is Lacan's claim, and it is at this point that we start to see the deeper connection between Reformation thought and psychoanalysis.

Lacan's project

We are dealing with the filiation between Freudian psychoanalysis and Protestantism. Elaborating Lacan's claim entails searching out convergences between Freudian psychoanalysis and early Reformation theology. We must, of course, take Lacan's own psychoanalytic thought into consideration. His thought might be best characterized by its strong resistance to most post-Freudian psychoanalysis, notably, ego psychology with its strong moralizing tendencies, its emphasis on the development of self consciousness: the formation of a responsible, integrated individual being capable of adapting to social norms and values. Beginning in the early 1950s Lacan calls for a *retour à Freud*, arguing that Freudian psychoanalysis primarily concerns the subject's alienation, disharmony, and disunity, its inabilities to adjust and adapt. Lacan aims at the re-evaluation of Freud's work, including the intellectual traditions this work represents, to re-root psychoanalysis in Freudian soil (compare Needleman Armintor, 2004). It is in this context that he turns to the Western intellectual tradition, criticizing, for example, the Cartesian *cogito* – the supposed starting point of a turn to a rational, self-conscious, autonomous subject – but also begins searching out an intellectual tradition that could be identified as the cultural paternity of Freudian thought.

Lacan's project is Freudian insofar as he attempts to further think through human subjectivity in terms of psychoanalysis' perspective of pathology in relation to the philosophical tradition. He follows in Freud's fascination of religious authorities (the "great man" such as Moses and Saint Paul), the study of religion and culture as well as their moral and philosophical implications, and the tendency in Freud's writings to refer to certain philosophers as – what Viktor Tausk has called – "pre-psychoanalytic thinkers" (Tausk, 1814, p. 127). Yet in Lacan's writings the relationship with philosophy is more profound, despite the fact that his texts certainly cannot be characterized by strict logical argumentation. At the core of his theoretical framework we find, in the first place, a combination of psychoanalysis, Ferdinand de Saussure's philosophy of language, and Claude Lévy-Strauss structuralism. This results, at least partly, in the transcription of psychoanalytic concepts into philosophical ones. The combination of psychoanalysis and philosophy is probably the most important Lacanian innovation, although it is also an elaboration of the Freudian claim that psychoanalysis is situated between biology and philosophy (Freud, 1938).

The fact that Lacan clearly states the subject of psychoanalysis is the Cartesian *cogito* shows that he realizes Freudian psychoanalysis can only be fully understood in view of an intellectual tradition in which philosophy plays a leading role. The subject of psychoanalysis has an "inaugural moment" at the "beginning of the seventeenth century", says Lacan referring to Descartes (1596–1650) (Lacan, 1998b, p. 223). We should notice here that Lacan's view on Descartes is rather ambiguous. The Cartesian *cogito* points towards both the inauguration of the self-conscious, autonomous ego that Freud criticizes in, for example, his case studies, and the ego promoted by ego psychology. By inciting the formation of a strong, self conscious, responsible ego, and defending precisely the type of autonomy Freud criticizes, it is clear to Lacan that ego psychology is simply a betrayal of psychoanalysis. Freud's case studies provide the basis of these criticisms. In *Studies on Hysteria* (1896a) Freud shows that the hysterics' moral characters are only a façade behind which amoral drives rule. The case of the Rat Man is another convincing example: the troubled young patient is certain he loves his father until Freud confronts him with the repressed truth: at the same time he intensely hates his father. On the other hand, says Lacan, not only does the Cartesian ego provoke a new perspective regarding what "causes" and guarantees this ego, but also that which undermines and calls it into question (Evans, 1996, p. 26). Descartes points towards this when reflecting on the imperfection of doubt (thought) and the ability to think of something more perfect (Descartes, 1637). This leads him to assume that this ability is caused by something more perfect, that is, by God from whom everything "in us" originates. It is precisely this divine cause that undermines the ego, says Lacan, since Descartes follows in the tradition of an Augustinian inspired voluntarism[8] and gives primacy to the will of God, which makes conscious thought depend on eternal verities as God decrees them. It is precisely this dependence on God as the "subject who is supposed to know" that makes every "I think" merely a transient fading point, an effect of the Other's desire (Lacan, 1998b, pp. 224–225). What Descartes calls "God" Lacan refers to as the subject of psychoanalysis or "the subject of the unconscious" – in short, "God is unconscious" (Idem, p. 59). According to Lacan, Descartes is the first to have scientifically elaborated the fact that every "I think" has its place in a network of autonomous unconscious signifiers, i.e. that every "I think" is in fact an "it (Id) thinks", that every thought is preceded and caused by something else: "the dark God" whose desire cannot be comprehended (Idem, p. 225). It is in this sense that Freud's work could be called "Cartesian" (Juranville, 1984). In the next chapter I show that Lacan's interpretation of Descartes is Spinozistic in nature.

The inaugural moment of the modern subject

The "inaugural moment" of the subject of psychoanalysis need not be limited to Descartes. The radical inwardness characteristic of Descartes' philosophy is shared by many systems of thought in his age, and Descartes is not the only one to reflect on the relation between doubt, certainty, and existence. The very notion "that I can have no knowledge of what is outside me except by means of the ideas I have within me" (Taylor, 1989, p. 144) has a certain affinity with the religious notion that a truthful assessment of what exists outside oneself is only possible through faith, that is to say, through a correct, inner conscious religious disposition. This line of thought is evident in the intellectual environment in which Descartes carries out his philosophical project, which results in his *Discourse on Method* and the *Meditations*: the long period he lived in the predominantly Calvinist Republic (Watson, 2007). Here we only need be reminded of the fact that Descartes' mentor Isaac Beeckman (1588–1637) – a philosopher and natural scientist who supported Descartes' reflections on doubt and certainty – was also an elder in the congregation where one of the most important protagonists of the radical Dutch Reformation, Willem Teellinck (1579–1629), was a minister. In his later mystical writings, Teellinck focuses on the need to doubt the truthfulness of all human faculties and representations to establish a true foundation for certainty and the assurance of faith, namely, God (Westerink, 2002). This is the radical expression of an idea that dominates Calvinist religious life: a truthful assessment of existence and the assurance of faith and salvation are only possible on the basis of a conscious, radical reformation of inner life. As advanced by Luther and Calvin this issue is "*the* central philosophical issue for Descartes" (Bordo, 1987, p. 38). Hence, there is good reason to date modern subjectivity's inaugural moment somewhat earlier, regarding Descartes as a single landmark among others that contribute to the formulation of modern subjectivity.

We need of course to establish what are generally considered to be the characteristics of Cartesian thought that make it this supposed inaugural moment. There is much literature on this issue, of which I can only mention some landmarks. In the 1950s Alexandre Koyré – whose philosophical thought influenced Lacan – describes the relation between Cartesian thought and the origins of modernity in terms of a split between the world as extension and matter on the one hand, and the "interior locus" as pure mind able to grasp the idea of God on the other hand (Koyré, 1957, pp. 74f). Among others, Charles Taylor argues that the confinement of thoughts and feelings (the psychological) to the subject – hence, that thoughts and feelings are no longer part of an order of things located in the world – is established in Descartes' era (Taylor, 1989, ch. 11). Richard Rorty calls this modern, individual mind the inner arena, indicating the inner "mental" space in which sensations, perceptions, ideas, moral codes bodily and are reviewed by an inner observer (Rorty, 1979, p. 50). The term arena indicates a distinction between the realm of the subject's "inside" and that of the world as "outside". This subject is aware of the fact that it is no longer belongs to a natural universal order, and that its inner life can only be subjected to an inner authority, an inner life that remains inaccessible to others. Hence, the subject as defined by this inwardness is also always dislocated, alienated, and disconnected from the objective outside (Bordo, 1987; Brennan, 1993). The modern subject must first of all position itself in relation to – or even in opposition to – the world. Hence, by turning inward it takes an outside, eccentric position. This dislocation is relevant not only in reflecting on the modern subject-object-dichotomy from a philosophical perspective, but also preludes themes in the writings of both Freud and Lacan.

These are as follows. First, there is the fundamental helplessness of the child and its reaction formations in response to the disintegration of an original organic unity with the motherly environment. Second, the inner dynamic of the psychic apparatus is neither mirrored in the outside world nor naturally attuned to the demands of culture. Third, because the subject is ruled by the pleasure principle it is mentally maladapted to reality, and needs, therefore, to develop a number of tools such as rational thought, fantasy or technical crafts in order to pursue postponed pleasure – the work of the reality principle. Fourth, there is Lacan's notion of the ultimate object of desire, which results in a desire that resists normal social codes and procedures.

But the question with which I began is whether this subject is first established in Cartesian philosophy, and whether modernity should to be understood in terms of the inauguration of a self-conscious, rational, and autonomous subject. The contributions of early modern theological thought are decisive here, not the least because this thought moved the masses as opposed to being confined to an intellectual elite. The modern subject's dislocation is centrally related to religious thought, i.e. the conceptualization of the estrangement between the individual sinner and God, and of the estrangement of the true believer and godly in this idle, sinful world. Their inner struggles, desire for rebirth, and the call for conversion all point in the same direction: turning away from the world and sin to reconnect with God, from dislocation to reconnection.

Michel de Certeau should be mentioned here as a pioneer in the investigation of the subject of psychoanalysis' inaugural moment. He argues that Lacan's references to Hadewijch of Antwerp (thirteenth century) and Theresa of Avila (1515–1582) not only betrays a certain affinity for religious movements such as mysticism lacking in Freud's work, but also shows that the modern subject's inaugural moment is situated in the field of religion (Lacan, 1999, p. 76). De Certeau's interest concerns the way in which the Lacanian distinction between the subject of the speech-act and the subject of the statement has its roots in sixteenth and seventeenth-century mysticism (De Certeau, 1986, 1992). Mysticism of this type can no longer be characterized by a contemplative attitude towards a hidden divinity in outside reality, but is completely preoccupied with inner experience, i.e., the mystic's inner life as interior locus of divine speech. This is the case in the mysticism of, for example, Theresa of Avila and John of the Cross (1542–1591). To make possible an inner dialogue with the divine as "it who speaks", through an act of the will the mystic must create an inner space for the "it" to speak. Hence, a mysticism of this type hangs on a free-floating desire to hear the other speak. In this way De Certeau points at a cultural paternity between mysticism and Lacanian thought – a thesis that seems to sustain the suspicion that Lacanian thought is nothing other than Catholicism in psychoanalytic guise. Of interest to us is De Certeau's claim that modern mysticism's most radical form is evident in the "nomad" Jean de Labadie (1610–1674) – the impossible mystic who goes from being a Jesuit via Jansenism and Calvinism to becoming a "Labadist" without being able to fix a place for "it" to speak (Idem, p. 293). When De Certeau writes of Anna Maria van Schurman (1607–1678) – De Labadie's kindred soul, participant in the main intellectual circles (including correspondence with Descartes, Richelieu, and Constantine Huygens), and an the erudite student of one of the Dutch Reformation's main protagonists, Gisbertus Voetius (1589–1676) – he makes an interesting connection between hatred and radical orthodox Calvinist thought. Without further contextualizing this hatred or tracing it back to Luther, De Certeau writes the following:

> She plots a course set upon the 'hatred' that prompts God to act, as if all things spoke to her in the language of solitary and inconsolable fury,

> to which the response was an unrequited love. (…) This God who 'comes out', but for a struggle to the death with his disappointing creation, a god outside of himself, on the boundary where he is exiled both from himself and from the world, furious with a desire lacking an object – perhaps he resembles Labadie in his last days.
>
> (Idem, p. 285)

De Certeau says that Schurman describes in a radical fashion the rage and disappointment of a God who wants to save all, but finds none worthy of saving (Van Schurman, 1678). It is the God who – as Teellinck writes in 1627, some years of the Synod of Dordrecht – wanders through the night like "a strange man", a "hero who fails", and a "giant who can't help". Disappointed and full of wrath, God turns away from the world and man, and calls into the dark, longing for someone to hear him (Teellinck, 1627).

As I show in later chapters, we find in this literature a connection between the so-called "dislocated subject" and a reflection on the reason for this dislocation, namely, original sin and God's hatred and wrath. Teellinck and Schurman stand in a particular Protestant tradition that reflects on this sin and hatred, as well as related issues such as predestination and despair, and the reformation of inner life through a reorientation of conscience. This tradition has its spokesmen in every generation, and for the most part there is a direct influence from one onto the other, although it all begins with Luther.

Does modernity then begin with Luther, and does his thought mark the inaugural moment of modern subjectivity? Moreover, the terms "modern" and "modernity" refer to a much-discussed era regarded by some scholars as breaking radically with the past, specifically, the medieval intellectual traditions. Some scholars focus on the relation between faith and reason, arguing that modernity is the result of secularization, which becomes visible in the Enlightenment's critique of religion. Others focus on the emergence of modern identity, man's self-perception, and its characteristic aspects in relation to the world and others. Marcel Gauchet, for example, writes that the major break of modernity "came with the breakdown of the hierarchical structured continuity between the human and divine sphere". This "resulted in a radical change of the perception of human fallibility and the world's imperfection". The birth of modern subjectivity is then understood as coinciding with a gradual process of culpabilization, the attribution of evil to human nature and moral choice, a process through which the origin of sin is internalized and becomes the model of subjectivity (Gauchet, 1997, pp. 167–168). This view is supported by extensive studies concerning the emergence of Western guilt culture (Delumeau, 1990).

Lacan speaks of Luther's place in history as the beginning of a new direction in thought, one that occurs near the beginning of the sixteenth century and appears at a break (*point de fracture*). But what does this "break" describe? When we look at a similar proclamation by Lacan concerning Descartes – that regarding the subject of psychoanalysis and its inaugural moment at the beginning of the seventeenth century – we find our answer. Although Descartes does indeed establish a new direction in thought concerning subjectivity through his meditations on the *cogito*, Lacan never highlights the influence of either Etienne Gilson's authoritative reading of Aquinas' influence on Descartes, or that of his teacher Koyré regarding the scholastic and Augustinian origins of Cartesian philosophy (Koyré, 1922; Gilson, 1930; Roudinesco, 1997, pp. 88ff). These scholars convincingly show that the origins of modernity cannot be understood in terms of a radical break initiated by a single philosophical genius. From this perspective Descartes' work can be seen as an inaugural moment in the development of modern, enlightened, emancipated subjectivity that is nonetheless contextualized – which is to say that Descartes' thought is itself working through an intellectual tradition and reflecting the consequences of this tradition. It is an important moment in the evolution of ideas.

This is all the more true with Luther. His work marks a new way of thinking. Although Lacan does not refer to Lucien Febvre's *Martin Luther, un destin* written in 1928, it is likely that this book influences his view on Luther and his place in history (Febvre, 1928; Roudinesco, 1997, pp. 92–94). Febvre approaches history in a manner similar to Koyré: A history of ideas should not be constructed in terms of continual progress but new and rediscovered directions and models in thought, produced by real persons living in specific circumstances, available to structure the lives and thoughts of people – hence, the directions of thought-framing mentalities. Febvre writes of Luther's discovery of original sin, justification, and predestination as one of the foundational moments in modernity as well as a rediscovery – or even repetition – of Paul's thought and that of others. The general contours of Febvre`s view on Luther are recognizable in Lacan's evaluation of Luther's place in history.

Luther is "modern" because he stands within and reformulates a tradition of *via moderna* and *schola Augustiniana moderna*. At the same time he defines what Koyré would have called a new conceptual structure, an innovative model for the interpretation and organization of people's lives and thoughts (Roudinesco, 1997, p. 94; Gillespie, 2008, pp. 4–19), a new model for a theology of piety that emerges from, transforms and breaks with late-medieval religiosity and pastoral conceptions (Hamm, 2004). We can indeed locate the origins of modernity here, since it is Luther who, confronted with the decomposition of the Aristotelian universe as order in which every living being has its place, value, meaning and telos, redefined human subjectivity in terms of an inner divided mental site – man as dislocated sinner and conscientious believer (Schürmann, 2003, p. 353; Taylor, 2007, ch. 2; Mjaaland, 2009). God's Word first constitutes self-consciousness as the *locus* where faith, religious thought, and speech make a (justified) sinner conscious of his state. This assessment is thoroughly convincing given the abovementioned focus on inner convictions, etc. among Descartes' Calvinist contemporaries, all the more so when one recognizes the contextually-situated nature of this moment. The breakdown of an external order based on essence (form) gives way to the centrality of this inner, conscious site, where the sinful subject inclined to evil is re-constituted in and through symbolic language and conscience formation. In my view this shift produces a side effect, a disruptive outcome with which Luther has to deal, namely, determining the place and meaning of the creator of this site. This creator is the hidden God (*Deus absconditus*) who wills as he pleases and whose essence is incognizable. In the following paragraphs and chapter I show how Lacan deals with this issue.

The ethics of psychoanalysis

For Lacan, in his seminar on the ethics of psychoanalysis (Moyaert, 1994; De Kesel, 2009; Moyaert, 2012), it is clear that the problem of God's eternal hatred appears at the beginning of modernity. It is certainly not a coincidence that Luther is the one who articulates this hatred in a radical fashion: he represents a schism in a unified church that had been a concrete instantiation of a universal order. In the first place this order was of all a rational, moral nature, one that crumbled in the late medieval debates between scholasticism and nominalism. In the medieval universe man's being is naturally embedded in an order created and guaranteed by God. The purpose of life is to actualize in thought and action potentialities that are part of human nature.

Central to scholastic Aristotelianism as represented by, for example, Thomas Aquinas, is the claim that through reason and a natural desire for the good man can comprehend God's eternal decrees as revealed in Scripture, since these decrees are themselves reasonable and beneficent. When dealing with morality in the *Summa theologica*, Aquinas says that, "reason is the rule and measure of what is done" (Gilson, 1994, p. 265). The moral law is bound to reason, and since man is inclined to do the good (in the sense of pursuing his own good) and avoiding evil, as well as seeking the Supreme Good (God), the moral law is attuned to both custom and universal conscience. "There is in man an inclination to good, according to the nature of his reason, which nature is proper to him; thus man has a natural inclination to know the truth about God, and to live in society" (Aquinas, 1984, I.II.94).

Written in our nature, this natural inclination to do good and avoid evil is thus called natural law. The fundamental thesis affirmed by Aquinas is that the natural law participates in the eternal law, i.e. the rational order of creation. Hence, man desires to do good, and the ultimate object of desire is the Supreme Good itself. Of course, as we have seen, original sin causes corruption that incites some to persist in evil, but rational persons nevertheless freely choose the good. The law is good and because it is good the law is willed by God. God's will is bound to that which is reasonable and good (Lottin, 1949; Bradley, 1997; Schneewind, 1998).

The claim that God's will is grounded in reason is a point of much debate in late medieval thought, notably in the traditions of *via moderna* (nominalism) and *schola Augustiniana moderna* (McGrath, 1987). Luther stands in the middle of these traditions when he writes, on the one hand, that God's will is essentially incognizable and, on the other, argues that man is so fundamentally corrupted by sin that a natural inclination or capacity to be or do good is unthinkable. These two claims share in the more basic supposition that man's inclination to do evil (sin) is the effect of an evil motive (hatred) in God – we take a closer look at this issue in the next chapter. This is Lacan's interest when dealing with the ethics of psychoanalysis. He begins with the premise that the moral law cannot be understood as either founded in the natural order of being, a natural human desire for the universal good, or the pursuit of that which is generally regarded as reasonable, beneficent, useful, or needed from the perspective of social consensus. At this point it also becomes clear that in his view psychoanalysis cannot be harmonized with a utilitarian ethics, one in which the desire for happiness is regarded as being pursued through a combination of rational choice and functionality, efficiency and/or social consensus.

Luther preludes a fundamentally Freudian insight when he questions both the natural inclination of man's desire and the supposed goodness of the desirable object – man is inclined to evil and there is an eternal hatred in God. Freud indeed poses the question of whether the object that gives pleasure is morally good. Those who, especially in the 1960s, interpret Freud as advocating a more liberal view on sexual morality, i.e. as an emancipator of sexuality and champion of liberal society that gives room to individuals to freely unfold their potentialities and pursue their ideals, will probably answer in the affirmative. Certainly ego psychologists, who relate the aim of the individual's mental development – psychic integration – to society's aim of adaptation to shared norms and values, will interpret Freud as presenting a theory in which desire and the morally good are attuned. According to Lacan, however, such a view, one in which psychoanalysis supports society's moral conventions is a betrayal of Freudian thought. Freud's starting point is the individual, the neurotic who suffers from acting and behaving in conformity with society's demands, hence, one who suffers from not being able to live according to his desire. As early as 1880, when he was translating John Stuart Mill's *The Subjection of Women*, Freud is already sceptical of an ethics based on the pursuit of happiness. In a letter to his fiancée he writes that civilized man does not pursue pleasure; man merely controls the drives and subjects enjoyment to the cultural ideal of refinement (Westerink, 2009b, pp. 2–6). This pre-analytic intuition is maintained throughout Freud's writings. Freud expresses this in *Civilization and Its Discontents* when he forgoes asking, "how can we realize the desire for happiness?", but starts from, "why is it, that people are so unhappy?" Freud's answer can be summarized as follows: there is something that stops people from striving for happiness in a calculated and rational way – being happy "is not included in the plan of Creation". The object of desire is something other than that which is generally understood as morally desirable. And yet there is a relation that Freud describes as "contrast" – enjoyment presupposes a restriction that is either given in our constitution or by the outside world (Freud, 1930, pp. 76–77). Restriction, however, implies that the "programme of becoming happy cannot be fulfilled". Freud adds: "yet we must not – indeed, we cannot – give up our efforts to bring it nearer to fulfillment by some means or other". There is no way to obtain all that one desires, and thus "every man must find out for himself in what particular fashion he can be saved" (Idem, p. 83).

Lacan makes this dialectic between desire and limitation the cornerstone of his seminar on the ethics of psychoanalysis. Desire can only be conceived in relation to restriction. Lacan picks up Freud's claim that the individual's desire for happiness cannot be given up despite remaining unfulfilled, notably in the final chapter of his text on the ethics of psychoanalysis where he writes that "from an analytical point of view, the only thing of which one can be guilty is of having given ground relative to one's desire", that is to say, having betrayed one's desire "for a good motive or even for the best of motives", such as one's social duty or economic profit (Lacan, 1992, p. 319).

A short note on Lacan's concept of desire (*désir*) is necessary since the German-language equivalents, *Verlangen* or *Begehren*, play only a minor role in Freud's vocabulary. Its closest concepts are *Begierde* and *Wunsch*, and Lacan's conception of desire is indeed related to these. It has been rightfully suggested that this conception of desire is also related to a theological-philosophical tradition in which desire points at an endless, boundless, and ultimately unfulfillable desire (Moyaert, 1994, p. 15). The question then is of what specific theologies come to mind here. In my opinion we need not only think of modern mysticism, but certainly also of Saint Augustine and those who are influenced by him, such as Reformation theologians and also the Catholic Reformer Cornelius Jansenius (1585–1638) with his thought on desire (*delectatio*) of God as opposed to sinful libidinal desire (*libido*).[9] In terms of philosophy, Lacan's references are more explicit. In his sixth seminar on desire he mentions Baruch Spinoza (1632–1677) side by side with the Puritan poet John Donne (1572–1631) as one of the few precursors to Freud. Spinoza's formula "desire is the very essence of man" (Lacan, 2000, p. 16; Spinoza, 1677, III, prop.59, def. 1)[10] is quoted as a formula that captures Lacan's own notion of desire. In the context of our study, I will show that Spinoza's thought is an important inspiration to Lacan's psychoanalysis, notably his thoughts on immanent causation and the relation between cause and effect (see the next chapter). Spinoza's philosophy is also of importance because he pictures a quiet, intellectual desire for God that, in a sense, dismisses and is in opposition to the radical, desperate desire for salvation and existential fear of God's wrathful condemnation endemic to the orthodox Calvinism of Spinoza's time.

Desire, the law and the Thing

Just as Freud thinks that enjoyment and happiness are only possible in terms of contrast and restriction, Lacan starts from the premise that desire should be conceived in terms of limitation. Desire is always a counterforce evoked by limitation. This limitation is conceived by Lacan as a prohibiting law. What he expresses here is an elaboration of Freud's analysis of the categorical imperative in *Totem and Taboo*.

As can already be inferred from the introduction to his essay on totemism and taboo, Freud is particularly interested in answering unsolved problems related to social psychology,[11] such as the relation between totemism and exogamy, and the relation between totemism and taboo. He writes that the taboo, unlike features of totemism, still has its place in Western civilization – Kant's categorical imperative as a moral rule that functions in a compulsive manner and rejects conscious motivation, is essentially a taboo (Freud, 1912–1913, pp. xiii–xiv). He is particularly interested in reconstructing the unconscious motives that give the taboo its strength and status. The problem he addresses here has – as we have already seen – deep roots in his clinical writings. When he discovers in his earliest analyses of obsessional neurosis that the core conflict of neurosis is between an interiorized cultural morality, on the one hand, and inner drives and infantile wishes, on the other hand, the question arises as to what motivates the internalization of this morality in the first place. When the inner forces of libido are strong enough, according to Freud, cultural morality is simply rejected, which is surely the case in the mental lives of perverts (Freud, 1896c). The motive he discovers is a sense of guilt not to be regarded as the effect of transgressing an internalized morality, but one evoked by an inner conflict between love and hate that precedes this internalization. In his great case study of obsessional neurosis, that of the Rat Man, Freud shows that the conflict between love and hate is in fact a conflict within the sphere of love, since "the essence of love" includes a sadistic component (hate) (Freud, 1909, pp. 238–239).[12] Here we find the unconscious motive that gives taboo and morality its strength. The individual does not accept cultural morality because of a natural inclination to recognize a certain morality as good and/or useful, but because of an inner dynamic between hate, love, and a sense of guilt that connects with that morality. In *Totem and Taboo* this model of obsessional neurosis is applied to culture and religion, which are themselves understood as manifestations of, and vehicles to, inculcate morality. Freud's reconstruction of primal history, in which the dialectic of love and hate leads to the murder of, and identification with, the tyrannical primal father, is basically a description of this process: when an inner constitutional conflict is related to the first object choices, a dynamics of identification and sense of guilt lead to the first moral-religious and cultural institutions, such as taboos and totemic social structures. Although the categorical imperative rejects any conscious, rational motivation on Freud's interpretation, it can still be said to follow from unconscious motives. The law's (taboo's) task is to obstruct direct access to that which is prohibited. This is the point of Freud's interpretation of religion as morality: it both represses and stages (hence, repeats) an inner dynamic of love, hate, and sense of guilt.

Lacan's approach is dialectical: He reconstructs the law from desire and vice versa, saying the law evokes desire. At the basis of this account stand his views concerning the imaginary and symbolic order.[13] According to Lacan, the first identity-forming stage of life is called imaginary. It is characterized by the dual relationship of child and mother, and what Lacan calls the mirror stage. This stage gives rise to one's first sense of identity through identification with an image of oneself. In the mirror the child's bodily unity is reflected, a reflection that implies alienation since the image is different from the original – the image as ego ideal does not exist (Lacan, 1978, pp. 61–77).[14] For all later identifications this model is an elaboration of Freud's theory of narcissism, as well as a critique of those psychoanalytic theories insisting on ego-integration or self-realization. The next stage begins with symbolic castration. The father confronts the child with a prohibition on the mother as an exclusive object of possession and to be possessed (devoured) by.[15] The child is thus confronted by the fact that it cannot possess everything it and the mother want. For this reason the child will have to specify its desires in its own unique way. The father thus introduces the child into the cultural world in which it seeks the fulfillment of specified desires in a symbolic way.[16] It is in this context that we can situate the relation between law and desire. The transition from the imaginary to the symbolic as depicted in Lacan's version of the Oedipus complex is marked by a prohibition – the law of the father – on the mutually possessive relation of the child with the mother, one in which the selfish satisfaction of needs is central. Entrance into the symbolic order entails the introduction of a fundamental lack – something is prohibited. It is from this lack that desire emanates.

In *The Ethics of Psychoanalysis* Lacan argues that the child's relationship with the mother is one of ambivalence, like that of each and every relationship with one's fellow human beings, with the *Nebenmensch*. Here he is referring to a short passage in Freud's *Project for a Scientific Psychology* regarding memory and judgment. According to Freud, the child perceives certain traits of the other as familiar when it succeeds in recognizing and associating these traits, via memory, with one's own traits and movements of the body. Not every trait of the other can, however, be understood. There is always an aspect that remains "strange" – the other as other. This otherness makes an impression as it ties together the recognizable traits in an obscure unity. Freud refers to this incognizable other as *Ding* (Freud, 1895, p. 331).[17] Lacan picks up on this idea and regards this complex as a model for the perception of all objects: "The *Ding* is the element that is initially isolated by the subject in his experience of the *Nebenmensch* as being by its very nature alien, *Fremde*" (Lacan, 1992, p. 52; Juranville, 1984, pp. 215–232; Boothby, 2001, ch. 4; Moyaert, 2002, ch. 4;

Moyaert, 2012). Every object is thus both familiar and strange: on the one hand an object is perceived as coinciding with needs and interests, wishes and expectations (caring, protecting) and qualified by its attributes, and on the other it also reveals itself as an essentially incognizable non-attribute. In every object there is a kernel that resists representation, symbolization, and hence socialization.

Lacan argues that the Thing (*la Chose*) is the ultimate object of desire, a focal point around which are organized representations and desire regulated by the pleasure principle – the Thing is a non-symbolized, unimaginable object there like a black hole in the centre of the universe. This Thing has affinities with the Kantian *Ding*, a reference that can be traced back to *Totem and Taboo* and Freud's analysis of the categorical imperative: the *Ding* "is a forbidden good". It is the "foundation of the moral law" – and at the same time desire for the Thing should be understood as an effect of the law; the Thing gains weight and importance in light of the fact it is forbidden (Lacan, 1992, p. 70). According to Lacan, desire for the Thing is a melancholic desire always aimed at (re-)finding that which is regarded as the good *par excellance* (the Sovereign Good) that provides enjoyment (*jouissance*). The mother as the object of incestuous desire and as prehistoric Other could represent this good. It is precisely the object of this incestuous desire that gives us a clear indication of the cause of desire, as well as why Lacan names this cause the foundation of the moral law. This object is the forbidden object of desire – a prohibition introduced by the father. Desire is thus a reaction to limitation – it is caused by the law of the father.

A person "cannot stand the extreme good that *das Ding* may bring him", says Lacan (Idem, p. 73). Attaining this Thing implies a transgression of the pleasure principle and the law that prohibits access to enjoyment, shielding the subject from against the self-destructive inclinations of egocentricity since, according to Lacan, "jouissance is evil", "it is suffering", it is pain. Lacan here invokes Freud's notion of the death drive as depicted in *Beyond the Pleasure Principle*. Not only are the drives organized in terms of the pleasure principle, procuring pleasure as an avoidance of displeasure and release of tension, but they also incite a kind of compulsion to repeat (trauma), stage painful experiences, or resist a cure (negative therapeutic reaction). Within Freudian thought his conception of the death drive is highly speculative, but shows at the very least that something within the human being resists personal development, integration, and growth. In this sense it expresses a moral conviction, namely, that there exists a drive towards a primal state in which neither love nor hate are tamed, one in which the primal self-destructive drives are neither yet organized nor controlled by civilization (Westerink, 2009b, pp. 167–174). The death instinct is not for Lacan a separate drive distinguished from Eros but an aspect of every drive. It is thus also an aspect of desire.

Not all desires aim directly at an ultimate object, nor is the Thing desire's only object. The desire that law, lack, and limitation evoke moves in two directions. The law organizes a number of desires within certain limits, for example, doing good works and being virtuous, which is to say, caring for oneself and others, pursuing socially acceptable ideals, and finding a form of satisfaction in the profitable *Ersatzobjekte* as determined by culture, and last but certainly not least, finding pleasure in the articulation of one's own identity ("I am …"). Socialization brings about certain advantages that Freud emphasizes time and again when he argues that culture is a necessary protection against a variety of inner and outer threats – although culture is unlikely to provide happiness at least it protects against unhappiness. Likewise, neither does Lacan deny advantages associated with the individual's socialization in a cultural environment that demands social duties (Lacan, 1992, p. 324; Moyaert, 2012). On the contrary, by organizing desire the symbolic order liberates the individual from the imaginary's devouring entanglement. The law of the father signals the possibility of desire's expression within the parameters of the symbolic (Boothby, 2001, p. 174). It offers the possibility of expressing one's individuality. But individuality is more than just an effect of socialization – there always remains an essential aspect that resists adaptation, one that resists integration in a cultural field where people have a role or function used for the common welfare and, as such, are thus interchangeable–exchangeable.[18] Desire for the Thing shows that man's natural tendency to take up moral and cultural obligations and useful social rules is by no means self-evident.[19] There is a pure desire unencumbered by care for oneself or others – unrestricted, unconditional, absolute (*absolvere* means "to free", "to let go" or "to complete") that can be seen in the great classic tragedies where desire is pushed to its limits (the tragic hero's death instead of adjustment or compromise), in mysticism (the mystic's exlusive longing for union with the one divine object), as well as in the stubborn, even unreasonable defence of theological and moral positions against all odds (Moyaert, 1994, pp. 27–28). Hence, this desire is recognizable in Luther's disavowal of church practices and authorities, and all the medieval *Sautheologen* before him.

On this point Lacan reverses the Freudian relation between religion and morality. Freud tends to reduce religion when his focus is on religion as the representation or expression of morality, regarding religion primarily as the outcome and playground of guilt. Lacan supplements the field of morality with reference to religion, in order to point at what lies beyond the domain of the law. Although religion is certainly situated within the symbolic order, when discussing the ultimate object of desire – that which falls outside the symbolic and beyond the law – religion has for Lacan a privileged reference: religion is capable of conceptualizing the relation between law and desire, as well as the Thing as object of desire.

This reading and short presentation of Lacan's thoughts on desire and the Thing, as both desired good and strangely evil, is necessary to understand some of his references to religion in the seminar on the ethics of psychoanalysis.[20] In the passage used as our starting point to investigate the cultural paternity between Reformation thought and Freud, Lacan mentions, after all, the Thing and its relation to law. According to Lacan, Luther "published his *De servo arbitrio* in order to emphasize both the fundamentally bad character of the relations between men and the fact that at the heart of man's destiny is the *Ding*". A few sentences later he writes:

> That hatred which existed even before the world was created is the correlative of the relationship that exists between a certain influence of the law as such and a certain conception of *das Ding* as the fundamental problem, in a word, as the problem of evil.
>
> (Lacan, 1992, p. 97)

Freud shows that hatred is indeed, argues Lacan, the constant factor in the relationship between law and the Thing. In *Totem and Taboo* it is the tyrant of the primitive horde that, by his example, evokes both a desire for the horde's women and hatred against him. It is this tyrant that "for that very reason introduced the order, essence, and foundation of the domain of the law" (Idem).

Lacan claims that Luther recognizes, "that at the heart of man's destiny is the *Ding*". This remark is intriguing. It expresses his view that the Thing is cause – *la chose* means the cause – of desire, as well as desire's ultimate yet prohibited object. This Thing is indeed a destiny, as the constitutive cause of and that around which the symbolic coalesces, and although the symbolic law is capable of binding a large part of desire, the Thing always exerts its presence and calls into question the law. "That is why Christians in their most routine observances", says Lacan, "are never at peace". Whenever one is seriously called to do the good and avoid evil, the question arises "for the good of whom?" or "at what price?" It is here that the Thing appears as a question mark in the field of social regulations and duties, as the object of a transgressive desire.

It is the above mentioned dialectic of law and Thing that Lacan addresses when noting a correlation between the "evil", prohibited Thing and law, and Luther's thought on the created world and God's preceding hatred. We address this in detail in the proceeding chapters. In *The Ethics of Psychoanalysis* Luther is not the only religious author in whose thought Lacan finds a correlation. The same procedure is evident in his interpretation of Saint Paul's *Epistle to the Romans*, Chapter 7. The relationship between the Thing and law is nowhere better defined than by Paul in his epistle, says Lacan, arguing that what Paul calls sin – *ἁμαρτία*, sin, means "lack" or "want" – is equivalent to the Thing (Idem, pp. 83–84; Lacan, 2005, p. 29). Lacan says this epistle is a text in which Paul demonstrates that 1) we only know sin and desire through the law (Rom 7:7), 2) without law sin is powerless (Rom 7:8), and 3) through the law sin comes to life, gains importance, and becomes excessive – a coming to life that eventually leads to death (Rom 7:9–10). To protect against sin and guarantee pleasure within its parameters the law is introduced, and yet it is only through law that sin takes on an excessive, transgressive character: the conscious believer rather than the ignorant sinner is one who knows himself to be a sinner. Lacan asserts that this psychological truth is revealed by Paul.[21] At the heart of human destiny lies sin. It is this sin that comes to light in relation to the law, which, says Lacan, leads Luther to emphasize a hatred that flames up in relation to the law, that is to say, a desire that goes beyond faith, a fundamental passion that exists before the world is created, and that, infused in man, distorts all relations between man and God.

It is worth noting that Lacan's interpretation of Paul's *Epistle to the Romans* is remarkably close to Luther's. Luther points out repeatedly that only a promulgated law, i.e. one transmitted orally or written down, is "an opportunity for sinning". Moses' only intention, says Luther, was "through the law to reveal sin", and he says that Paul expresses the same: "Through the law comes nothing more than knowledge of sin" (Luther, 1523/1545, III-242). In an introduction to the *Epistle to the Romans*, Luther says that, "the law increases sin" (Luther, 1522/1546, III-367).[22] And in *The Bondage of the Will* he repeats this sentiment: the function and effect of law is to disclose "sickness, sin, evil, death, hell, the wrath of God, though it affords no help and brings no deliverance from these" to the ignorant (Luther, 1525a, III-262). Hence, the law not only reveals sin and increases its weight, but it also reveals God's wrath. It thereby discloses a "twofold evil", one "inward" and the other "outward", namely, human nature's corruption and the evil inflicted by God in the form of wrath, respectively.[23] Through the law these two forms of evil are closely related, and it is precisely this connection between evil as cause of the law (God's hatred) and as effect of the law (sin) that are united in Lacan's view on the relation between Thing and law. In the next chapter we further reflect on this relationship between cause and effect.

Moses' and Kant's Thing

There is another important reference to religion that, in my opinion, brings us once again to Luther via a detour. At a certain point in his seminar, Lacan argues that Freud's essay on Moses and monotheism "is founded on the notion of Moses the Egyptian and of Moses the Midianite" (Lacan, 1992, p. 173). Moses the Egyptian is a prince who chooses a people for himself, a people to continue the monotheistic project pharaoh Akhenaton begins. This figure represents a kind of moral and rational thought – the type of intellectuality Judaism later advances in and through identification with this great, enlightened man. Moses the Egyptian is a lawgiver. Moses the Midianite only takes a position of prominence after Moses the Egyptian is murdered by the Semitic tribes who wander through the desert, finally joining other Semitic tribes at Kadesh. The Midianite Moses is an obscurantist, a priest-like shaman figure belonging to a barbaric cult that worships the volcano god Jahve. It is this

Moses that, says both Freud and Lacan, can be related to God's revelation in the burning bush, that is to say, not the God who provides Moses with a social duty to free his people from slavery, but the God who reveals himself as "I am what I am" (Ex 3:14), "a God who introduces himself as an essentially hidden God". Lacan refers to this revelation as "Moses's Thing" (Idem, pp. 173–174).[24] This part of the revelation concerns neither law-giving nor social order; it does not refer to attributes with which man can relate or comprehend. This self-revelation points, in fact, towards the hidden and inaccessible essence of God. Anyone who reads the Exodus text will notice that Moses is not obliged to fulfill his task in the name of this God – not the least because Moses is ineloquent. The reason for this can be found in the fact that his calling makes Moses an eccentric, one who will probably be rejected by both his own people and the Egyptian court. In other words, Moses is asked to sacrifice his relatively secure life as shepherd in the service of his father-in-law Jethro for a life that is only guaranteed by a God who promises safety (Ex 4: 19) and yet also threatens to kill him (Ex 4:24–26). In his seminar on the four fundamental concepts of psychoanalysis, Lacan refers to the revelation of this God "who is" when reflecting on the issue of sacrifice, specifically, the suffering one is willing to undergo "for the presence of the desire of this Other that I call here *the dark God*" (Lacan, 1998b, p. 275). Moses' Thing is indeed depicted by Lacan as "dark God", one whose desires and demands are not restricted by a rational law – the fact that this God reveals himself as the God of Abraham, Isaak, and Jacob already points in this direction. It is a God who not only promises the fulfillment of desire but also demands an obedience that leads to possible suffering and death – we need only think of Abraham's obedience when asked to sacrifice his son Isaak.

But is this dark God to which Lacan refers an idea actually dating from the time Exodus was compiled and edited? The answer to this question is not really. The story of Moses' calling and God's revelation as "who is" reflects the intentions of its main composers. The Jahvist tradition stresses the universality of God's lasting bond with creation and his people, and presents Jahve as a God who leads his people out of Egypt to the Promised Land. The Elohist tradition, regarded as responsible for accounts of God's self-revelation, stresses God's transcendence and presents Moses as his medium of liberation (Schmidt, 1989, pp. 72–90). The distinction between a God who reveals himself in a cognizable way and a God who hides his essence is, in fact, an idea that emerges in medieval nominalism. For example, we find it in the work of William of Ockham (?1287–1347) when he reflects on the distinction between *potentia ordinata* and *potentia absoluta*. Luther provides a new interpretation and application of this distinction in *The Bondage of the Will*, when he writes of *Deus praedicatus* (*Deus revelatus*) and *Deus absconditus*. We therefore find the first conceptualization of a dark, hidden God precisely where we would have expected, at the moment when nominalism critiques Aristotelian-Thomistic theology, when the view that man's natural and rational inclinations are in harmony with a reasonable-moral order established by the Supreme Good is called into question.[25]

Traces of Luther's conception of God as revealing but at the same time fundamentally hidden can also be found in Lacan's reading of Immanuel Kant (1724–1804). Lacan says that Kant represents a Christian tradition that pays "little attention to God's jouissance". This is "how Kant makes palatable his voluntarism of Law-for-Law's sake". Lacan argues that Kant decides on his doctrine of the categorical imperative – commanding that one should do one's duty for the sake of doing one's duty – because he feels pressured by "some nearby mystic", namely, Emanuel Swedenborg (1688–1772), who glimpses what lies beyond the law: the *Grimmigkeit* of a faceless God, says Lacan, or in the words of Sade a "supreme-evil-being" (Lacan, 2006, pp. 772–773). Kant thereby avoids conceptualizing God's *jouissance*, being raised as he was in a strict, pietistic Lutheran environment, one from which he distanced himself. Lacan nevertheless links this *jouissance* to *das Ding* as *la Chose*, the cause that lies behind all that which can be perceived, a "dumb reality" that commands and regulates (Lacan, 1992, p. 55). This is precisely what Kant wants to exclude, *Religionsschwärmereien*, "a way of rediscovering", says Lacan, "the relationship to *das Ding* somewhere beyond the law" (Idem, p. 84). Swedenborg *avec* Kant: two Lutherans reflecting in their own ways on the relation between the law's influence and a conception of *das Ding*. That Kant pays little attention to God's *jouissance* is contiguous with an important aspect of Luther's thought: from a philosophical perspective he warns of the hidden God's will. As we will see, such inquiry causes melancholia and despair – it opposes faith, says Luther, and opposes reason, says Kant. And yet, in Swedenborg a complementary aspect of Luther's thought becomes visible: this hidden God as cause of the created world and revelation is always present beyond his works and words – he cannot be avoided, he has to be glimpsed (David-Ménard, 1990).

Double government

Conscience is an important psychological element of Luther's thought. His teachings on sin and the will's bondage, critique of good merits, and rejection of the scholastic views concerning *synderesis* and conscience are important because of the theological and psychological innovations they initiate, as well as the roles they play in the development of theories of conscience in Reformation thought (Baylor, 1977; Langston, 2001).[26] In Chapter 4 we look more closely at the crucial role Luther and Calvin play in the transformation of the concept of conscience. In scholasticism and late medieval thought, conscience was generally considered the application of *synderesis* – the natural innate habit of practical reason by which man could apprehend moral principles – in everyday judgment and moral action. Luther argues that conscience should not be understood as a power to act but one to judge the sinful inner state of man before God. What conscience judges, first and foremost, is that human nature as completely corrupted by original sin.

Although both Luther and Calvin reject *synderesis*, they do not completely reject natural law for several reasons (Pearson, 2010) but they will give the concept a new meaning. Calvin argues that sin indicates a state in which man is deprived of natural knowledge of the good. Only through an act of grace does a person receive the faith necessary to truly obey God's law. The fact that just sinners doing good works exist is a sign of the fact that God might curb "the perverseness of nature, preventing it from breaking forth into action, yet without rendering it inwardly pure" (Calvin, 1559a, 2.3.3).[27] These virtues indicate that God limits sinfulness for the sake of maintaining basic social structures, since society's existence would be unimaginable if everybody simply acted on his or her sinfulness. Beside this function of natural law, there is also a spiritual conscience that Calvin defines as an inner knowledge of God's will that accuses and excuses man's inner state, according to God's judgment (Calvin, 1559a, 3.19.15–16, 4.10.3). Calvin calls this construct the "double government" of outer behaviour and inner spiritual life. Whereas reason guides common conscience and only demands self-control for the sake of social life, spiritual conscience is tyrannically scrutinizing, admonishing and testifying against sin: "They [sinners, H.W.] are terrified and confused by conscience, which is the most agonizing of all torments and the most cruel of all executioners" (Bouwsma, 1988, p. 41).

We thus see the emergence of a completely new view regarding conscience, namely, as a psychic faculty with two functions: the government of both outer (social) and inner (spiritual) affairs. It is my view that this distinction reappears in Lacanian psychoanalysis, in the filiation between Luther/Calvin and Lacan. Elaborating on Freud's theories concerning the superego's formation, Lacan argues for the existence of an oedipal conscience that forms through an identification with the father's authority. This conscience, which he refers to as "collective", organizes desire in the symbolic order by demanding desire's fulfillment in socially-acceptable ideals and aims (Lacan, 2006, p. 137).[28] However, Lacan follows Klein and others in presuming pre-oedipal conscience formation. In short, not only is there a collective superego inciting us to pursue socially acceptable, moral goals but also a more primitive superego that pushes desire for the ultimate object, which does not provide pleasure as the reduction in tension but *jouissance* as a painful enjoyment (Idem; Lacan, 1975, pp. 164–165; Moyaert, 2012). It has no interest in curbing the perverseness of nature to maintain social structures or pursue pragmatic consensus. Instead it presses the individual to a Thing that absorbs him and alienates him from others.

The key words

We began investigating the cultural paternity between Luther and Freud by examining Freud's scepticism regarding liberal Protestant thought. We ended with a thesis regarding a filiation between Calvin and Lacan –Lacan's reading of Luther's *The Bondage of the Will*, one that emphasizes God's eternal hatred – a hatred "that existed even before the world was created" – might in fact be called a Calvinist reading of Luther (Lacan, 1992, p. 97).[29] These two points framed a discussion of theological themes that connect Reformation thought with both Freudian and Lacanian thought. The key issues to be discussed in the next chapters are the following: supralapsarian predestination and the will's bondage; God's hatred, original sin, and the knowledge thereof; natural and divine law; common as well as spiritual conscience.

Chapter 2

The will and the hidden God

Luther's theology represents an inaugural moment in a new direction of thought that influences the lives and thoughts of people that at the same time continues a number of intellectual debates that began in the Middle Ages. In order to understand Reformation thought's commitment regarding predestination, God's hidden will and hatred, the denial of human free will, man's inclination towards evil, and the disavowal of good works (the main topics of this chapter) the medieval roots of these commitments have to be considered. It is against this backdrop that we will be able to see in which ways Reformation thought can be regarded as a new direction of thought, one that anticipates the hardcore of psychoanalytic thought. Central to this chapter then, is Lacan's claim that Luther's concept of a "hatred which existed even before the world was created" is the correlative of the relationship Freud discovers at the heart of both individual and cultural life. This is the relationship "between a certain influence of the law as such and a certain conception of *das Ding* as the fundamental problem, in a word, as the problem of evil", in other words, a dialectic between a divine cause beyond good and evil on the one hand, and everything created or revealed as good on the other hand.

The emergence of the dark God

Medieval scholastic theology is based on two main pillars. First, there is the unified Catholic Church with its strict hierarchical order that provides authority to theological and moral thought. Second, scholastic thought is largely realist in the medieval sense of the term, that is to say, it is based on a belief in the existence of universals of which particular things or individual human beings are actualizations, expressions, or appearances. Through either divine revelation or an investigation of nature the individual comes to know these universals, these abstract principles and ideas. These two pillars are representative of the same fundamental commitment: natural order and purpose reflect God's reason and goodness. This is the broader metaphysical framework in which moral thought is embedded. God is the Supreme Good and, as such, can be neither the cause nor source of evil – evil is conceived as the absence of good. In the writings of Aquinas *synderesis* indicates the naturally innate habit or disposition of practical reason through which man apprehends both basic and general moral principles of natural law. Conscience is the application and regulation of this intuitive moral knowledge in every day judgments and actions. Reason is, therefore, the rule and measure of both what is and what should be done – with respect to people's knowledge of these Scripture it is largely negligible (Aquinas, 1984, I.II.94; Lottin, 1949; Greene, 1997; Pope, 2002). Hence, scholastic thought is based on reason and authority, and it is precisely at this point, at its very roots, that this world starts breaking down and new theological models appear.

Taken together, a focus on reason, the rise of universities and intellectual scholarship, and subsequent intellectual debates and their corresponding schools inevitably gave rise to questions concerning the predominant theological systems and their basic premises. This is the broader context for the rise of two schools – often intertwined – that are of importance to us: nominalism (*via moderna*) and the renaissance of Augustinian thought (*schola Augustiniana moderna*). The first movement is primarily associated with William of Ockham, as well as the Franciscan order, and various forms and schools at different universities such as Paris, Heidelberg, and Tübingen. The second movement is related to the Augustinian order and universities such as Oxford (Thomas Bradwardine) and Paris (Gregory of Rimini). Two aspects of nominalism deserve our attention: Ockham's distinction between *potentia absoluta* and *potentia ordinata*, and his voluntarism. Concerning Augustinian thought our focus will be on the doctrine of predestination.

Nominalism's fearsome God

Behind Ockham's distinction between *potentia absoluta* and *potentia ordinata* stands a basic question, namely, whether "God could be said to act reliably without simultaneously implying that he acted of necessity" (McGrath, 1987, p. 78). This issue is fundamental as it calls into question God's omnipotence. If God acts reliably then he cannot be said to act arbitrarily; if he acts out of necessity then his actions are determined by external constraints. Ockham defends God's omnipotence, arguing that God is capable and has the freedom to actualize any hypothetical possibility provided this possibility is not self-contradictory. He assumes that God has actualized a number of possibilities and that – for reasons known only to God – other possibilities remain unactualized. With respect to all initial possibilities God is absolutely free and omnipotent – *potentia absoluta*. Given his choice of actualizations – his ordained power, *potentia ordinata* – God is also reliable, as he imposes on himself an obligation to respect the established order. This is sealed with a covenant, a "contract" between man and God, which not only guarantees God's reliability but also includes a promise of justification as reward to those who have put forth a sufficient moral effort (*facientibus*-principle). Those that sufficiently avoid evil and do good will be saved. As in scholastic thought, it is assumed that people are knowledgeable of basic moral principles and free to choose either good or evil (Idem, pp. 75ff; Miethke, 1969, pp. 137–163).

Heiko Oberman rightfully describes Ockham's nominalism as follows: "What is often called Ockham's razor is the slashing away of the hierarchy of being, of ideas and concepts, which sheer speculation had invented" (Oberman, 1992, p. 27). Ockham indeed insists "on the full reality of our experienced world", which means that – from a psychological point of view – issues such as God's reliability, the assurance of grace and salvation, obedience to God, and moral effort are no longer situated within a larger ontological framework, but bound to human experience. Since Ockham relates salvation and justification to divine reliability and a covenant, and seeks to reconcile man's capacity to apprehend moral principles, the free will of man and God, and God's omnipotence, his teachings seem to provide a steady basis for faith's assurance.

And yet Ockham's thought is a new source of major uncertainty. For example, what do "sufficiently moral efforts" consist of? How can a person be assured of salvation? In his teachings on predestination and reprobation he argues that what is true eternally can be false temporally, since any proposition regarding a future event is contingent by nature. A future event is contingent if, and only if, it is possible both that the event will and will not occur. Propositions are only necessarily true once they have occurred in reality. Any proposition regarding a person's predestination to either salvation or damnation is, thus, only necessarily true once the person is actually saved or damned. Whether God will actually save or damn a person does not necessarily depend on anything a person does or does not do, since there is nothing intrinsic to sin that brings about damnation. Salvation can thus be based on merit, but it can also be the exclusive effect of God's grace – God can justify a person without contrition. Reprobation is caused by man's sins, yet God can also annihilate a man despite his good works or even command a believer to hate him. In this way Ockham secures God's omnipotence; his will is neither bound to the will and acts of a person nor obstructed by a person's future choices. God is not indebted to anyone and, logically, he has the power to interact with that which he creates when and how he wants. The choices God makes do not depend on criteria that seem morally appropriate from a human perspective but on whether they serve his hidden purposes (Ockham, 1983; Leff, 1957; Halverson, 1998, pp. 113–122; McCord Adams, 1999; Levi, 2002, p. 56). Ockham's teaching stresses the necessity of contingency on logical grounds without thereby equating contingency and unreliability, and his doctrine on the covenant seems to guarantee salvation through good works based on knowledge of moral principles (Oberman, 1992, p. 27). However, from a logical point of view, the gains he makes on this front are "negated by their [Ockham and his followers, H.W.] commitment to a divine power that determined everything absolutely but did so in an utterly arbitrary and therefore unpredictable way" (Gillespie, 2008, p. 29). A person is asked to do that of which he is capable (*facientibus*-principle) but he can never know whether he has done so sufficiently, nor is he ever sure of justification. This raises feelings of anxiety, incapacity, and deficiency (Hamm, 2004, ch. 3).

Some of Ockham's followers, such as Robert Holcot (?1290–1349), accept the inevitable consequences of assuming that God's will determines that which is good and that which is not: only God determines what counts as sin and merit. A person should act in a moral manner, to the extent that he is capable, simply because such behaviour is appropriate, although God could still either condemn or reward a person regardless of how they lived (Leff, 1957, pp. 216–227; Oberman, 1992, pp. 84–93). The conclusions of John of Mirecourt (?1300–?1349) are more radical. He argues that God's will "is necessary for every event and is always efficacious, causes not only the physical human act which is sinful, but even the moral specification of the sinful act precisely as sinful". In other words, what God wills to be sin is sin, and in this sense God is the cause (although not the author) of sin (Levi, 2002, p. 64). The nominalist Adam of Wodeham (?1300–1358) thought through Ockham's position to its limits. In his view God's will is bound by neither obligation nor contract. God simply wills what he wants, unrestrained by principles, laws, rules, or even his own Word. He can thus elect sinners and condemn believers: there is no relation between human moral action and divine reward. God can even deceive and mislead, go against his own beliefs and sin, since his will is not subjected to anything, not even his own knowledge of moral principles. Thinking through God's *potentia absoluta* Wodeham thus eliminates the relationship between transcendence and creation. What remains is the free will of God on the one hand, and the human capacity to will and do good on the other (Leff, 1957, pp. 241–254).

These nominalists understand God's righteousness as depending on the arbitrary decision of his will, and God's righteousness and goodness are consequently undermined. Good and evil thoughts and acts are those that God arbitrarily decides to be good and evil. Consequently, it is no longer possible to comprehend God's supposed goodness since he can demand that which seems unreasonable and contrary to basic moral ideas and promises. Michael Gillespie is thus correct when he writes:

> Nominalism sought to tear the rationalistic veil from the face of God in order to found a true Christianity, but in doing so it revealed a capricious God, fearsome in his power, unknowable, unpredictable, unconstrained by nature and reason, and indifferent to good and evil.
>
> (Gillespie, 2008, p. 29)

In terms of its speculative consequences nominalism undoubtedly undermines not only a Thomistic view on humanity's participation in the divine via the mediation of natural law, but also its conception of an absolutely free and indifferent God with the potential of turning universal order to insecure chaos. But whether this "dark God of nominalism" is the cause of profound uncertainty among believers is open to question (Idem). As we will see in the next section the immediate response was primarily academic.

A fifteenth century follower of Ockham, Gabriel Biel (?1415–1495) – whose thought had a profound influence on scholars at the University of Wittenberg, including Luther – is more moderate, less academic, and more pastorally theological (Oberman, 1963, p. 424), than Ockham's abovementioned early followers. Biel also believes that God's will precedes any and all moral principles, and that God can thus overrule any established moral norm, thereby doing something that seems unjust. For any act of God is indeed its own justification. Hence, God's will determines that which is just, and he can do whatever he wants without ever being unjust (Idem, pp. 96ff). Yet, according to Biel, God's reliability need not be doubted since God imposes on himself an obligation to respect the established order. The radical consequences of nominalist thought are thus only logical, merely academic thought constructs. God could indeed command a believer to hate him, for example, but He would not establish an order in which such a command would be needed; this logical possibility is merely speculative (Idem, pp. 93–95).

The Augustinian way: far from loving all mankind

In the previous chapter I mentioned Aquinas as a representative of the scholastic view on predestination. God is neither the cause nor source of evil. He shows his goodness in a twofold manner – mercy for the elect and justice for the reprobates. No person is condemned to punishment except by reason of his own iniquity. Damnation is thus the effect of human beings freely choosing evil and persisting in sin. God's punishment is a just response – punishment understood in the sense of ignoring the reprobates, thereby leaving them to effect their own exclusion from salvation. "Lack" of election corresponds to a lack of goodness on the part of the reprobate. We have also seen that Ockham both emphasizes human free will and divine omnipotence. The very idea that sinners are punished and others saved, the plan of predestination, is a matter of God's free choice. And since there is nothing intrinsic to sin that necessarily leads to damnation, Ockham can insist that God saves only through an act of divine grace, and can damn a virtuous person (*potentia absoluta*). Yet he emphasizes the fact that reprobation is the effect of freely choosing evil and persisting in sin. As it happens (*potentia ordinata*), sin precedes God's punishment and merit precedes God's reward.

The fourteenth century saw the rice of academic Augustinianism, especially at the universities of Oxford and Paris. This movement is based mainly on Augustine's late writings against the semi-Pelagians. Ockham and his followers are now labelled "modern Pelagians". There are two main problems: the Ockhamist interpretation of 1) *potentia absoluta* as the realm of past, present, and future possibilities; and 2) *potentia ordinata* as the realm of experience and perception, and of the established moral order and natural law in and through which a person is free to choose good or evil. In its extreme versions these two orders act independently of one another. According to the Augustinian opponents, the modern Pelagians indeed reveal a capricious God, unknowable, unpredictable, unconstrained by either nature or reason, and indifferent to good and evil. God is so unknowable, free, and omnipotent that it is impossible to detect any constant order in his actions. There is no correspondence or causal relation between his will and man's deeds, nor is there any empirically certain knowledge of God. God simply transcends every human action and established moral order. This moral order is thus "the most fleeting of contingencies" (Leff, 1957, p. 132; Oberman, 1957, pp. 34–43). Their introduction of the so-called *facientibus*-principle – that a person should make sufficient moral effort to be rewarded with salvation – does not obviate the logical conclusion that "man was made virtually independent of God" (Leff, 1957, p. 135).

Like Ockham, the archbishop of Canterbury Thomas Bradwardine (?1290–1349) also emphasizes God's omnipotence. Instead of focusing on absolute and arbitrary possibilities, however, he stresses God's constant operation – God's will is the cause of the human will's movement, both at the moment and for the duration of time a person is willing (or desiring) something (Oberman, 1957, p. 110). There is thus an immediate connection between God's will and the human will This connection is desirable and good since man's natural condition is so weak that without grace any and all people, says Bradwardine, would sin continually (Leff, 1957, p. 59). His defence of God's sovereignty and the grace he bestows to protect humans against their own sinfully-inclined autonomy is reflected in Bradwardine's doctrine of predestination: "predestination does not happen on account of human works, but on account of the gracious will of God" (Idem, p. 115). For the elect this means that grace, faith, and – consequently – merit lead to reward and salvation. As to reprobation, he argues that by sinning man introduces damnation, that is to say, by refusing to accept grace man condemns himself. Because of this refusal God further withholds his efficient grace, which would result in salvation. Hence, God does not actively damn a sinner, and yet given the fact that, according to Bradwardine, God's permission is always also an act, and that God is constantly and actively participating in his creation (Idem, pp. 58–59), this refusal can be interpreted as a positive act. Since God is the cause of all that exists, he is also the cause of sin. God permits sin "as an agent for good" by contrast since only through contrast can goodness be conceived (Leff, 1957, p. 60; Wilks Dolnikowski, 1995, p. 200).

Bradwardine's direct influence on Reformation thought must, however, be doubted.[1] He is nonetheless an important scholar in terms of his revival of Augustinian thought in opposition to the supposed Pelagianism of Ockham, and in his anticipation of Luther in the absolute denial of merit and free will. The work of Gregory of Rimini more directly influences Luther, whom Luther praises as his sole companion against all scholastic scholars (Luther, 1519).

Rather than rejecting *via moderna* – as Bradwardine does – Rimini upholds central tenets of Ockham's thought (Leff, 1961a, b; Santos Noya, 1990; Bermon, 2007). He agrees to the distinction between *potentia absoluta* and *potentia ordinata*, not for the sake of speculating on God's free will and arbitrariness, but to reset these in order to be compatible with God's nature. He agrees with Ockham that creation is contingent and God can overrule the natural order if he so wills, but disagrees with Ockham's claim that God's will is the only criterion for determining good and evil. God is good and just, and for this reason he can neither act in an evil manner nor be unjust. Hence, he cannot mislead, lie, nor demand that a person hate him. If He were to do so then he would not be God, and to suggest that God can do evil and be unjust, e.g. be the author of a sinful act, is a denial of his nature. Qualities such as goodness and justice do not depend on God's will but are attributes of his nature. Given these attributes God would not will something in opposition to this nature. In fact, it is via God's will that human beings have knowledge of his nature, since God's nature can only be grasped through the laws and commandments that he reveals. In this way it is clear that Rimini gives more weight to Scripture than his nominalist opponents.

These revealed laws and commandments have to be obeyed. Rimini does not follow Bradwardine on this point, in radically rejecting man's free will and emphasizing a general human weakness. Instead he turns to Augustine's interpretation of the Fall and original sin. Concupiscence leads to moral impotence, a fundamental distortion of the natural inclination to good. Human beings are still capable of performing moral duties (with the aid of God's habitual grace), but to be morally good and free from sin requires a special, efficacious grace that infuses God's love as the *sine qua non* of moral goodness. This efficacious grace precedes the habitual, sufficient grace needed to establish cooperation between the human will and God. The Fall is thus a crucial moment in the history of salvation (McGrath, 1987, pp. 91–92). Only the love of God and strict, subsequent obedience to his will are the basis of a morally good life.

Whether or not God gives his grace is independent of merit and demerit, but is grounded solely in a doctrine of predestination. Radicalizing Augustine's later views on double predestination, Rimini is the first to argue that before establishing the world God predestines some for eternal life and some for eternal damnation. He writes:

> Whoever is predestined has been predestined by the mercy and graciousness of the divine will alone... and neither is anyone predestined on account of good works or the good use of free choice, nor on account of a lack of sin or whatever else renders man unworthy of eternal life,

> which God foresaw as future; but rather these things follow from this predestination.
>
> (Halverson, 1998, p. 153)

According to Rimini, election and reprobation should be assessed according to the same criteria – God deals with the elect and the reprobates in the same just manner. If the elect are elected solely on the basis of God's mercy and grace (and not on account of merit) then the reprobates are equally damned by an act of God (and not on account of demerit).[2] Rimini's decisive argument, however, is Scriptural. He provides an exegesis of the *Epistle to the Romans* 9:13, where Paul writes, "Jacob I have loved, but Esau I have hated". Rimini claims that Esau is not hated because of evil acts he will commit in the future, but because he is a reprobate, because God decides not to have mercy on him even before the foundation of the world. "God, far from loving all mankind and desiring the salvation of all individuals, deliberately discriminated between them, choosing to elect some and damn others" (Leff, 1961b, p. 168).

What he ought to do, not what he can do

Thus far I have outlined late medieval positions for the sake of introducing issues Luther takes up and elaborates on in his own thought, supplementing aspects of these issues based on the historical context in which he found himself. Luther indeed follows in the footsteps of Gregory of Rimini, his sole companion against all scholastic theologians. Luther agrees with Rimini that Augustine is the most eminent theological authority after Paul: "Augustine did not quite reach the thought and sense of Saint Paul, although he came far nearer to it than the scholastics" (Delumeau, 1990, p. 263). Luther praises Augustine as the best interpreter of Scripture, the wisest among the Church Fathers, and above all as a "defender of grace" and radical opponent of Pelagianism.[3] Augustine makes it perfectly clear, says Luther, that good works and merit are meaningless, that salvation does not in any way depend on man's will but solely on God's grace. God punishes those that deserve punishment and shows mercy to those that do not deserve it. Without grace a person's will is enslaved to sin and, because of the Fall, all are in this state of enslavement. The idea of free will is a sinful illusion, empty and idle, with neither content nor reality (Forde, 2005, pp. 47ff). Augustine already made this clear, says Luther, in his opposition to Pelagius and Cassian, arguing that defending free will does not make sense given that a sinful person cannot perform a righteous act. Only a God who demands obedience can set the will free.

Whereas Paul, Augustine, and Gregory of Rimini are among the few truly enlightened and trustworthy authorities in matters of faith, sin, grace, and the enslaved will, the opponents are many. "All scholastic scholars" have erred in these matters, not the least by making Aristotelian thought the basis of their theologies and ethics. In his *Disputation against Scholastic Theology* Luther writes: "Virtually the entire *Ethics* of Aristotle is the worst enemy of grace" and "it is an error to maintain that Aristotle's statement concerning happiness does not contradict Catholic doctrine" (Luther, 1517a, IV-12). Luther presents Aristotle mainly as a philosopher that defends the ability of the individual to be righteous through virtuous action; a person can earn his salvation through good works. Luther argues on the other hand that only through faith is justification possible: "Works contribute nothing to justification. (...) His justification by faith in Christ is sufficient to him" (Luther, 1518, IV-56). Luther also refers to Aristotle as a heathen that defends a natural knowledge of God's essence and claims that man's desire naturally aims towards the Supreme Good while detesting evil (Kusukawa, 1995, pp. 32ff).[4] These so-called Aristotelian characteristics of scholasticism apply not only to *via antiqua* (Aquinas, Duns Scotus) but also *via moderna*.[5] Most scholastic scholars favor the idea of salvation through merit, a conception of *synderesis*, man's natural desire for the good, and man's freedom of the will. Luther disagrees.[6]

Nominalism is indeed a major point of reference for Luther. He was educated at the University of Erfurt (1501–1505) where he was taught scholastic thought via a nominalist approach. When appointed to teach philosophical ethics at the University of Wittenberg (1508), once again Luther found himself in an institute representative of *via moderna*.[7] His critique of nominalism – notably, those regarding man's free will and reason – grows steadily over the years. He expresses this critique in the above-mentioned disputations as well as other texts (McGrath, 1987; Oberman, 1989, 1992). In *The Bondage of the Will* Luther expresses his critique of nominalism implicitly when Erasmus is construed as a "sceptic" who speculates on God's essence, defends free will (and thus Pelagian thought) and merit, and errs around in thought constructs that, according to Luther, are typical for nominalist shrewdness.[8] Erasmus indeed worries that if one excludes the will's freedom then there will be no room for merit. In *De libero arbitrio* he basically argues for a mild Augustinian view on freedom of the will, saying that as it concerns the process of salvation and justification, divine grace is the primal cause of cooperation between the free human will and divine grace. Interestingly, this position is quite close to Rimini's: grace initiates both the desire and power to achieve good in cooperation with grace (Erasmus & Luther, 2006, pp. 18–21; Reinhuber, 2001). Yet in the midst of his furious dispute Luther associates Erasmus with Rimini's opponents.

It is now Scripture that provides Luther with an answer to Erasmus, since Paul himself writes: "There is no such thing as merit, but all who are justified, are justified freely (*gratis*), and this is to be ascribed to nothing but the grace of God" (Luther, 1525a, III-267; Gerrish, 1973). By denying free will and merit Luther implicitly distances himself from the problems the *facientibus*-principle raises. If the human will is free then a person would be in constant despair regarding his spiritual status – he could never be certain he had done enough to please God. However, this does not imply that man is totally unfree in his daily life and daily actions. It means that neither human freedom nor merit secures his justification or has significant bearing "in matters pertaining to eternal salvation" (Luther, 1525a, III-32). There is only limited freedom regarding choices and actions irrelevant with respect to salvation and justification. On the whole actions considered free are negligible, such that Luther assumes a general doctrine of divine determinism.

Luther discusses this issue at the very beginning of *The Bondage of the Will* and it provides the basis for what follows. Luther's question is "whether God foreknows anything contingently, and whether we do everything of necessity" (Idem, III-36). Luther answers, "that he foresees and purposes and does all things by his immutable, eternal, and infallible will" (Idem, III-37). The argument here recalls Rimini: if God is by nature good and just then he is immutably good and just. The same goes for other divine attributes, including God's prescience. If he knows as he wills then his will is eternal and unchanging (because so too is his nature), and if he wills as he knows then his knowledge is eternal and unchanging (because so too is his nature) (Idem). God thus works willingly and knowingly "all in all":

"From this it follows irrefutably that everything we do, everything that happens, even if it seems to us to happen mutably and contingently, happens in fact nonetheless necessarily and immutably, if you have regard to the will of God" (Idem, III-38).

Luther says that this idea is fundamental:

> Christian faith is entirely extinguished, the promises of God and the whole gospel are completely destroyed, if we teach and believe that it is not for us to know the necessary foreknowledge of God and the necessity of the things that are to come to pass.
>
> (Idem, III-43)

The will of God and the actions that follow necessarily can be neither resisted nor obstructed by anything. Luther thus defends determinism. Everything a person does only appears as contingent and mutable, that is to say, only appears as the effect of free will – a sinful illusion.

This divine determinism is part of Luther's view regarding the enslaved will of man. The main problem he addresses in *The Bondage of the Will* is indeed the *servo arbitrio*, the enslaved will, i.e. the will inclined to evil. Like Rimini before him, Luther gives full weight to Augustine's doctrine of original sin. The only act of the human will that was ever truly free is that which leads to Adam's fall. Luther sees Adam's sin as a selfish desire, a general disobedience that takes the form of a desire for self-interest and advantage in a proud and bold manner. Self-love is a perversion of that love which is oriented towards one's fellow – as Christ commands. This disposition necessarily leads to a variety of sinful acts. From original sin stems all the evils prohibited in the Ten Commandments, such as idolatry, despair, false pride, impurity, hatefulness, laziness, theft, deceit, murder, etc. Because of this original sin, man's general disposition cannot be understood in terms of reason controlling desire, a natural inclination towards the good, a natural disinclination towards evil, the ability to choose good freely while avoiding evil, or an inclination to love God and one's fellow man. In *The Bondage of the Will* we see this same line of thought at work: since all human beings are Adam's offspring, all suffer under sin and, hence, necessarily sin:

> Furthermore, seeing that through the one transgression of the one man, Adam, we are all under sin and damnation, how can we attempt anything that is not sinful and damnable? For when he says "all," he makes no exception either of the power of free choice or of any worker, but every man, whether he works or not, endeavors or not, is necessarily included among the "all." Not that we should sin or be damned through that one transgression of Adam if it were not our own transgression. For who could be damned for another's transgression, especially before God? It does not, however, become ours by any imitative doing of it ourselves, for then it would not be the one transgression of Adam, since it would be we and not Adam who committed it; but it becomes ours the moment we are born—a subject we must deal with some other time. Original sin itself, therefore, leaves free choice with no capacity to do anything but sin and be damned.
>
> (Idem, III-272)

Although human beings tend to believe that the choices they make and the acts of their will and reason are free choices and acts, reason and will are in fact enslaved by sin (MacIntyre, 2010, p. 118). A person cannot will the good, and worse still, Satan dominates him. Luther argues that the will is never in a state of indifference to either the good or God. Not willing the good does not imply that the will can withdraw into a position of neutrality or that it can simply refrain from willing anything specific. Being a sinner consists in being torn between Christ and the Antichrist: "the human will is placed between the two like a beast of burden" (Luther, 1525a, III-65).

The devil most certainly uses this opportunity not only to further enslave the will to its aim, infusing evil thoughts and deeds that oppose God, but also to add blindness to sinfulness. He does so by making people believe they are free and powerful. Only when God takes possession and control of the will is a person liberated from servitude of this type. Luther conceives of the devil primarily as God's eternal opponent, in an almost Manichaean sense (Taylor, 2007, p. 64). He is the Antichrist, the opponent of Christ who pushes man's sinful inclinations to extremes. The devil thereby completes that which is dispositionally human: an expulsion from the good and inclination to pursue evil (Oberman, 1990). What should not be overlooked in Luther's writings are his associations between this work by the devil and shit and dung, and his descriptions of humanity's corrupted state in terms of filth and rubbish. Luther indeed associates man's exclusion from a state of righteousness and expulsion into the world – and that his fallen, enslaved state deprives man of even an ounce of worth, although he proudly imagines himself as free, powerful, etc. – with images of humiliation and desolation. Man is waste product and the world is a cloaca or cesspool. Luther describes a helpless situation in which a person is dislocated – "dirt is matter in the wrong place" (Freud, 1908, pp. 172–173) – strictly dependant on God's mercy. But there is more to this. Luther wants to provoke opponents such as Erasmus (Brosché, 1978, pp. 58–61) with his scatological language, confronting them with the blind spot in their theological projects, specifically, their idle speculation regarding God's nature. Reason's overestimation is a sinful act precipitated by the devil, especially that of a theological nature without faith in Christ:

> "Yet with such a phantasmagoria Satan has frightened men away from reading the sacred writings and has made Holy Scripture contemptible, in order to enable the plagues he has bred from philosophy to prevail in the Church"
>
> (Luther, 1525a, III-25).

The blind spot of all scholastic scholars is precisely the nature of original sin, the very source from which their own thoughts and actions spring (Osmond, 1990, pp. 17–18). The model employed here is no longer that of the scholastic distinction between bodily desires as sinful on the one hand and the reasonable virtuous soul on the other hand. Instead the guiding thread here is that both the body and soul are united as sinful flesh, a unity that combats spirit. Hence, Luther's anal imagery is symptomatic of his conception of intellectual thought as part or product of the lowest bodily and instinctual inclinations – as waste matter. Not only does this recall Augustine's account of the causal relation between an unconscious desire rooted in the body and a conscious will and reason that attempt in vain to compensate for, control, and repress this desire. More importantly for us it also anticipates a core Freudian commitment: at the very root of one's being there exists bodily urges and drives that govern a person in terms of the mechanisms of the pleasure principle – pleasure as the reduction in bodily tension. Seemingly higher order intellectual activities that function by restraining the drives and provide them with a civilized character are, in fact, activities through which the pleasure principle attempts to realize its aims. Freud expresses this same idea in his second, topographical model, where the superego is described as not only functioning to repress the id, but also as the "expression of the most powerful impulses and most important libidinal vicissitudes of the id" casting the drives in a concretely ideal form – for example, the specific intellectual goal a person desires (Freud, 1911; Freud, 1923a, p. 36; Lacan, 1992, pp. 93–94). In this way then Freud presents consciousness and the body as unified, which stands in opposition to traditional body–mind dichotomies within philosophical thought that overemphasize the qualities and capacities of intellect and reason (Freud, 1938).[9] In his account of the flesh, original sin and its effects Luther anticipates this view in his critique of the scholastic views of man's ability to be rightly oriented towards God through conscious perceptions and reason.

On the other hand, God makes known to human beings how to be saved and what they should. Man "is warned and instructed as to what he ought to do, not what he is able to do; their purpose is that he may know his sin, not that he may believe himself to have any power" (Luther, 1525a, III-127). The law thus sets a standard for a good though unattainable moral life. The strength to obey this law comes only from faith, and faith is only effectuated by God's mercy. Luther formulates this as follows: "Free choice is defined as being so impotent that it can will nothing good without grace, but is forced to serve sin, though it possesses an endeavor that must not be ascribed to its own powers" (Idem, III-144). Obeying God consists in acting "against reason and against our natural will" (MacIntyre, 2010, p. 119). The worthiness of merits is a fact; salvation and justification are only possible by faith. Compared to Rimini Luther is more radical on this point. Whereas Rimini argues that God can neutralize sin with an efficacious act of grace, Luther holds that a person always remains a sinner, also when he is justified by faith – God does not expunge man's sinful disposition (Santos Noya, 1990, pp. 137–139). A believer is thus *simul iustus et peccator*: in the flesh a person is always a sinner, yet through faith in Christ, God already shows a person his mercy, and for this reason he does not punish a person because of a sinful disposition but continues to work in a person until this sin is mortified.

The notion of salvation and justification by faith is not entirely new. Augustine, Bradwardine, and Rimini also write on this. But the idea that only through faith (*sola fide*) can man be saved and justified is new. As a gift of grace this faith is infused through one's encounters with (reading, hearing) Scripture as the Word of God. Scripture not only teaches us what we ought to do (but cannot do and do not do) but it also helps us recognize sin as sin. It incites a search for forgiveness and salvation. A despair caused by the awareness of sinfulness (by law) drives us towards Christ as our saviour (the Gospel). God's Word ultimately reveals a single truth, namely, that Jesus Christ suffers and dies because of our sins, and is resurrected for our justification (Oberman, 1989, pp. 171–172; Gillespie, 2008, pp. 117–119). This is all a believer knows and needs to know:

> For what still sublimer thing can remain hidden in the Scriptures, now that the seals have been broken, the stone rolled from the door of the

> sepulcher, and the supreme mystery brought to light, namely, that Christ the Son of God has been made man, that God is three and one, that Christ has suffered for us and is to reign eternally? Are not these things known and sung even in the highways and byways? Take Christ out of the Scriptures, and what will you find left in them?
>
> (Luther, 1525a, III-26)

Faith alone saves and justifies, and God only gives it through an act of mercy. It arises exclusively from hearing the voice of God, that is, God's Word – Scripture. For this reason the Bible is more than a text that simply informs people of that which they are also capable of understanding through natural reason, specifically, a discernment between good and evil and instructions to act accordingly (as "all scholastic scholars" thought). Scripture is now the Word of God, the revealed will or solidified voice of God, which efficaciously calls to faith. God is *Deus revelatus*, ordaining his will, works, and promises in his Word (Oberman, 1989, pp. 223–225; Forde, 2005, pp. 26–30).

Below the words and works

Luther's critique of nominalism is inspired primarily by Augustinian thought and a return to that which scholastic scholars neglect: Scripture, regarded not as the momentary revelation of God who could reveal something else at any given moment, but the eternal Word of God, which calls a sinner to faith and proclaims salvation in Christ. Like Rimini, however, Luther also adopts aspects of nominalism: voluntarism – its focus on the will of God as absolutely free, an experience-oriented approach, and the distinction between *potentia absoluta* and *potentia ordinata*. Despite his constant criticisms of speculation and intellectual shrewdness, the fundamental distinction Luther makes in *The Bondage of the Will* between *Deus absconditus* and *Deus praedicatus* (*Deus revelatus*) is clearly a novel application of the distinction between the two potencies (Brosché, 1978; Oberman, 1994; Lohse, 1995; Pesch, 2004). Regarding this distinction between the hidden and revealed God, Luther writes the following: "The distinction I make—in order that I, too, may display a little rhetoric or dialectic—is this: God and the Scripture of God are two things, no less than the Creator and the creature are two things" (Luther, 1525a, III-25). We have already seen that Luther ultimately regards the Word of God as the revelation of Christ. Luther indeed argues that the incarnate son in whom all the treasures of the Godhead are hidden is God's ordained power. He thus gives a whole new meaning to *potentia ordinata*. It no longer refers to moral principles, laws, and duties intelligible to human beings that can be applied in freely willed moral actions. Luther radically rejects this model: salvation and justification are only possible though faith, i.e. believing Christ died for the sins of man and rose from the dead. Christ is thus the means to salvation, and from this perspective we can understand Luther's definition of God's ordained power as Christ, as well as his claim that "apart from faith in Christ there is nothing but sin and damnation" (Idem, III-274). God's Word is the only standard a faithful sinner has for self-assessment. As it concerns politics and authority, we are already familiar with the implications: Scripture is its own authority – its interpretation does not depend on an authoritative tradition of scholarly interpretations and church interventions, nor can its truth ever be measured in terms of exegetical consensus. Scripture is God's ordained will. It is the foundation on which Luther stands while he opposes the pope, emperor, Erasmus, and all scholastic scholars. The Word of God is also Luther's answer to problems created by nominalism. Before Luther the medieval Augustinians already criticize unsettling ideas such as an arbitrary God, deceiving and unreliable, as well as a human freedom disconnected from an invariant moral principle, which causes uncertainty and anxiety. Luther finds his own solution to these problems raised by nominalism. Through his ordained power God points in a single direction – Christ.

The assurance of faith and certainty of salvation require God's omnipotence and immutable will on the one hand, and man's sinful impotence and enslaved will on the other hand. However, Gillespie is right when he writes that these commitments also undermine the certainty Luther seeks. Assurance is gained by faith in Christ, yet God and his Word are two distinct things: "How can there be anything anywhere that is below, above, within, or without the word and work of God, except God himself?" (Idem, III-106). Behind Christ the saviour stands the immutable will of God. This is *Deus absconditus*, the hidden God that Luther also refers to as *Deus nudus*, the naked God. This is God insofar as he chooses to hide himself, revealing his will only in as far as he wants to reveal it (Idem, III-60; Gerrish, 1973; Paulsen, 1999; Gillespie, 2008, pp. 151–161). But the question inevitably arises while reading or listening to scripture "what, why, and how far" does God will what he wills (Luther, 1525a, III-140). This is the question that leads "below" the Word. The question of "why" and "where from" indicates that every *telos* (salvation, justification) also implies an *archè*, a source, cause, point of departure – the hidden God.

It is at this point that nominalism's capricious, unpredictable, and indifferent God resurfaces in all his awesome majesty and omnipotence. Beyond the Word, the nominalist's omnipotent God who wills as he pleases reappears as a terrifying non-figure, who Luther associates with an abyss, an empty place. Luther describes this God in sheer nominalist language:

> He is God, and for his will there is no cause or reason that can be laid down as a rule or measure for it, since there is nothing equal or superior to it, but it is itself the rule of all things. For if there were any rule or standard for it, either as cause or reason, it could no longer be the will of God. For it is not because he is or was obliged so to will that what he wills is right, but on the contrary, because he himself so wills, therefore what happens must be right. Cause and reason can be assigned for a creature's

> will, but not for the will of the Creator, unless you set up over him another creator.
>
> (Idem, III-181)

When Luther writes that God is hidden in the Word, one might be tempted to conclude that God's will is in strict conformity with the revealed Word. Yet this is not the case: The hidden will and essence of God and the Word of God are two distinct things, as I showed before. Luther further supports this position when he says that although Scripture does not portray God as wanting the sinner's death, in terms of his inscrutable will God, in fact, wants the sinner to die (Idem, III-137). In terms of his Word God is merciful and concerned for the fate of man, yet in terms of his immutable will he is indifferent to those whose fates he foresees and predestines to damnation. At this point Luther faces a serious problem. On the one hand he argues that at the heart of Christian faith and throughout the whole of the Gospel stands the necessity of God's foreknowledge regarding things that will come to pass, as well as his promises. On the other, Gospel seems to contradict God's inscrutable will – *Deus revelatus* and *Deus absconditus* do not coincide. The solution Luther proposes might be called "Luther's razor". The highest form of faith, he writes, is to believe God "merciful when he saves so few and damns so many, and to believe him righteous when by his own will he makes us necessarily damnable" (Idem, III-63). Although God seems to delight in the torments of the wretched and be worthier of hatred than love, this should not prevent us from having faith:

> It is enough to know simply that there is a certain inscrutable will in God, and as to what, why, and how far it wills, that is something we have no right whatever to inquire into, hanker after, care about, or meddle with, but only to fear and adore.
>
> (Idem, III-140)

Hence, in response to a slew of questions this account raises – e.g. why God saves so few and condemns so many (so many who cannot themselves be held personally responsible for the whole of humanity's sinful state), why God permits sin without giving human beings the chance of salvation through merit, or why he demands that men do that which they cannot (the impossible), in short, why God wills and predestines human beings and the rest of what he creates to be as they are – Luther responds, "it becomes us not to inquire" (Idem; Pesch, 2004, p. 137; Forde, 2005, pp. 34–35). The edge of faith is thus marked with what Freud would simply call a prohibition on thought: the obstruction of the epistemophilic drive and of intellectual inquiry. It is skeptical, intellectual questioning, says Luther, that undermines faith and trust in Christ. Faith as trust (*fiducia*) in God's Word is "the only 'solution' to the 'problem of God'" and "thus it bids us to stop before the supreme majesty of the hidden God" – Scripture reveals that God is hidden (Idem, p. 40). Luther has a clear warning for those who cross the line and desire to know the mystery that is God: Those proud men who seek to penetrate the abyss of divine predestination by reason, who compulsively question their salvation in vain, will certainly perish. Questions of "why" and "what", says Luther, fascinate those who speculate on them. Indeed, one can respond to these questions with fascination, i.e. being immovably bound to and intrigued by an all-absorbing uncanny object that both guarantees a person's life and threatens to destroy it (Thys, 2006, pp. 332ff; Paturet, 2008, pp. 37–38). But to question God's will is to doubt his very existence. Being confronted with God's inscrutable will – which lies below his Word – one can either fear and adore it, i.e. react with a kind of despair that eventually results in a strengthening of faith (trust), or pursue a philosophical line of reasoning motivated by the questions that arise from this account.[10] But is this then a free choice? The answer to this question is no. Rather, it is the moment *par excellance* in which one is either moved to faith and obedience to Scripture, or the moment is which one is incited by the devil. At the rim of this abyss one either falls to one's knees or simply falls. Faith thus consists of avoiding the abyssal emptiness of the Thing, the hidden God as the gravitational centre in Luther's thought (Lacan, 1992, p. 130).

To be the object of hatred rather than love

Luther's razor slashes away intellectual speculation regarding the question of why God wills as he does. Faith is the solution to the "problem of God". But what exactly is this problem?

Salvation through Christ might be understood as the *terminus ad quem* of faith's movement, of which *Deus absconditus* is *terminus a quo* (Gerrish, 1973). Indeed, salvation and justification through faith are the goals of a salvational history that begins even before the world's foundation. This does not mean, however, that this movement is one "away from the Hidden God" – a "flight" from God so to speak.[11] Faith's movement is less straightforward and more complex for the simple reason that God is always "below, above, within, or without the word and work of God". A "flight" from God would, therefore, always be a movement away from his Word. Luther's insistence that the faithful should focus on God's ordained power does not contradict this claim. On the contrary, by focusing on the Word – on Christ as Saviour – the believer is shielded from a direct view of what lies hidden behind – the "abyss" always there in the corner of one's eye. We should not overlook the implications of a conception of God as *Deus nudus*: the Word is like clothing that denies us a direct glimpse of God's nakedness. The believer does not flee in horror from God – he flees from sin and enslavement. In so doing not only does he catch a glimpse of Christ as the incarnate son who suffers for humanity, but he also hears the strange, threatening proclamations of a God who wants to be apprehended in a manner other than "perception or experience," who gives life by killing, justifies by making guilty. In short, the believer is always also confronted with the God who "hides his eternal goodness and mercy under eternal wrath, his righteousness under iniquity" (Luther, 1525a, III-62). The search for salvation promised by a loving and merciful God thus always also provokes a contrary experience – a person is shattered and terrified at the moment he finds himself *coram Deo* (Causse, 1999, p. 128). The Word always also points at its speaker, the hidden God who not only initiates but also endangers this movement of faith when he becomes its *terminus ad quem*.

God is the cause of faith's movement not only because he bestows faith through an efficacious act of grace, but also because he works "all in all". As we have seen, this is Luther's starting point in *The Bondage of the Will*: "Everything we do, everything that happens, even if it seems to us to happen mutably and contingently, happens in fact nonetheless necessarily and immutably, if you have regard to the will of God" (Luther, 1525a, III-38). Hence, we must assume God "works in us both good and evil", and that he consequently rewards "his own good works in us and punishes his evil works in us" (Idem, III-58). The only truly free will is that of God – God foresees and foreknows everything, and that which he foreknows he wills. Further, what he wills he wills immutably and from eternity: "He foresees and purposes and does all things by his immutable, eternal, and infallible will" (Idem, III-37). Consequently, Luther makes no attempt to distinguish between foreknowledge and predestination (Brosché, 1978). The question now is if God predestines only those elected for salvation, if God denies faith and eternal life to those that remain in sin, or if (more strongly) God strengthens and hardens the inclinations of sinners. It is clear at this point that Luther leaves no room for human free will, hence, even a sinner's persistence in sin cannot be explained by the sinner's will, since this would cause damnation to depend on a human act. He favours "a stark conception of reprobation, which derives the exclusion from grace from a direct decree of will on the part of God". (Idem, pp. 88–95). Luther is thus a follower of Rimini and a precursor to Calvin as it concerns a doctrine of double predestination. This is visible, for example, in Luther's interpretation of the hardening of Pharaoh's heart (Ex. 4:21) (Luther, 1525a, III-165ff; Forde, 2005, pp. 51–52). Erasmus also wrestles with the idea that Pharaoh's heart is hardened as the instrument of a just cause, the exodus of the Israelites. He argues that Pharaoh must at least have freely willed and (unknowingly) cooperated with God's will. Yet Luther rejects such cooperation, arguing instead that God alone hardens Pharaoh's heart for a single, merciful purpose –Biblical texts leave no room for another interpretation. The Pharaoh's behaviour is necessarily compulsive since it is willed by God. It is the actualization of God's immutable will. Another example is God's love of Jacob and hatred towards Esau – before Luther Rimini already reflects on Saint Paul's comment on this story in his *Epistle to the Romans* (Rom. 9:13), and as we see shortly Calvin also relates his views concerning predestination to precisely this text. Luther mentions Jacob and Esau as examples of people without wills of their own, who are either loved or hated by God in accord with his eternal and immutable nature (Luther, 1525a, III-195ff). It is according to God's eternal and immutable will that he loves Jacob and hates Esau.[12] Indeed, we find here a characteristic of the way in which God loves and hates that distinguishes it from the way in which humans do:

> We know quite well that God does not love or hate as we do, since we are mutable in both our loving and hating, whereas he loves and hates in accord with his eternal and immutable nature, so that passing moods and feelings do not arise in him.
>
> (Idem, III-199)

From this we might indeed infer a supralapsarian doctrine of double predestination. Despite the fact that Luther never explicitly writes that before the foundation of the world God creates sin and decides who will be condemned, the evidence that he held such a view cannot be overlooked. Given his anti-speculative attitude we need not be surprised that he does not offer a systematic account regarding his views on the subject of predestination. If one could comprehend that God can be both merciful and just, and at the same time appears full of wrath and iniquity, Luther says one need not have faith. One should simply believe that which is written in Scripture:

> Admittedly, it gives the greatest possible offense to common sense or natural reason that God by his own sheer will should abandon, harden, and damn men as if he enjoyed the sins and the vast, eternal torments of his wretched creatures, when he is preached as a God of such great mercy and goodness.
>
> (Idem, III-190).

That God both elects and condemns is a fact known from Scripture. But questions of how and why the hidden God damns so many – and according to what principles – is mere speculation. Such inquiry only leads to the very "depth and abyss of despair" – which should be avoided (Idem). A sinner who has neither faith nor a sense of the meaning of Christ's death and suffering cannot reflect on predestination without bringing God's wrath upon him. Predestination is "is a wonderfully sweet thing for those who have the Spirit, but a bitter thing and harsh above all things for the prudence of the flesh" (Luther, 1515–1516, 371). Instead God's immutable will should be the foundation of the Gospel's consolatory and joyful message to the faithful.

Luther's point of departure in reflecting on God's love is his original, immutable will, and the basic impossibility of distinguishing love from hate in his will (Causse, 1999, p. 128). There is both love in his wrath and righteousness in his apparent iniquity. Whatever his intellectual or spiritual capacities, a person should not question either God's motives – assuming he has them. The highest form of faith is, after all, to believe in God's mercy given that he saves so few and condemns so many – in other words, to be the object of love rather than hate. Hence, it is enough to know merely that God's will is inscrutable.

There is no limit to this inscrutability. We should not overlook here the fact that intellectual speculation signals more than its incitation by the devil as God's opponent. Compulsive thought regarding the cause of the devil's actions constitutes part of the abovementioned abyssal despair, since behind the devil stands God:

> Now, Satan and man, having fallen from God and been deserted by God, cannot will good, that is, things which please God or which God wills; but instead they are continually turned in the direction of their own desires, so that they are unable not to seek the things of self. This will and nature of theirs, therefore, which is thus averse from God, is not something nonexistent. For Satan and ungodly man are not nonexistent or possessed of no nature or will, although their nature is corrupt and averse from God. That remnant of nature, therefore, as we call it, in the ungodly man and Satan, as being the creature and work of God, is no less subject to divine omnipotence and activity than all other creatures and works of God.
>
> (Luther, 1525a, III-176)

Jean-Daniel Causse rightfully argues that *Deus absconditus* is in a sense "diabolical". Since the will of God does not coincide with his ordained Word, neither can God be entirely discerned from the devil. The work of the devil is nothing but an instrument (an extension) of God's will, one that not only fails to coincide with his revealed Word of salvation but also actually opposes it. Hence, in his exegesis of Psalm 117 Luther even writes that:

> God's faithfulness and truth always must first become a great lie before it becomes truth. The world calls this truth heresy. And we, too, are constantly tempted to believe that God would abandon us and not keep His Word; and in our hearts He begins to become a liar. In short, God cannot be God unless He first becomes a devil.
>
> (Luther, 1530, 31)

The model is the following: there exists God's immutable will that is then actualized in two opposed instruments, which are in fact part of one and the same will: his ordained Word and Satan. Elsewhere Luther expresses this in a simple formula: "Iam extra Iesum quaerere deum est diabolus" (Causse, 1999, pp. 147–152).

Concerning the diabolical in Luther's thought, Lacan is quick to point out that Freud "did not hesitate to mention and call by its name" the figure that preoccupied "both scientific and theological thought" in the period preceding the emergence of modern man, that is, the Cartesian subject. This preoccupation concerns "*Diabolus* himself", evident in a discourse in which "the symbolic is united with the diabolic" (Lacan, 1992, p. 92). According to Lacan Freud is once again concerned with an issue of heavy disputation during Luther's era that then disappears from the agenda. What is Lacan here talking about? At first this appears to be a reference to Freud's interpretations of the figure of the devil. In his study of the seventeenth century demonological neurosis of the painter Christoph Haitzmann Freud reasons as follows: God and the devil are originally identical, a unified figure that later split into "two figures with opposite attributes".[13] In the history of primal religion God has a clearly ambivalent character, both good and evil, thereby mirroring the primal father and his son's attitudes towards him:

> If the benevolent and righteous God is a substitute for his father, it is not to be wondered at that his hostile attitude to his father, too, which is one of hating and fearing him and of making complaints against him, should have come to expression in the creation of Satan.
>
> (Freud, 1923b, p. 86)

Freud thus focuses on the split between two sharply contrasting attributes – good and evil – originating from a primal ambivalence of the Godhead's character.

But Lacan's concern is not only with an original unity of opposed affects such as love and hate in the Godhead, mirroring as it does the character of the primal father. Freud also reflects, after all, on the problem of relating man's "evil" or "sin" – i.e. his dispositional inclination towards aggression and destruction – to the image of God as omnipotent, good, and the image in which man is created. He writes that the devil is an ideal supplement, as the evil opponent of God. Instead of cherishing the illusion of man's good, moral nature, Freud argues that the fundamentally "evil" character of human nature should not be disavowed. As a destructive force the death drive should be acknowledged. The question here is not how the devil's existence is to be explained psychologically but how man's nature is related to a principle of evil (Freud, 1930, pp. 120–121). This gives us a clear indication of what, according to Lacan, preoccupies Luther and is excavated by Freud. In the first place this concerns the issue of central importance to Lacan's claim regarding a cultural paternity between Luther and Freud, namely, an evil in both creator and human beings. (Not only does the devil personify evil aspects of the Godhead, but he is also a figure that mirrors man's evil nature.) Lacan thus recognizes that Luther anticipates a key aspect of Freudian thought: a fundamental hatred and evil exists from which culture (creation) emerges; religion – notably, its first sign (the totem) and the central symbol of Christianity (the cross) – substitutes the hidden father God for a symbolic body that obscures direct access to its enigmatic origin. At the same time, however, religion also theatrically stages this evil in the figure of the devil (Paturet, 2008, pp. 48ff). Second, whereas Jung – and Lacan refers to him explicitly – upholds an Aristotelian model of the universe characterized by a continuity between "our images and the world that surrounds us", and a "deep connection" in which evil has no positive content but is merely a projection or symbolization of what is lacking, Freud radically puts evil back into the place it belongs, namely, the human body. Here again Freud connects up with Luther, who envisioned sinful man as waste matter from the devil's anus (Lacan, 1992, pp. 92–93).

Lacan's comment on the body in Luther's thought that both the symbolic and the diabolic can be understood as united opens an interesting perspective with regard to Luther's devil. Is there a relation between the parts of the body and the role they play in Luther's imagery? He strongly associates the devil with bodily openings (anus, mouth), ones that demarcate a separation (or absorption) of an object from the body. Just as the body establishes a physical connection between several openings, Luther's metaphors regarding bodily openings also suggests a relationship. God speaks – the Word is his voice. He opens his mouth and reveals that which he wants to reveal. Whosoever desires to know more than is revealed and thereby questions God will, whoever, so to speak, focuses on the mouth from which the voice comes falls into the abyss. He finds himself in horror and despair, tormented by the problem of evil and predestination, yet without any hope of or faith in salvation. Is this not the proud intellectual eventually unmasked as waste matter from the devil's anus? This is merely a suggestion that seems logical when we consider the mouth as the empty space from which both the voice leaves the body and the void in which one is swallowed up and digested.[14] If so then this bodily imagery reflects the diabolical character of God.

The will, its object and cause

The problem of God is the problem of evil. Whoever moves beyond the principles of *sola fide*, *sola gratia* and *sola scriptura* and proceeds to question the "why" of God's will, inevitably becomes fascinated by an object that hides itself, willing both good and evil – a God not there to answer. Whoever fails to be satisfied by obedience to the law and trust in divine promises, but asks after God's motives, eventually despairs because of the admixture of both love and apparent iniquity, righteousness and wrath, in short, the essence of God that contains aspects of both love and hate.

One can argue that Luther's theological innovation basically consists in a movement *ad fontes* – a lot of Scripture and a bit of Augustine – and that Reformation starts by giving priority to the three abovementioned principles, as opposed to medieval scholasticism and an emphasis on obedience to church institutions. In this case one is likely to overlook the veiling character of Scripture that clothes the naked God. Both scripture and faith shield man from an abyss. The Word as both law and gospel keep at a distance the other movement *ad fontes* that gains importance as the source of the Word.

Lacan argues that this second movement *ad fontes* – that is to say, the desire to comprehend the cause of human nature and the whole of creation – establishes Luther as a precursor to Freud. To understand this claim we need to focus on an analogy between the Thing and law (language) in Lacan, and the enslaved will (desire), the hidden God, and his relation to the Word in Luther.

According to Luther, the concept of free will is "an empty sound" (Luther, 1525a, III-81). Gerhard Forde describes it as "a *no-thing*, a title without a referent, an oxymoron", a word without substance (Forde, 2005, p. 55). Only God has a truly free will (since even the devil only wills that which God wills him to will), and God's will is the cause of man's willing either that which is good or that which is evil. As we have seen, Luther is not the first to radically deny human free will. Bradwardine stresses God's participation in the act of human willing at the moment and for the duration of a person's willing (or desiring). In this divine determinism, however, original sin (man's natural inclination towards evil) hardly plays a role. This aspect of Luther's thought is more directly indebted to Rimini, that other influential interpreter of Augustine. But then again, Rimini does not advocate a conception of the human will that is completely enslaved. So as it concerns the human will, Luther poses this issue in far more a radical fashion than anyone before him. In so doing he anticipates a line of reasoning that, according to Lacan, reappears in Freud's thought. Two ideas are central. First, the will is not inclined towards the good – man does not desire the good. Second, God's will is the source of man's, such that the object of desire is determined by the desire of the Other. We should look more closely at each of these two issues.

The denial of the good

Freud's claim that the good is not the object of desire is related to his conception of the pleasure principle. Freud originally names this the "unpleasure principle", denoting the build-up and release of tension. Unpleasure here refers to an experience of the build-up of mental tension such that pleasure is the experience of this tension's being reduced. Individuals strive to avoid unpleasure and achieve pleasure (Freud, 1900, pp. 598–604). A definition such as this already implies that pleasure might also be experienced in the discharge of aggression. It is already clear at this point that we cannot equate pleasure with the good – only inner psychic life is served by this reduction in tension. This principle is untethered to its effects on the external world.

Reality does of course come into play when the satisfaction of needs is denied and subsequently causes unpleasure. A certain control over reality is necessary if the child is to gain "assured pleasure at a later time" (Freud, 1911, p. 223). Through thinking, fantasying, and remembering, children develop insights into the nature of reality for the sake of manipulating and employing external reality to obtain pleasure. The reality principle thus serves the pleasure principle. This claim might lead us to believe that pleasure is in some way harmonious with that which is regarded morally good – culture is then understood as the realm in which drives are sublimated and aim towards socially desirable, pleasurable goals. But this is only a part of Freud's thought. In *Civilization and Its Discontents* Freud writes – as we have seen – that happiness "is not included in the plan of Creation" – a statement reinforcing his earliest intuitions regarding culture's demand that the drives be repressed thereby denying happiness and thus provoking the build-up of psychic tension. Furthermore, in *Beyond the Pleasure Principle* Freud shows there is reason to believe – given the repetition of and fixation on traumatic events in soldiers' war neurosis, as well as the negative therapeutic reactions of patients who resist treatment and are inclined to cherish their misery – that not only does the psychic apparatus seek the avoidance of unpleasure. He confirms this intuition while witnessing a scene in which his grandson plays with a bobbin, repeatedly throwing it away and bringing it back. What Freud calls the *fort-da* game is supposed to be the staging of a painful experience, namely, the absence of the child's mother (*Fort!*). It is these phenomena that lead Freud to seek for another principle of psychic life, beyond the pleasure principle, which is not directed at the avoidance of unpleasure but the experience of a painful enjoyment (Freud, 1920, pp. 54–55). This is what Freud associates with the death instinct, a drive aiming at the maintenance of a primal state, thus resistant to development and the individual's further composition.

In his early writings Lacan argues that the death drive should be understood as a nostalgia for the fusional relation of oneself with the mother's body, which he describes as *une assimilation parfaite de la totalité à l'être* or *abîme mystique de la fusion affective* (Lacan, 1984, p. 35; Evans, 1996, pp. 32–33). It is thereby situated in what he calls the imaginary order, an order consisting in the dual entanglement of the child's desire with that of the mother. Later he says the death drive is present in every repetitive movement and, therefore, in every drive. The instincts of life and death are always two sides of the same coin. In *The Ethics of Psychoanalysis* he associates the death drive (desire for death) with the Thing as the *terminus ad quem* of pleasure's entire economy. Every drive has a tendency to move beyond the pleasure principle towards a domain in which enjoyment and pain coincide. The symbolic order hinders the realization of this tendency, protecting a person from being absorbed by the Thing (Lacan, 1992, pp. 211–213).

Of central importance is Lacan's interpretation of the Freudian death drive as fundamental to an ethics of psychoanalysis. This is in opposition to, for example, a traditional Christian ethics of Thomas Aquinas, developed "along the paths of an essentially hedonist problematic". Lacan means by this an ethics that relates the good to an experience of pleasure, not insofar as the good would be based on the discernment of "true pleasures from false" ones, but discerning "the true and false goods" on the basis of what "pleasure points to" (Lacan, 1992, p. 221). Since the core of Aquinas' view on *synderesis* and natural law is the convergence of knowledge of the good and pleasure to be obtained from desiring the good, this reference is telling.

In his sixth seminar Lacan critically reflects on this hedonist tradition and its identification of the good with pleasure (*convergence du plaisir et du bien*), adding that such an ethics could only be realized within the limits set by an authority (*morale du maître*), one disciplining and regulating the subject's habits. Such an ethics expels desire from its proper place in human nature, confining it to a realm of bestiality and perversion outside the moral order (Lacan, 2000, pp. 13–14). Not only does Spinoza's identification of desire as the essence of man – or John Donne's Puritan-ecstatic poetry – oppose this tradition, says Lacan, but so to does the thought of Luther. Not only does Luther question authority and merit, as well as locate desire in the body, but he also points towards the sinfulness of natural desire, its hate and transgression – i.e. the movement from adoration to horror and despair. Both Freud and Lacan associate this movement with the death drive.

Through his adoption of a radical view on original sin (see Chapter 3), Luther shows that human beings are inclined to evil, especially when they pursue selfish interests and experience pleasure in sinful actions and worldly objects: "everyone finds in himself displeasure in what is good and pleasure in what is bad" (Luther, 1522/1546, III-366). The Law makes us aware of this. This is an awareness that not only precipitates a revaluation of pleasurable experiences as ones eventually resulting in pain (damnation), but also incites suffering because the sinner experiences God abandoning him, as well as his own incapacity to do what he should:

> Time seems long to all who are afflicted; and on the other hand, it seems short to those who are happy. But it seems especially and immeasurably long to those who have that inner hurt of the soul, the feeling of being forsaken and rejected by God.
>
> (Luther, 1517b, 142)

In other words, at the moment a sinner discovers the good the realization also occurs that his life is one of suffering – this is mirrored in Christ: God becomes man *qua* suffering figure. Hence, suffering is a crucial reference in the life of the faithful sinner. This is an even greater issue as it concerns the intellectual's movement from faithful adoration into inquiry regarding God's majesty. When he transgresses the prohibition concerning God's will he is confronted by the "abyss of hell", horror and despair. In other words, one's natural inclination towards evil ends by being swallowed up in a void, precisely the point at which the hidden God is always not found, hell – we should not here overlook Luther's use of the word "abyss" to refer to both hell and the realm in which the hidden God supposedly hides ("abyss of his father heart and unspeakable love"; "abyss of God's goodness"; "abyss of divine predestination"). It is precisely when a natural inclination reaches its limit at transgression that we see the coincidence of enjoyment with pain.

Luther regards this excess as the work of the devil. The devil stands at the abyss' rim as a combatant who incites one to transgress the border between the works of God and his Word on the one hand, and their hidden cause (and essence) on the other hand. He acts as God's instrument, pushing the damned towards damnation and strengthening the faith of the elect through spiritual combat. His ominous presence is already enough to direct one's entire focus towards the figure of Christ. There is reason to relate Luther's conception of the devil to his personal experiences. We know, after all, that he experienced the devil's presence vividly: Luther's accounts of his nightly fear when yelling and arguing with the devil ("Lick my arse!"), hearing the devil wander through the corridors of the Augustinian monastery at Erfurt and the Wartburg, and when Luther found the devil sleeping in his bed (Oberman, 1989, p. 105; Muchembled, 2003, pp. 111–112). We should be careful here, however, not to reduce Luther's conception of the devil to an amalgamation of his personal experiences alone, which could all too easily be interpreted in terms of either an anal phase in Luther's spiritual development or an almost pathological obsession. Such interpretations detract from the question regarding what precisely is so dangerous about inquiry into God's will. In other words, what is the nature of this excessive preoccupation the devil incites?

Intellectual inquiry into the hidden God, raising unanswerable questions concerning the "what, why and how far" of God's will, questioning the nature of God's essence, motives, and will that creates both good and evil, might all be characterized as a compelling desire to know a fascinating, uncanny object – the ultimate object of desire. This is not simply a matter of Luther's personal preoccupations. The importance of this object cannot be explained in terms of personal interest alone. This object is important as the cause and source of the whole of creation while at the same time failing to coincide with this creation. It thus gains its importance in terms of its theological weight – a weight inherited from medieval theology. The decomposition of a universal medieval order, one in which the Supreme Good is present and cognizable, and the subsequent problem of the nominalist's dark God, untrustworthy and detached from creation, precipitates Luther's turn to both Scripture and grace as constitutive of the sinner's self-conscious faith. However, the centrality of God's Word becomes so important that its source, the hidden God, becomes of even greater importance. Rooting faith (*fiducia*) in Scripture and grace, moreover, increases the potential for a novel uncertainty whenever the adoration turns to desperate questioning regarding God's will. In other words, because Luther's solution to theological problems becomes so important to believers – salvation: a matter of life or death – unanswerable questions regarding the "what, why and how far" of God's will become especially important as well. Since the foundation of a universal order is lost this foundation becomes all the more important when an order of faith is established in the life of an individual. Hence, the problem with questioning the essence and motives of God – i.e. the problem with intellectual inquiry – is that it undermines faith, searching for a lost foundation that is out of sight; that is, one that is fundamentally uncognizable. This is the point at which Luther's conceptions of the abyss and hiddenness coincide: God is not there – he gave his Word as a substitute since he is himself essentially lost, out of sight. In this sense then a compelling desire to know the will and majesty of God, compulsively questioning his motives, can be understood as a compelling desire for a lost object and, consequently, a refusal to accept this loss. The inquiry of God's hiddenness is synonymous with a refusal to accept the Word and faith. If forced to label this refusal of both loss and reality then we could do no better than what Freud means by melancholia, clinging to a lost loved object (Freud, 1917).

Desire is not restricted to any pleasurable good but ultimately aims at a lost object, one that Lacan describes in terms of the strange, prehistoric, and absolutely Other – the Thing. This is visible in Luther's when the desire for salvation strays beyond its proper object (Christ) into the terrible abyss of the ever-hidden God who desires the death of the sinner, "according to that inscrutable will of his" (Luther, 1525a, III-140).

The desire of the Other

Lacan not only argues that Luther denies "the good as such", the good as object of desire, but also that the "mad man from Wittenberg" indicates "that at the heart of man's destiny is the *Ding*, the *causa*", which is to say, something at the heart of psychic life that does not belong to us (Lacan, 1992, pp. 96–97).[15] For Luther this is God as the ultimate source of every person's will and desire, whether for good or evil. The will's enslavement and bondage indicates that neither will nor desire are either "neutral" things or independent and "unattached" faculties in the human mind (Forde, 2005, p. 55). On the contrary, what a person wills is determined by his relation to others/objects as well as his predetermined place in history.

What we call the object of desire, Lacan argues, is in fact always the object of another's desire. With this formula Lacan expresses, in the first place, a central Freudian thesis, namely, that the initial object of a child's desire (the mother) is an object of desire because she is also already the object of the father's desire. In his study on group psychology Freud elucidates this claim, arguing that "bonding to another person" is based on primary narcissistic identification – i.e. identification with an ideal represented by the father in the proceeding phase (Freud, 1921, pp. 106–107; Westerink, 2009b, pp. 180ff). Identification thereby precedes object love: becoming like the ideal (the father) is preceded by a desire to have what the ideal desires (the mother). In this way then the father is not only an admired ideal but also a hated rival. Inner feelings of both love and hate are thus bound in an ambivalent attitude towards the father figure. This is already a foundational claim in *Totem and Taboo*. It is not because the primal father possesses women that he is both admired and hated but because identification with him evokes an analogous desire to possess these women. Hence, at the root of culture lies not the desire to possess women but a pairing of love with hate to the father figure, which results in a sense of guilt and the first prohibitions (taboos) and social-religious institutions (totemism) after his murder.

Following Klein's project of focusing on pre-oedipal developments, Lacan elaborates what he calls this dialectic of desire (Fink, 1995; Van Haute, 2002). On the one hand, a desire exists in the relationship between the mother and child. The mother is there to satisfy the child's needs, although the child eventually discovers the mother is not always there to do so. In the child's mind her absence raises a question regarding what else she could desire aside from satisfying the child. The child's only response is to desire to become this other object of the mother's desire. This is, however, impossible as the child cannot get a grip on what it is its mother desires. Her behaviour is unpredictable – she comes and goes (*Fort! Da!*) – and what it is she really wants is incomprehensible. The child is thus at mercy of a capricious, primal Other who wills and does as she pleases. This captivation of the child's desperate desire evokes in it a desire to be freed from this omnipotent, devouring mother.

On the other hand, Lacan never fails to state that desire arises from lack, a lack that results from the father's prohibition on the mother as an exclusive object to possess and be possessed by. In this way he introduces the child to the order of language. In this order the child is now capable of expressing its own desires. But this liberating possibility of the expression of desire does not imply freedom. Desire is always expressed in language, which – as Lacan indicates – is *le discours de l'Autre*. The words a person uses to express himself are never based on one's free choice. From the multitude of possibilities that acquired language offers the words and expressions as child uses to express themself are never consciously, freely, and independently chosen. Rather, the child is always already situated in the discourse of its parents and culture; that is, in a complex of desires, aspirations, expectations, and references to others. This complex structures the child's unconscious like a chain or matrix of signifiers over which it has no control – *l'inconscient est le discours de l'Autre*. It is an internalized language given by the father.

This brief outline concerning Lacan's views on desire, the imaginary, and the symbolic is sufficient for us to understand what he means when he refers to the filiation between Freudian thought and Luther's account of the human will. The subject's desire is always a desire of the Other: "it is merely at the level of the desire of the Other that man can recognize his desire ... that the subject's desire is constituted" (Lacan, 1998b, p. 235). Whether we speak of the child's desire for the mother in which it is held hostage, or a desire that emanates from lack, which results from a prohibition and is expressed through the Other's discourse, there is no such thing as the autonomous desire of an individual. Desire is always bound to both a cause and object that are external to the subject, expressed in a language given from without.[16]

On Luther's account the human will is always determined by God's will. At first sight though it seems as if willing evil is a disobedience, a pursuit of self-interests that could be interpreted as willing freely, desiring in a fashion that flies in the face of the Other's desire, God's will. Yet according to Luther this is an illusion, since sinners cannot pursue anything other than their own sinful interests. God wills the human will's bondage to evil because of disobedience. This is determined by God even before the foundation of the world. "He works evil in us" just as he wills the hardening of Pharaoh's heart. But this is not the only way in which God works evil. The fact that the faithful sinner should accept his incapacity to penetrate God's majesty, that he should focus solely on the incarnate son and express himself as a believer by means of the revealed Word, implies that a desire exists that always tends to transgress this prohibition into the realm of that which is prohibited. At this point the devil acts as God's instrument to incite the desire to transgress the abyss' rim, thereby undermining the revealed order by calling into question God's essence and motives. As it concerns faith, any desire for the good – any desire that conforms to the commandments and promises of both the law and gospel – is evidently willed by God. Luther's commitments regarding the entire salvational economy of grace, Scripture and faith, and a radical rejection of free will, express the view that the human will is moved by the Other's desire.

Luther's Thing

The difference between *Deus absconditus* and *Deus revelatus* is nothing other than the difference between God and his Word. We already sketched the context for, and main problem with, which Luther takes this to be a solution: nominalism's fearsome God. As the fundamental aim of Luther's life and work, the revealed Word is the answer to "his desire to find a merciful God" (Oberman, 1989, p. 127). The solution to the problem of the nominalist God is the introduction of the *sola scriptura*-principle: God reveals himself as good and merciful in his Word – God here expresses that which he wants, namely, to save all men.

God's Word – as the message of grace and thus the source of faith – is a key concept in Luther's theology. But the Word actually consists of two parts, law and gospel, which are best characterized in terms of Scripture's two functions. Even in his early writings Luther argues that the law teaches human beings what they ought to do but are yet are incapable of doing (Luther, 1513, p. 292). The law teaches that human beings are sinners by nature. This law is not confined to the Mosaic law *strictu sensu* but more broadly includes the Old Testament in its totality, showing what human beings lack, namely, faith and salvation. The law is an ordeal since it judges the sinner as worldly, despicable, and damnable, showing a person's disobedience and selfish interest. It thus humbles a person. This is beneficiary because the humble receive grace. Not only does the law expose sin but it also functions to make distinctions between good and evil, right and wrong, the elect and damned. In this way then not only is the law an ordeal for the individual but it also demonstrates God's justice. All these aspects coalesce in the figure of Christ, in whom the Word becomes flesh and through whom the law is fulfilled. Luther expresses this view in *The Bondage of the Will* when he writes of the law as a preparation for the grace and salvation through faith in Christ (Luther, 1525a, III-131). The law gives a person both an awareness and knowledge of sin, says Luther, and an awareness regarding one's incapacity to do or will that which one should. The law's promises, threats, and do not lead to a freely willed reorientation to life but only the humble suffering of one abandoned by God who, nonetheless, needs his grace for salvation.

Scripture is the revealed Word of God. This is revealed through a speech act on God's part, which presents both his laws and promises in language, through which a person enters into a new relationship with himself, Christ, his fellow man, history, and the world. For the believer this revelation is the sole means through which the sinful, dislocated individual can be reoriented in both his spiritual and worldly life. This is guidance given by God. Only through grace can a person redirect his desire from selfish interest to love of one's fellow (Raunio, 2006). Scripture transforms people, binding them in new relationships and to an order that implies a radical shift in perspective regarding the nature of life. It gives life new meaning, one beyond purely selfish and contingent ends, even beyond those determined by the existing social and ecclesiastical orders. Hence, it is a religious language that restructures a person's life and identity. The desire of the believer, *simul iustus et peccator*, is organized and bound by Scripture, turning one's full attention towards Christ not only as object of faithful adoration but also its significance for both social and ecclesiastical structures – Christ's church as the communion or body of believers.

Scripture functions here in the same manner as what Lacan calls the symbolic order, indicating the cultural realm of language in which a person expresses his desires symbolically through inter-subjective relations. In his role as castrator/frustrator the father initiates this order, which says Lacan, can be characterized in terms of two key notions: law and desire. The father prohibits the abovementioned imaginary entanglement of desire between the child and mother. In this act of prohibition the father divides (child and mother) and binds (law and language). This prohibiting liberation comes at a price, however, which consists in the acknowledgement of lack. No longer can a person possess that which he ultimately wants, and of equal importance, he is only capable of expressing himself imperfectly in "the discourse of the Other". Each and every expression by the self is incomplete, and although individual expressions may be both true and authentic, each and every expression also veils another possible truth about oneself. This prohibition and discourse of the father/Other lie at the heart of both symbolization and subjectivity. But not everything can be symbolized or expressed in discourse. An imaginary loss is suffered that cannot be described. There is the absolute Other whose discourse is "in us" but whose essence we can grasp in neither images nor language.

This is precisely where Lacan leads his readers in *The Ethics of Psychoanalysis*. There he associates law, limitation, and discourse with creation, which acts as a pole in the dialectic between the Thing and law. In this context the principle of *creatio ex nihilo* receives a new meaning: creation can be described as *creatio ex nihilo* because we do not know the God responsible for it. He is a hidden God, a God who chooses to hide himself, who chooses not to exist for human beings (Lacan, 1992, pp. 213–214). At this point Lacan's references to Luther come into play. The fundamental human passion has a cause. In other words, the Other's desire causes man's desires, and yet this Other is a stranger, hidden in and below his discourse. The Other is the *nihil* from which creation originates, the ever-hidden Other who is, thus, not there. Lacan illuminates this claim in the context of a religious metaphor regarding the nature of a pot or vase: making a vase consists in fashioning matter around a hole, in making an object that represents "the existence of the emptiness at the centre of the real that is called the Thing" (Idem, p. 121). In this case fashioning a signifier is synonymous with introducing a gap or hole, and this is further analogous to the relation between revelation and the abyss. The vase (revealed) is good in terms of the way it functions, works, and can be used in the world. However, is it not precisely the function or work of creation that Luther denies? Lacan answers in the affirmative. Indeed, according to Lacan, Luther's thought confronts us with the question of how to conceive of a vase – what it is – if not in terms of its usefulness (Idem, p. 122).[17]

In the previous chapter I claimed that Freud begins with an analysis of the categorical imperative for the sake of discovering the primal sources of religion, morality, and social institutions. Lacan makes a similar move when he says the Thing is "the beyond-of-the-signified" (Idem, p. 54). He describes desire's ultimate object in terms of a lack in the symbolic order, i.e. the symbolic law that excludes the Thing from the matrix of signifiers. A prohibition determines the Thing's importance as the ultimate, overvalued object of desire. In this way then the Thing is itself a revelation brought about by the prohibitive law. I argued before that identification precedes object choice, and here we see the same logic at work: that which is ultimately desired only receives its importance because of the father and his prohibition.

On this basis we might be tempted to conclude that the Thing is nothing other than the incestuously desired "mythic body of the mother" as conceived by Melanie Klein. This is not, however, what Lacan argues. He says instead that Klein's conception of the mythic body of the mother is situated "at the central place of *das Ding*" (Idem, p. 106). In Kleinian thought then, the mythic body of the mother represents the Thing, the ultimate object of desire that is lost.

In *The Bondage of the Will* the hidden God represents the Thing. This is obviously not to say that God is synonymous with the mythic body of the mother, although they function in the same manner. The hidden God gains his importance as the Thing precisely because of the fact that contemplating him is prohibited, i.e. by the fact that God chose to hide his essence and will (Paturet, 2008, p. 66). Because *Deus absconditus* and *Deus revelatus* do not coincide something is lost. It is precisely this lost piece that becomes the Thing, desire's ultimate object for the intellectual – the oracle from which he expects answers to the questions "what, why and how far".

When Luther discusses the difference between *Deus absconditus* and *Deus revelatus*, his focus is clearly on the moral features of this difference. God the son, revealed in incarnation, is good and wants to save all men, while God the father, the hidden God, has a diabolical character uniting in him good and evil, righteousness and iniquity, love and hate. It is the God of predestination who chooses the elect and damned even before the foundation of the world, the God who wills what he wills without limitation. Lacan mentions these features when discussing the filiation between Luther and Freud, which concerns two main issues. First, Luther's conception of the revealed Word as law and its underlying, hidden cause on the one hand, and Freud's conception of taboo (law) and its relation to a primal prehistoric father. Second, this filiation concerns the ambivalent characters of both the hidden God and the primal father, and their being the cause of evil and hatred. Luther expresses this in his theology when he claims that God wills everything, including hatred and evil. In Freud the sons identify with the tyrant who reigns according to his natural, unrestrained inclinations.

This filiation is not, however, an equation, an anachronistic reduction of one to the other that neglects differences in discourse and meaning. Luther's *Deus absconditus* is not Freud's primal father. As it concerns a cultural paternity, the crucial point is that in Luther's voluntarism not only the divine law but also man's inclinations (as caused by God) that are to be restrained by this law, appear to be grounded in an unreasonable act of a divine will that goes beyond a human understanding of good and evil. Man's original sin is thereby grounded in the incognizable will of God. The contours of this idea are recognizable in Freud's analysis of the categorical imperative, as a moral restraint and its source, an identification with and murder of the father – man's primal crime results from the father's tyranny. This is what Lacan points towards in *The Ethics of Psychoanalysis*.

The first cause and predestination

In a letter to Heinrich Bullinger, written 25 November 1544, Calvin gives us an impression of Luther's character. It is a characterization that matches *The Bondage of the Will*'s spirit, a furious, rage-fueled attack against Erasmus. Calvin writes the following:

> I hear that Luther has at length broken forth in fierce invective, not so much against you as against the whole of us.(...) I must acknowledge him to be an illustrious servant of God. But while he is endued with rare and excellent virtues, he labors at the same time under serious faults. Would that he had rather studied to curb this restless, uneasy temperament which is so apt to boil over in every direction.
>
> (Calvin, 1544)

Although Calvin and Luther never met in person, in many respects Calvin followed Luther – seemingly he had more difficulties with Luther's temperament than his theology, which Calvin admired. Despite a difference in views on key issues such as free will and predestination, Calvin and Philip Melanchthon (1497–1560) – a collaborator of Luther – had a friendly relationship, not the least because the latter's character was the opposite of Luther's – mild and reasonable (Bouwsma, 1988, p. 18, 232; Selderhuis, 2009, pp. 57–62; McGrath, 1993, p. 151).

An intellectual leader of the early Reformation movement at the University of Wittenberg, Melanchthon defended Luther's *The Bondage of the Will* against Erasmus in the 1520s. At this time Melanchthon's own theological ideas were closest to Luther's.[18] Although in his later commitments regarding human will and reason – notably in later versions of *Loci communes* – Melanchthon comes closer to Erasmus than Luther. Beginning in the 1540s Melanchthon argues that human beings possess natural knowledge of God as both creator and lawgiver, organizing man's relationships with both the divine and his fellow man. He defends *synderesis* as an innate principle regulating basic forms of civil moral conduct as well as enabling people to cooperate and participate in their own salvation (Delumeau, 1990, pp. 536–537; Raunio, 2006). Hence, in his later writings Melanchthon affirms a minimum degree of free will and breaks from Luther's strict determinism. In matters regarding God's hiddenness, predestination, the enslaved will, and the denial of merit, Calvin is eventually closer to Luther.[19]

Like Luther, Calvin proposes a distinction between God's hiddenness and his revealed will (word) (Gerrish, 1973). This revelation serves not only to bridge the gap between the sinner and God but also veils God's essence and denies direct access to his majesty. From time to time, "God showed the presence of his divine majesty by definite signs", but all these signs also "clearly told men of his incomprehensible essence", restraining their minds "from attempting to penetrate too deeply" (Calvin, 1559a, 1.11.3). In addition, like Luther, Calvin also associates a desire to penetrate God's hiddenness with idle philosophical speculation, such as that practiced by "the sophists of Sorbon" who identify God's *potentia absoluta* as lawless and unpredictable (Calvin, 1552, p. 118; Muller, 2000, p. 47; Steinmetz, 1995, pp. 40–52). He associates this speculation with shameless blasphemy, describing it as the indulgence of useless, confused, and dangerous curiosity (Calvin, 1559a, 1.14.1, 3.21.1). Speculation regarding God's hiddenness concerns issues related to predestination (Idem, 3.21–24) and determinism, the origin of evil (Idem, 1.15.8), and the providential use of the wicked (since all men are submitted to God's will) (Idem, 1.17.2). In his discussion of such themes Calvin often refers to God's "secret" and "incomprehensible" plans and decrees that are "hidden" from us. He makes frequent use of the same concepts Luther employs, notably his conception of the "abyss".

> But if they do not admit that whatever happens in the universe is governed by God's incomprehensible plans, let them answer to what end Scripture says that his judgments are a deep abyss [Psalm 36:6]. For since Moses proclaims that the will of God is to be sought not far off in the clouds or in abysses, because it has been set forth familiarly in the law [Deuteronomy 30:11–14], it follows that he has another hidden will which may be compared to a deep abyss.
>
> (Idem)

Yet whereas Luther argues that God and his Word do not coincide, and that God seems to have two wills, one hidden and the other revealed, one in which, for example, God desires the sinner's death and another in which he wants all to be saved, or one in which he is indifferent to those he damns and another in which he is merciful, Calvin stresses the fact that there is no difference between these two wills. When he refers to the hiddenness of God or God's hidden will, Calvin only refers to the "first cause" of God's acts, the "cause of causes" – which is to say – God's "will and pleasure" as the source of all he wills (Idem, 1.16.9, 3.23.2; Calvin, 1554, p. 459; Calvin, 1552, pp. 121–122, 190, 192). Defending against "allegations" that he (and Luther) ascribe to a doctrine of "two contrary wills in God", Calvin writes the following:

> I everywhere teach, that the most perfect harmony subsists between God's hidden counsel, and the outward word of his doctrine. I grant that Augustine mentions different wills; but these are so harmonious with each other, that the last day will demonstrate how consistent he was in all his complicated modes of action.
>
> (Calvin, 1558, p. 44)

As is well known, Calvin ascribes to a doctrine of double predestination. He defines predestination (McGrath, 1993; Muller, 2008; Selderhuis, 2009) as God's "eternal decree, by which he compacted with himself what he willed to become of each man. For all are not created in equal condition; rather, eternal life is foreordained for some, eternal damnation for others" (Calvin, 1559a, 3.15.5). According to Calvin, God does not damn certain people because he hates them as human beings. Rather, God hates sin and because he foresees that some will sin he hates them as sinners. Esau is thus hated even before he is born, because God foresees that Esau will be unworthy of grace. In other words, Esau is hated because God can see nothing good in Esau "except what he had already determined to bestow by the benefit of his election" (Idem, 3.22.4-5; Calvin, 1552, pp. 75–76).

Adam's original transgression of righteousness is, therefore, also foreseen and permitted.[20] Calvin makes clear that there is no distinction between this permission and divine will (Calvin, 1559a, 3.23.8). What God permits he wills. Hence, the fact that Adam sins, acting against God's will, is in fact the will of God. The divine, "marvelous and ineffable plan of operation" is thereby carried out (Calvin, 1552, p. 44). God's will constitutes the necessity of things, says Calvin, even those things that seem to run contrary to his will – whatever happens or changes in the world is a product of the secret stirring of God's hand, and whatever God has determined to happen must necessarily take place (Calvin, 1559a, 1.16.19). God is thus "the cause and the author" of those to be saved and those to be damned. For this reason God is indeed the author of sin, in the sense that he permits/wills Adam to sin, choosing not to prevent (not to will) it. Man is responsible for sin insofar as he freely chooses to transgress God's will, which is only possible because God permits/wills it. Thus by not preventing sin God's hatred towards the reprobate takes on a somewhat nuanced character, although God's wrath also makes Calvin uncomfortable, as is evident in his tendency to apologize for God's cruel actions. Calvin says that Jericho's slaughter, for example, in the process of which women and children are also butchered, is both cruel and severe but not unjust as it constitutes the punishment for centuries of sinful actions. Predestination is indeed a "dreadful" decree if one focuses on God as the cause of sin and author of wrath (Bouwsma, 1988, p. 106). Calvin stresses, however, that this double decree of predestination is righteous – "God's will is the rule of righteousness"; whatever God wills must be considered righteous because of the very fact that God wills it (Calvin, 1559a, 3.23.2). Ultimately this brings about something good: not only God's glorification but also an acknowledgement and trust by believers that salvation is grounded solely in Christ and God's mercy (Calvin, 1552, p. 89). Towards this end the wicked are mere instruments: "what men do perversely is of God, and ruled by his hidden providence". Although God wills those works committed by wicked people (such as Judas), through their sins these people transgress the will of God such that "the rebellion of the people is rightly condemned because against God's will they revolted" (Calvin, 1559a, 1.18.4). This instrumentalization of the wicked and the damned points at a certain immutable rationale in God's will, which provides the doctrines with its psychological meaning, namely, the avoidance of the confrontation with a pure unreasonable capricious will of God. Moreover, this is the point of distinction between the attitudes of adoration and despair.

Calvin thus follows Luther in arguing that God is the first cause of both love and hate. The case of Jacob and Esau serves as an example. The two brothers are "branches of a sacred root" (Idem, 3.21.6). The ultimate question then is "Why God hates Esau?" According to Calvin it is impossible to answer this question, penetrating the wisdom and righteousness of God. We must content ourselves with pronouncements from Scripture: God hates Esau even before the foundation of the world (Calvin, 1551, p. 50).

Although Luther explicitly writes of the hatred of God as the cause of the hatred of man, implicitly ascribing to a doctrine of double predestination, we should note that Lacan's interpretation of Luther's *The Bondage of the Will* is, in fact, a "Calvinist" reading. More so than Luther it is Calvin who clearly defines and defends a doctrine of supralapsarian double predestination, and the case of Esau makes clear that God hates man even before the foundation of the world. Most although not all subsequent Lutherans tend to recoil from the consequences of Luther's thought regarding God's hatred and predestination. Calvin was in fact uncompromising (Martinich, 1992, p. 273) in his elaboration of these issues, coaxed into so doing during debates with opponents, more systematically than Luther while at the same time not falling into speculation. This uncompromising aspect of early Reformation thought seems to appeal to Lacan.

The inclinations of animals

Calvin repeatedly stresses that human beings are mere "vessels" of either God's mercy or wrath, for the purpose of glorifying and honoring God (Calvin, 1552, p. 76; Calvin, 1559a, 3.23.1). Human beings are vessels because man is an object of either the inherited sinful traits of Adam or of God's mercy that redirects the sinner's life towards the glorification of God. (As we have already seen, it is precisely this metaphor of the vessel or vase that Lacan puts to use to argue that both Luther and psychoanalysis show that fashioning a signifier (the Word) is identical with the introduction of a hole, an emptiness around which a world or something else is created. This metaphor concerns not the creation of a functional object but *creatio ex nihilo*, i.e. the relation between the Real and the symbolic (or the hidden God and his Word).) Calvin's focus is also on the vessel's emptiness rather than its usefulness in the world. His defence of supralapsarian double predestination is closely related to his anthropology, one in which man inherits from Adam an inclination towards evil and hatred of God. Man is originally created in God's image and "the individual parts of his soul were formed to uprightness, the soundness of his mind stood firm, and his will was free to choose the good". Yet, from the fallen Adam his whole posterity derived his corrupted state contracting "from him a hereditary taint" (Idem, 1.15.8). Corrupted by original sin human beings are unable to will or do anything good, as they are enslaved to sinful inclinations. On this point Calvin agrees with Rimini, arguing that God deals with reprobates in a fashion parallel to the way in which he deals with the elect. Hence, since the foundation of predestination proves that being elected is not a matter of doing good works, one has to assume the following:

> For as Jacob, deserving nothing by good works, is taken into grace, so Esau, as yet undefiled by any crime, is hated [Romans 9:13]. If we turn our eyes to works, we wrong the apostle, as if he did not see what is quite clear to us! Now it is proved that he did not see it, since he specifically emphasizes the point that when as yet they had done nothing good or evil, one was chosen, the other rejected.
>
> (Idem, 3.21.11)

For Calvin the crucial point is to secure God as the point of origination of all glory, thereby excluding all free will and human merit, "all works either past or future" (Calvin, 1552, p. 64).

Parallels between the thought of Luther and Calvin regarding the denial of free will and merit have already been dealt with sufficiently.[21] There are, however, significant points of difference in their respective accounts. For example, whereas Luther strongly ties man's sinful inclinations to the work of the devil Calvin prefers different imagery.[22] Not only does he regularly speak of vessels and pottery – empty material instruments of either divine wrath or mercy – but he also links human existence and behaviours to those of animals. For Calvin this makes sense because of human nature's fundamental depravity – a depravity so deep that a few virtues and little sense of purpose in one's life (honouring God and meditating on the heavenly life) cannot begin to compensate for (Calvin, 1559a, 1.5.4, 1.15.6). Because of this depravity, lack of goodness, inclination towards evil, and malicious denial of the divine, Calvin's comparison of humans with animals becomes prominent. This is evident in remarks comparing men to "grubs crawling upon the earth" and five-footed worms (Idem, 2.6.4).[23] In his sermons on predestination Calvin calls ignorant sinners "hogs" and "brute beasts", unconcerned by their fates (Calvin, 1551, pp. 50–51; Calvin, 1559a, 2.2.5). In the *Institutes* sinners are regularly described as "brute", "stupid", "mad", and "fanatical" beasts (Idem, 1.3.3, 2.1.1, 2.3.3, 2.10.3, 3.9.1, 4.1.2, 4.4.5; Huff, 1999). Most importantly, his association of man with animal is apparent in Calvin's depictions of man's natural inclinations and appetites. Calvin says the true and complete happiness of man depends on mercy, since happiness is to be found only in contemplation of those good things belonging to God. This relation between the good, God, and happiness is his point of departure in the *Institutes*. The "philosophers" have always taught "that all things seek good through a natural instinct, and this view is received with general consent". But what is the nature of this good in light of man's sinful inclinations? Calvin writes the following:

> If you consider the character of this natural desire of good in man, you will find that he has it in common with animals. For, they also desire their own well-being; and when some sort of good that can move their sense appears, they follow it.
>
> (Calvin, 1559a, 1.1.1)

Reason does not overrule these desires in man, but rather, "like an animal he follows the inclination of his nature, without reason, without deliberation".[24] This appetite, desire, or inclination of his nature has nothing to do with a free act of the will (since it results from an enslaved will), nor does "some sort of good" refer to either virtue or justice, but to a "condition" of well-being that certainly does not coincide with the protection and promotion of the well-being of others (Idem, 2.9.46; Hoitenga, 1997, pp. 76–78). This well-being does not even coincide with man's true happiness since happiness is included in neither the life nor aims of sinners.

We have already discussed an interpretation of the Freudian pleasure principle in which the object of desire does not coincide with the good. As it concerns the origins of this principle, Freud is primarily indebted to his teachers in neurophysics and the medical sciences. These disciplines are characterized by positivism and materialism, and in large measure gain inspiration from Darwin's views concerning the evolution of species. This background places its stamp on Freud's early work not only in the lab studying the human brain and eel genitals, but also his initial interest in hysteria as a disease proving difficult to explain in terms of either brain damage or the nervous system malfunctioning.

Freud's early psychoanalytic writings regarding a conception of the "primary ego" or "primary processes" dominated by the pleasure principle is clearly influenced by his teacher Theodor Meynert. Meynert develops a conception of the development of morality that departs from a Darwinian perspective that life consists in a struggle for survival. Meynert considers every organism essentially "evil" and "parasitical", as it lives on that which it can take from others to survive. This is apparent not only in animal but also human life, e.g. the need of the child to seek satisfaction that is provided by others. Conscious thought and the brain's development are only "secondary". In this respect then human beings are different from animals not only because of their rationality but also their ability to control these parasitic, egoistic impulses through conscience (Westerink, 2009b, pp. 49–55). Freud applies this theory in his own work to make clear that a child is fundamentally amoral – unaware of any moral principle – an idea he later generalizes when discussing "the undeniable existence of evil" in human nature" (Freud, 1930, p. 120). The "secondary processes" indicate rational, moral capacities.[25]

When Freud later positions the unconscious between the body and consciousness, and psychoanalysis between biology and philosophy, neither the body nor biology are necessarily limited to the study of human physiology. Man cannot be distinguished from animals at the level of either the body or natural mechanisms and principles, according to which the psyche functions. A strict distinction is never made between man and animal in the biological theories to which Freud refers throughout his writings. In *Three Essays*, for example, Freud writes on sexual excitation in terms of toxic and physiological processes found in both human beings and animals (Freud, 1905, p. 216). Neither is August Weismann's theory on germ cells to which Freud refers in *Beyond the Pleasure Principle* limited to human beings. Weismann's germ cell theory concerns the immortality and inheritance of a core molecular structure, unchanging and carrying the characteristics of either the species or family group – be it man or animal (Westerink, 2009b, p. 169).

Philosophical sources inspire Freud's thought regarding human instincts and cultural morality as well. Adolf Storfer's 1911 study of patricide anticipates Freud's *Totem and Taboo* as well as subsequent writings on culture that relate psychoanalysis to both ethics and law (Storfer, 1911). An early follower of Freud, Storfer describes in Hobbesian terms how the war of all against all is exchanged for primitive communities in which the advantage is a greater chance of satisfying one's needs at the cost of personal freedom. In both *Totem and Taboo* and *Civilization and Its Discontents* Freud stands close to Hobbes when asserting that culture restrains the aggression of the egoistic individual (Rieff, 1961, pp. 242ff).

In Hobbes' writings we can detect an important source of Freud's pleasure principle, including its association with animals. Hobbes begins his chapter on the passions in *Leviathan*, after all, with the vital and voluntary motions of animals (such as an appetite for food), of which man's motions appear as mere derivatives (Hobbes, 1651, pp. 84–87). Objects are not desired because a person thinks they are good but because – as in animal life – motion (desire) and aversion are basically causal forces, originating from an interaction between the body and an external chain of events. In this context Hobbes discusses the relation between good and evil on the one hand, and pleasure and unpleasure on the other hand. He defines good and evil in terms of objects of desire and objects of aversion, since neither good nor evil are related to the nature of objects, but are based on the relation between a person and an object. The good is relative to desire – something is good because a person wants it. A person's desires and behaviours are motivated by egoistic impulses. Hobbes goes on to describe pleasure as the result of obtaining a desired object, and displeasure as the effect of the appearance of an object of aversion. This scheme of the "simple passions" is then followed by a list of psychological concepts, which he defines by means of his notions of desire (self-interested appetite) and aversion. Higher mental functions such as the will, pity, and deliberation – functions Freud would relate to secondary processes – are thus not located in civilized man and characterized in contradistinction to his more primitive impulses, but are deduced from these primary passions. As in Freud's thought, the higher mental functions are governed by primitive mechanisms – and not vice versa.

Through Hobbes Freud's thought can be linked to a body of Calvinist thought. A relation between Calvin and Hobbes is easy to establish as Hobbes is deeply influenced by Puritanism – the English branch of Reformed orthodoxy. Key issues in his thought on human nature, such as lack of a natural predisposition towards religion and his conception of the primal state of war, match up with Puritan thought concerning its understanding of man as "atheist" and "murderer".[26] Hobbes is committed to the Calvinist doctrine of predestination, a commitment expressed in *Leviathan* when he defines God as the "first cause of all things", and when he argues that God is the cause (but not the author) of evil (Idem, p. 77; Martinich, 1992, p. 274; Schneewind, 1998, pp. 96–100). Hobbes defends Calvinist conceptions of predestination, determinism, and a denial of free will in his debate on these issues with Bishop Bramhall, who basically repeats the position of Erasmus and Arminius by defending (a minimum degree of) free will (Damrosch, 1979; Martinich, 1992, pp. 273–278; Gillespie, 2008). However, in Hobbes' thought predestination receives a new meaning: God is nothing more than the "first mover" of what Hobbes refers to as "nature", the cause and motions of events that can be described in terms of mechanical causality. He thus argues that "every act of mans will, and every desire, and inclination proceedeth from some cause, and that from another cause, in a continuall chaine, (whose first link is in the hand of God the first cause of all causes,) they proceed from necessity" (Hobbes, 1651, pp. 146–147). Hence, everything man wills – either good or evil – is caused by God's will as the first mover of a continuous, providential chain of events that cannot be influenced by human beings. From this point of view Hobbes argues that God wills nothing more that the continuation of this "chain". Applied to human nature, Hobbes writes that all men are created equal, striving to preserve their lives, and that from this equality arises competitive desires and conflicts, i.e. the war of all against all. This "ill condition" is a natural one (and for this reason need no longer be called "sin") that causes human beings to seek peace by means of a social contract to preserve their lives. The fundamental "laws of nature" (seek peace, be content with limited liberty) – expressed in divine law as well[27] – are thereby the result of man's natural condition, and in this sense they are also willed by God (Idem, pp. 86–100).

We see here how Calvinist thought regarding God's creative omnipotence and will, predestination, the human will, sin, and determinism prepares the way for secular theories of politics, ethics, and society. Placed in a natural condition through the absence and indifference of a divine first mover,[28] by imitation man must create artificial bonds and an "artificial animal" named Leviathan (the state) that protects these bonds (Shulman, 1988; MacIntyre, 2010, pp. 125–135). No longer do good and evil signify merely shifting appetites and aversions determined by principles of pleasure and unpleasure. They become fixed in contract through consensus. Peace is a good for all, and for this reason laws that secure peace are good – the state thus becomes the measure of good and evil (Hobbes, 1651, p. 469).

We can also recognize here aspects of Freud's though that stand close to Hobbes': the central importance of desire (appetite) and aversion, and pleasure and unpleasure, to psychic life; a denial of an absolute or greatest good; the ways law and social organization restrain aggressive impulses; the way in which the fundamental law of nature and the initial social contract explain the emergence and development of social norms also expressed in religious commandments. But there are also undoubtedly differences between Hobbes and Freud. For example, they have different views concerning desire's object. According to Hobbes man desires power to secure his life, whereas for Freud desire is conceived primarily as sexual in nature (although in *Totem and Taboo* Freud emphasizes the sons' identification with the father's aggression and power). Freud's reconstruction of primal history to explain culture is also, in part, the reconstruction of a primal social contract. The main difference between Hobbes and Freud on this point is that whereas Hobbes conceives of the contract as the outcome of a rational, conscious choice, Freud argues that the contract between the murdering sons is based on the unconscious motives of identification, hate, and guilt.

The immanent cause

Hobbes plays a crucial role in transforming Calvin's variant of the pleasure principle, describing man's sinful condition and inclinations in terms of psychic mechanism that regulate lower as well as higher mental functions. Freud's conception of the pleasure principle is rooted in this tradition. These similarities between Hobbes and Freud should not, however, lead one to interpret Lacan's claim regarding a filiation between Freud and Luther on "the *cause* of the most fundamental human passion" (my italics) in a Hobbesian fashion. This cause (Luther's God) is not a first cause in the way Hobbes means it – a prime mover who sets in motion a continuous chain of secondary causes and effects without further interference. This is not the kind of mechanical determinism Lacan has in mind. His is closer to the determinism of Hobbes' contemporary, Spinoza.

Spinoza (Lloyd, 1996; De Dijn, 2009) denies the Hobbesian distinction between a first cause and subsequent chains of secondary causation. God should not be thought of apart from nature. On the contrary, God is the created world (*Deus sive Natura*). Consequently, Spinoza argues that "God is the immanent but not the transitive cause of all things" (Spinoza, 1677, I prop. 18; Kiarina Kordela, 2007, p. 31). Lacan avoids interpreting such propositions in pantheistic or ontological terms: "what, quite wrongly, has been thought of in Spinoza as pantheism is simply the reduction of the field of God to the universality of the signifier" (Lacan, 1998b, p. 275). As opposed to pantheism, here Lacan's point of departure is Spinoza's idea that human thought be conceived as the aimless creative thought of God, since the human mind is part of God's infinite intellect: "When we say that the human mind perceives this or that, we are simply saying that God – (...) in so far as he constitutes the essence of the human mind – has this or that idea" (Spinoza, 1677, II prop. 11). The elaboration of this idea is evident in Lacan's conception of the unconscious as a reservoir of signifiers, as well as the distinction he makes between the subject of the statement ("ego") and the subject of enunciation (the subject of the unconscious). He argues the subject is essentially the effect of language. The subject only "exists" by expressing and defining itself in language – the birth of Freudian psychoanalysis takes place, after all, with Anna O's "talking cure" and it subsequently develops as the analysis of thoughts articulated in language.[29] For Lacan each and every statement is caused by and originates from something else or other ("the discourse of the Other") that does not coincide with these statements. Lacan's dictum that "God is unconscious" can be understood as an amalgamation of his conception of the unconscious as a reservoir of signifiers and Spinoza's conception of human thought as (immanently) caused by God's (Kiarina Kordela, 2007, pp. 17–18). Spinoza indeed anticipates the idea of an unconscious when he explains the illusion of human freedom in terms of conscious actions the causes of which one is ignorant. "Experience, no less clearly than reason", he writes, "teaches us that men believe themselves to be free by virtue of this cause alone: that they are conscious of their actions and ignorant of the causes by which they are determined" (Spinoza, 1677, III prop. 2).

But in what sense can this Spinozistic unconscious be understood as a "cause"? In Spinoza's thought cause is synonymous with effect, i.e. cause does not precede effect. A cause appears as such at the moment of the appearance of its effect. The equation of cause with effect (*Deus sive Natura*), and of substance with properties (in the sense that each of substance's infinite attributes constitutes and expresses substance's essence such that no substance exists behind its attributes (Idem, I def. 6, I prop. 11) is also apparent in Spinoza's commitments regarding an understanding of mind and body as expressions of two attributes belonging to the same substance. This is the cornerstone of Spinoza's criticism of Descartes' *cogito ergo sum*. Descartes' formula is based on a false distinction between transitive cause and effect, between thinking substance and extended substance. Spinoza bases his alternative on an immanent cause: *ego sum cogitans*, "I am thinking" (Kiarina Kordela, 2007, pp. 29–32). Lacan's analysis of the *cogito* moves in this same direction when he writes that every

"I think" is in fact an "it (Id) thinks". The unconscious God precedes and immanently causes each and every thought.

This dialectic of cause and effect captures Lacan's interpretation of the Freudian unconscious. Not only is the unconscious the cause of conscious expressions, but also the effect of repression – that is to say – an effect of conscious articulation: "repression and the return of the repressed are one and the same thing, the front and back of a single process" (Lacan, 1993, p. 60).[30]This dialectic of cause and effect, of repression and the return of the repressed, makes essentialism impossible. The unconscious does not exist apart from its effects, is not an essence under the surface of appearance, just as in Spinoza's thought regarding *Deus sive Natura* no substance exists apart from its endless attributes and appearances. Lacan's train of thought regarding the Thing also reflects, in my opinion, a Spinozistic influence. The Thing causes the fundamental human passion, a cause already "there" even before creation that can be identified with the introduction of "the order, essence, and foundation of the domain of law" (Lacan, 1992, p. 97). But it is also the effect of law as it gains its importance from being forbidden and since it is through the "fabricated signifier" that the "beyond-of-the-signified" enters the world. Lacan detects the same logic in Luther: *Deus absconditus* only appears as hidden on the basis of self-revelation in words and works, as the beyond-of-the-revealed (Idem, p. 54, 120). Hence, the Thing appears as both cause and effect at the moment it appears as effect.

The repercussions of a new direction of thought

These investigations of Hobbes and Spinoza take us deep into the seventeenth century. Their philosophies mark the beginning of an era in which metaphysics and religion lose ground relative to the natural sciences, rational Enlightenment thought, and the growing belief that man is free and autonomous. Yet there is more. As Michel de Certeau later describes it, the end of the seventeenth century is also the period in which a shift occurs with respect to thought on religion, from a concern with religion as dogmatic systems towards one in which religion is conceived as an ethics, as a guarantor of civil morality through its organization of behavioral modes used for political, social, and moral ends (De Certeau, 1988, ch. 4). Religion thus becomes synonymous with morality, and insofar as elements of religion cannot be reconciled with these social functions religion becomes highly suspect – traits of excessive religiosity thus fall to the domains of medical doctors and psychiatrists. That is, until Freud – a natural scientist *par excellence* – rediscovers the importance of prominent psychoanalytic themes to everyday life: the irrational, the unconscious, constitutional hatred, the hysteric's body as the locus of thoughts' expression through conversion, infantile helplessness, religion as the staging of a psychological drama, etc. Freud thereby rediscovers the intimate relation between religion as morality (symbolic order and law) and the repressed realm of instincts, inclinations, needs, and wishes. This is what I believe Lacan has in mind when points towards a filiation between Freud and a new direction in thought "whose repercussions are felt up to the end of the seventeenth century". Freudian thought connects up with a pre-enlightenment period that begins with Luther (Lacan, 1992, p. 97).

What are the repercussions of this new direction in thought that begins with Luther? According to Lacan these are predestination and the will's bondage, denial of the good and man's pursuit of evil, and God's eternal hatred. Reconstructing a theological history to witness developments and shifts in various views on these issues in the sixteenth and seventeenth century is unnecessary. Jean Delumeau rightfully asserts:"It is not so important to know whether Calvin put predestination at the center of his theology or not, but rather to observe that this doctrine was hotly contested within Protestantism itself, while Calvin's successors tended to magnify this aspect of Protestant theology" (Delumeau, 1990, p. 538). There are of course new developments, such as the integration of Calvin's thought on predestination with Protestant scholasticism by Theodore Beza (1519–1605), Calvin's successor in Geneva. His 1555 *Tabula praedestinationes* divides humanity into two strictly separate groups, two histories that begin with God's decree before the world's foundation (Bray, 1975; Muller, 2008, ch. 4). This view is taken up in William Perkins' 1590 *Armilla aurea*, where he gives an equally precise account of double destiny: one is either eternally loved or eternally hated by God, who elects and rejects even before the foundation of the world.[31] In these writings the doctrine of double predestination is treated systematically, evidencing speculative scholastic tendencies both Luther and Calvin tried to avoid, although both Beza and Perkins (1558–1602) stress the incomprehensibility of God's motives. At the turn of the century Perkins' doctrine of predestination is the starting point of a dispute between the Leiden professors Jacob Arminius (1559–1609) and Francis Gomarus regarding predestination, free will, and grace. This dispute soon split Dutch Calvinism into two opposing parties, remonstrants and counter-remonstrants. An (inter-)national church assembly, the Synod of Dordrecht (1618–1619), was necessary to force the condemnation of Arminius' teachings. Soon the canon of the synod would serve as a promising starting point for further reformation (Teelinck, 1627). Now that orthodoxy was secured, Calvinist teaching should become lived religiosity. The English Puritans had already shown way with a bulk of literature on doctrine and its applications in daily life.

In the second half of the sixteenth century Lutherans had their own disputes regarding the nature of predestination and human will (Kolb, 2005), as did the Catholics.[32] Among these debates by Lutherans, Catholics, and – not the least – Calvinists, the same theological concepts that play a dominant role in the debate between Luther and Erasmus are again discussed in their mutual interdependence. One of the most significant differences between the

Luther–Erasmus debate and the Arminian controversy concerns less the contents of the debate than the fact the latter dispute gains importance in the context of an already established Protestantism in which little was needed to widen the gap between various factions. In other words, at that time Calvinism was already a lived religion and academic controversies served only to further ignite flames of preexisting difference. Personal documents and biographies show that theological concepts such as predestination, reprobation, free will, and original sin provide structures in which to interpret the character of individual inner life and daily experience (Weaver, 1985; Frijhoff, 1995).

But further reformation of Dutch society at large envisioned by Teellinck, for example, never takes place. Radical Calvinism appeals to a largely world-avoiding sub-culture that flourishes in the second half of the seventeenth and eighteenth century but loses both its political significance and connection to enlightenment theology and philosophy. In England there are attempts to establish a radical Puritan society (1649–1660) under Oliver Cromwell's leadership, but Hobbes already foresees their outcomes in *De Cive* (1642): better to obey established authority than turn society into bloody chaos (Shulman, 1988). The political and social repercussions of this new direction in thought fade away in the second half of the seventeenth century.

As it concerns the issue of God's hatred as articulated in Luther's *The Bondage of the Will*, Lacan can hardly have been aware that in the course of debates on predestination and human will, God's hatred as "cause of the most fundamental human passion" is a delicate issue treated with care and consideration. The problem of the origin of evil and its relation to double predestination continues to be a central problem, especially in Puritan and orthodox Reformed teachings. Arminius' critique of Perkins' and Gomarus' doctrine of predestination, for example, concerns precisely the issue of God as the cause or author of evil. It is telling that, despite rejecting Arminius' teachings at the Synod of Dordrecht, the assembly, aware of the problem of the cause of evil and its possible pastoral consequences, does not accept a supralapsarian doctrine either. The assembly thus implicitly avoids the possibility that too much attention be drawn to the eternal hatred of *Deus absconditus* (Westerink, 2002, pp. 29–33).[33] This does not mean, however, that God's hatred is no longer expressed. On the contrary, authors such as Teellinck colourfully describe God's "sword of wrath", his hatred and revenge because of humanity's corruption, and his use of both pestilence and war to press individuals and governments alike to obey God and renew the covenant (Teellinck, 1624). Conceptions of God's hatred as wrath are widespread in Puritan and Reformed orthodox discourse. The question of whether one is elected or damned, and the related problem of despair, remain key issues in the *praxis pietatis* of the Calvinists who, during the seventeenth century, increasingly become a subculture focused primarily on inner signs of faith and salvation, and on resistance to sins of the world and flesh. Anna Maria van Schurman is a radical example of this.

(To what extent Spinoza's thought on obedience to biblical commandments, critique of an anthropomorphic image of God as Judge, and the general character of his work – the movement away from despair towards serene wisdom – might be understood as an answer to, or way out of, the pastoral problems and theological discourses that so profoundly influence Dutch religious mentality in the seventeenth century is an open question for further research.)

Chapter 3

Original sin and moral responsibility

Whereas the previous chapter focused on Lacan's claim of filiation between Freudian psychoanalysis and Reformation thought primarily in terms of issues dealing with origination and causation – supralapsarian predestination, the cause of the fundamental human passions, the bondage of the will, and the desire of the Other – in this chapter we further explore this claim of paternity from the perspective of human nature, an understanding and valuation of human nature shared by both Reformation thought and psychoanalysis. Psychological awareness regarding this naturally human disposition – as well as man's "evil" nature – brings us to the heart of an ethics of psychoanalysis, a Spinozistic ethics that consists in the honest recognition of desire's causes, objects, and vicissitudes, taking responsibility for one's desires i.e. desire as the locus of the moral subject.

Original sin: the many-headed Hydra

In previous chapters we saw that Augustine defines original sin in terms of concupiscence or libido, referring to sinful desires that distort man's natural inclination to the good – in other words, a freely willed disobedience to God. He rejects the semi-Pelagian view in which human beings are thought to be capable of controlling sin and cooperating in salvation. We noticed that Luther follows Augustine, notably in his later writings on predestination and his denial of free will, contrary to scholastic thought (including nominalism). Luther makes use of Augustine in his disputations to oppose scholastic thought. This separation is not, however, unproblematic. Among others, Thomas Aquinas holds Augustine in high esteem, often quoting his writings and referring to the latter's theological positions. This is also the case in Aquinas' *quaestiones* on original sin (Aquinas, 1984, II.I.82-83). He agrees with major aspects of Augustine's thought on the matter, notably, the idea that original sin is formally caused by disobedience to God's will, materially it consists in concupiscence (libido), corrupts the will, and is transmitted by procreation and not imitation. But Augustine is not the only important voice in Aquinas' theology. The other is Aristotle. Here we find a strategic reason for Luther to oppose Augustine to scholasticism, one that connects up with discussions in the late Middle Ages between the various *schola*: Luther's movement *ad fontes* includes an attempt to purify Augustinian theology of what he considers redundant philosophical speculation.[1]

According to Aquinas, original sin is the privation of an original justice, one that causes corruption to the soul's concupiscible powers and in turn causes the soul to go beyond the limits set by reason. Human beings thus become "evil" in the sense that there is an absence of good, defined in terms of a disorder of the soul's natural powers. In good, virtuous people reason takes precedence and rules over both the will and passions, whereas in other people the lower parts of the soul take control of the higher intellectual functions. The crucial point here is that evil is simply a privation, a lack or absence of the good. Evil is thus defined negatively and has neither an essence nor a reality of its own. This lack of good does not mean though that all good has disappeared – the natural tendency towards virtue has been disrupted, but neither knowledge of the good nor the capacity to control sinful inclinations (Idem, II.I.85; Gilson, 1994, pp. 155–158). Original sin causes a corruption that incites some to persist in evil. Nevertheless, rational persons freely choose the good, not the least because the good (God) is that towards which desire naturally tends. Since human beings are rational beings with knowledge of basic moral principles and capable of advancement in virtue, the issue of moral responsibility is clear: a person can and must act in conformity with God's reasonable will. A person is morally responsible for his or her advancement in a virtuous life, and morally blameworthy for acts that result from a persistence in evil. In short one's moral acts are the criteria for determining whether a person should be regarded as either good or bad.

Luther repeatedly argues that scholastic definitions of original sin are inadequate, not because they are wrong but because they are too "weak". The scholastic definition of original sin is based on Aristotelian philosophy: original sin is a privation or lack of original righteousness. Yet according to Luther this definition is incomplete and must be supplemented with a biblical-Augustinian view.

> On top of all this, it is a propensity toward evil. It is a nausea toward the good, a loathing of light and wisdom, and a delight in error and darkness, a flight from and an abomination of all good works, a pursuit of evil. (...) Therefore, as the ancient holy fathers so correctly said, this original sin is the very tinder of sin, the law of the flesh, the law of the members, the weakness of our nature, the tyrant, the original sickness, etc. For it is like a sick man whose mortal illness is not only the loss of health of one of his members, but it is, in addition to the lack of health in all his members, the weakness of all of his senses and powers, culminating even in his disdain for those things which are healthful and in his desire for those

> things which make him sick. Thus this is Hydra, a many-headed and most tenacious monster, with which we struggle in the Lernean Swamp of this life till the very day of our death.
>
> (Luther, 1515–1516, 299)

Evil is thus not only a privation of good but also has a substance and reality of its own. It can be described as an active pursuit of evil, an active resistance to the Holy Spirit, an "inborn disposition" or "an innate evil" (Luther, 1536b, III-165, 187). As stated above it is a condition that can be described as an illness, an "original sickness". It is this disposition that makes human beings sinners, "even though they have done no evil deed" (Luther, 1515–1516, 45). Luther describes it as a sickness, poison, or venom that exists even in healthy persons.

Crucial here is the distinction between this innate disposition and the actual sins that result from it – it is on this point that Luther refutes the Aristotelian–Thomistic logic wherein a person becomes unjust or bad by performing unjust or evil acts. According to Luther, "inborn evil makes acts evil. That is the condition, that is to say, original sin is the root of actual sins" (Luther, 1536b, III-191). This disposition is inborn or innate. Neither can it be completely controlled nor destroyed in this life. After all, the destruction of this disposition, of this *conditio humana* dating from Adam's sin, implies the destruction of the subject. By focusing on original sin rather than actual sins, and criticizing scholastic theologians for disregarding the total nature of sin, Luther emphasizes truth: one should recognize the whole truth of one's sinful disposition. Only through law is the truth of original sin's recognition possible. The law shows persons their disobedience, unbelief, and sinful selfish interests.[2] Only the law can do this:

> Before the Law was given, the revelation of the Law through Moses, original sin was in the world, that is, in the men of the world, but sin, original sin itself, even though the actual sins were certainly reckoned, was not counted, or reckoned, indeed, it was ignored, when there was no law, which actually did exist, but it was not recognized.
>
> (Luther, 1515–1516, 45)[3]

In other words, knowledge of original sin is not obtained through knowledge of actual sins. A person who commits evil deeds is counted for his crimes, but does not necessarily recognize himself as a sinner – such a person might identify his evil deeds as evil deeds but remain ignorant regarding the source from which these deeds originate unless he knows the law.

Luther thus clearly distinguishes between original sin as a human disposition or condition on the one hand, and actual sin as specific moral failings and immoral acts on the other. According to Luther the scholastics are basically ignorant of original sin and, thus, of the distinction between original and actual sin as well. They focus on actual sins – their presence or absence; the struggle by the virtuous against them – without taking into consideration the seriousness of the original, lasting, and persisting cause of these sins. The reason for this neglect, says Luther, is that "the scholastics do not want sin to be of such a kind, because it casts us away from the eyes of God" (Luther, 1536b, III-165). As an inborn evil, original sin makes us guilty before God and consequently subject to divine wrath and eternal death – scholastic theologians apparently exclude from reflection – or repress from conscious thought – such a conception. They deny that man is cast away, or vice versa, that man existentially lacks the supreme object of knowledge and desire.

But can a person be guilty of having an inborn disposition? Luther thinks so, and his critique of scholasticism gives us an important clue as to why. If original sin is considered merely a lack of righteousness that can be restored or compensated, then such a view gives occasion to pride and presumptuousness and eradicates the authority and fear of God. A person is then guilty of believing themmself to be free of sin, and such a belief is precisely the core of original sin. In other words, a person is not guilty because of an inborn disposition that results from Adam's ancient act, but is guilty of self-deceit, of denying this disposition – and the denial of this disposition is precisely what constitutes it. It is natural for an individual to be proud and radically self-centred, to desire only selfish ends, and think oneself free of sin, hence, God-like or at the very least not in need of either grace or spiritual help. It is precisely this unbelief that constitutes original sin.

> It is no small matter to say that man is ignorant of God and despises God, for these are the sources of all crimes, the sink of all sins, nay, the hell of all evils. Could any evil not be there where there is ignorance and contempt of God? In short, the reign of Satan in men could not have been described in fewer or more expressive terms than by his saying that they are ignorant of God and despisers of God. That betokens unbelief, it betokens disobedience, sacrilege, and blasphemy toward God.
>
> (Luther, 1525a, III-256)

Hence, original sin concerns less a moral guilt towards other persons and more a religious-existential guilt that results from a lack of fear, trust, and love of God. From this we can understand why knowledge of original sin does not result from contemplating either actual sins or virtuous behaviours but only the law prescribing God's will.

Closely related to this question is if human beings are in some way responsible for being sinners. In the previous chapter we saw that Luther says God works good and evil in human beings. Before Luther, Erasmus is already aware of and worried about the consequences of this assertion, which might discourage people from taking responsibility for their behaviour or initiative in moral conduct (Gillespie, 2008, pp. 149–151). But Luther says a person should take responsibility for being a sinner, not only in view of one's resulting sinful acts but also because awareness of sin is the first step towards salvation. Faith starts when the individual acknowledges he or she is a sinner, accepting this sinful disposition as one's own. To understand the importance of obedience to God's will and of justification *sola fide* a sinner should take responsibility for his or her sinful disposition, i.e. the fact that a person is exiled from the Supreme good (Kolb, 2005).

Calvin is even more explicit. He clearly rejects the idea that man should be relieved of moral responsibility because of God's omnipotence and will. The ancient Greeks defend fatalism as a consequence of divine determinism, and they express this in their tragedies and myths when blame for one's own wickedness is laid on the gods: "I am not the cause, but Zeus and fate" (Calvin, 1559a, 1.17.3). Instead of covering up one's own evil deeds by invoking the name of "God", that is to say, instead of taking a fatalistic position human beings should follow what is written in Scripture and actively strive for spiritual guidance. For Calvin the reason is obvious:

> He who has set the limits to our life has at the same time entrusted to us its care (…) It is very clear what our duty is: thus, if the Lord has committed to us the protection of our life, our duty is to protect it.
>
> (Idem, 1.17.4)

The eternal decrees of God do not thus hinder human beings from taking matters into their own hands, be it always a submission to God's will.

Before Calvin discusses in detail the nature and effects of original sin in the second book of the *Institutes*, he argues that self-knowledge inevitably confront us with original sin, discouraging and humiliating human efforts. Utterly deprived of self-assurance, this knowledge incites the sinner to consider the purpose of creation, to consider his own (lack of) abilities and, consequently, recognize "the nature of his duty" and "the extent of his ability to carry it out" (Idem, 2.1.3). An awareness of sin thus leads to the recognition that salvation depends on God's grace, which should then result in an eagerness to seek God through obedience. In short, a person should take responsibility for his life – recognizing his sinful disposition and his life's purpose – and accordingly live in conformity with God's will, while at the same time recognizing that such obedience will always be disrupted by sinful inclinations, and that he thus depends on an act of grace. This responsibility should not be confused with merit – the ability to carry out one's duties is defined within the parameters of grace and faith. It is, after all, precisely because of the unreliability and uncertainty that follows from the *facientibus*-principle, and the critique of merit, that moral responsibility is defined in a new way. In other words, moral responsibility is disconnected from an ethics that centers on merit, outer social behaviour, and custom. Calvin's conception of responsibility might be described best as the frank recognition of a human disposition characterized by egocentric indifference, disruptive to the relation with God and one's fellow man, which entails a recognition of the importance of a desire for salvation and one's need for grace.

A similar line of thought regarding original sin runs throughout Calvin's writings. Adam has the best of motives to control his passions, practice righteousness, and obey God's will, since these things secure the ultimate goal of life, to be loved by God and live in his presence. Creation can be described as if it were the lost, divine universe of the Middle Ages: a harmonious order between God and man, who is created in the image of God, honouring God through cheerful and willing obedience. Man's unfaithfulness and disobedience result from entirely selfish desires that lie at the root of his fall, the reason for his estrangement from God that causes "the depravation of a nature previously good and pure" (Idem, 2.1.5). Adam's rebellion against God – permitted by and hence willed by God himself – causes the perversion of his nature in the process of which God withdraws his own image from Adam's soul and thus severs man's participation in God. Although there are "remaining traces of the image of God, which distinguish the entire human race from the other creatures", Calvin argues the soul is utterly devoid of any good once it is "plunged in the deadly abyss" of original sin since this "Hydra" then "lurks in the breast of each" (Idem, 2.2.17, 2.3.2).

Like Luther Calvin argues that original sin is not propagated by imitation but carried as an "inborn defect from our mother's womb" – Adam's descendants are all infected with the same contamination, the same illness.

> Therefore, after the heavenly image was obliterated in him, he was not the only one to suffer this punishment – that, in place of wisdom, virtue, holiness, truth, and justice, with which adornments he had been clad, there came forth the most filthy plagues, blindness, impotence, impurity, vanity, and injustice – but he also entangled and immersed his offspring in the same miseries.
>
> (Idem, 2.1.5)

Calvin thus defines original sin as "a hereditary depravity and corruption of our nature, diffused into all parts of the soul, which first makes us liable to God's wrath, then also brings forth in us those works which Scripture calls 'works of the flesh'" (Idem, 2.1.8). As Luther before him Calvin states explicitly that original sin is more than a mere lack of goodness. It has a content and reality of its own that he calls "concupiscence", sinful desire in the broadest sense of the word – total depravity or perversion of human nature; corruption of all the soul's powers, of reason and will alike. He distinguishes original from actual sin and depraved customs that result from original sin, although he admits that Paul does not seem to make such a distinction. Original sin makes human beings guilty before God, not in the sense that human beings innocently bear responsibility for Adam's sin, but in the sense that human beings share in this guilt (or "curse") and are thus incapable of declaring themselves innocent – a person cannot point his finger at another claiming he or she is guilty; transgressive desire is part of a common, human nature and, hence, belongs to each and every individual (Idem).

With the breakdown of a hierarchically structured continuity between the human and divine spheres a new, more pessimistic perspective on human beings and the world arises. The theological consequences of nominalist thought are crucial here: an emphasis on God's absolute omnipotence and free will eventually undermines a harmonious relation between reality and transcendence. With regard to one's knowledge of universal moral principles, no longer is there a steady, secure point of departure in either the outside world or the individual – attempts to defend *synderesis* or God's reliability hardly alleviate the revolutionary potential of nominalist thought on this point. According to Luther only a radical Augustinian theology provides a way out of the problems nominalist thought creates. Moreover, the order of nature (including human nature) is no longer guided by an innate, cognizable moral law – if God is the sole norm of goodness then nature lacks goodness. This lack is quickly filled with a negative content: the human being's innate, sinful disposition.

Luther is a crucial figure in the gradual process of culpabilization, the internalization of evil's origins as the foundation of a new conception of subjectivity. The subject is understood as an inner arena wherein every thought and mood – mental and moral effects – is reviewed by an inner conscious and conscientious observer. The inner life of the subject is the *locus* where God's Word constitutes faith, religious thought, and speech, redirecting the subject's aims and life from the "inside". The subject is defined by its inwardness, by the consciousness of one's wicked nature and its consequences, subsequently subjected to an inner authority given *sola gratia* that remains inaccessible to others – thus a shift from the medieval harmonization of oneself with "external" realities and spheres. The Reformation is a clear sign of this movement, away from an understanding of salvation in terms of the individual's proper participation in an external order to one in which salvation depends on the individual's internal state alone. It is in this context that original sin – caused by someone else and inherited from another – can be understood as "mine". All people share in the "curse" that defines *conditio humana*. Acceptance of this condition is *sine qua non* for a fundamental reorientation of life. It is the *terminus a quo* that should neither paralyze nor discourage, but, as Calvin writes, be accepted in recognition that one is naked and empty-handed and, thus, has to "flee" towards God's mercy – by accusing and admonishing the law moves the individual to flee and seek (Idem, 2.7.8-9).[4] Only through acceptance of original sin as "mine" does it follow that he who died for all men also died for "me".

Evil nature

The question now becomes in what sense – and what not – early Reformation thought on original sin can be related to psychoanalysis. In Chapter 1 we saw that aside from Lacan several other scholars such as Taubes, Thurneysen, Reik, and Tillich recognize the familiarity between Christianity and psychoanalysis. Elaborating on this familiarity was, in some sense, obligatory since Freud himself explicitly associates the religious notion of original sin with the sense of guilt he situates at the centre of both neurotic and normal life. The Christian notion of original sin is in fact a condensed expression of this sense of guilt (Freud, 1915, p. 292) that Freud at times explains as an inherited psychic disposition traceable back to primal patricide. Freud's psycho-Lamarckism thus points towards a certain commonality with the notion of original sin as a hereditary disposition.

As it concerns Freud's psycho-Lamarckism in *Totem and Taboo*, it is clear that the content of inherited psychic dispositions is indeed none other than the sense of guilt he also refers to as original sin. But this psycho-Lamarckism is not without its problems. When explaining the emergence of Christianity in terms of Saint Paul's reassessment of a Jewish sense of guilt in *Moses and Monotheism*, a crucial moment in Freud's analysis is the claim that Christianity gained momentum because this sense of guilt spread "as a dull malaise" across large areas of the Mediterranean world (Freud, 1939, p. 135). Although Freud fails to further expand on this claim, it seems unlikely that the inheritance of psychic dispositions alone can account for this spread. The transmission of unconscious contents is more likely explained in terms of what Freud calls "tradition", by which he means the oral transmission of contents that survive among people despite their exclusion from official written records. We should therefore be careful when considering Freud's association of original sin with this sense of guilt. Psycho-Lamarckism not only confronts us with an aspect of Freudian thought that Freud himself further nuances in his Moses text, but which is also rejected by many of Freud's followers – including Lacan (Freud, 1912–1913, p. 158; Freud, 1939, p. 69).[5]

The inheritance of psychic dispositions does not itself lie at the heart of Freud's writings on religion. It is a typical aspect of the positivistic and naturalistic approaches Freud employs his applied psychoanalysis to relate the origins of individual morality to collective historical developments. This idea can hardly be defended though at the level of psychoanalytic practice. On the contrary, in the first place the trajectory of Freud's psychoanalytic practice and theory is opposed to a medical tradition in which neurosis (or neurasthenia) can be explained by weaknesses in the nervous system or the brain's malfunctioning, often regarded as an inherited abnormality. In the second place psychoanalytic therapy aims at delegitimizing the logic involved in projecting one's own "evil" or "guilt" onto someone else in the outside world. The Dora case is a beautiful example of this. It involves the difficulty of analysing mutual accusations between the main actors of Dora's stories and confronting the patient with her own "evil" wishes – Dora breaks off therapy at the moment she has to accept that her reproaches against her father only veil self-reproaches and sexual wishes (Westerink, 2009b, pp. 32–33).[6] In other words, at the moment a person should take responsibility for their own thoughts and wishes no longer does a past or present other exist who can be blamed. Consequently, no longer can one call upon some ancestor as responsible for a person's specific inherited inclinations and thoughts.

Elaborating the commonality between Christianity and psychoanalysis is problematic on another point as well, namely, Freud's interpretation of original sin as a sense of guilt – i.e. the identification of cause (disobedience) and effect (sense of guilt). Like so many theologians Freud loses track of the fact that, theologically speaking, not only does original sin need to be distinguished from actual sin but also from moral conflict. Luther expresses this in his telling metaphor of original sin as the Hydra with whom men struggle in the Lernean Swamp of this life. Only through law is original sin known as a disposition. This struggle with the Hydra is a struggle of the believer who knows the law rather than that of the ignorant. As a "curse" original sin expresses not a conflict between drive and morality but a disposition characterized by both a "lack" of righteousness and the "pursuit of evil". For this reason neither can original sin be reduced to sexual desire nor aggressive impulses – Augustine was already aware that libido has to be defined in a broader sense, one referring to all desires that express the disavowal of God's will. Adam's sin is his disobedience, the renunciation of a principle that had thus far organized the entirety of his mental life and behaviour. Hence, his fall indicates the inaugural moment of a new disposition, one in which man ceases to be naturally inclined towards obedience to God.[7] A sense of guilt then is only an effect of this fall. It expresses an inner conflict that only arises when a moral principle (law) is accepted as guidance and gives extra weight to original sin.

Although Freud is clear that morality is not innate but arises at a certain time as a result of reaction formations, identification, etc. he neglects the difference between disposition and conflict when conflating original sin and a sense of guilt. On this point then Lacan's interpretations of sin when reflecting on the filiation between Christianity and psychoanalysis seem more accurate than Freud's. Lacan focuses on the father-God as a pre-historic, pre-worldly tyrant that infuses his sons with his own hate. Hence, Lacan's focus is on the *causa pathomenon*. It is this "evil" that subsequently wills to destroy the father principle, a disavowal of both *Nom-* and *Non-du-Père*. According to Lacan, the fundamental problem that both Luther and Freud address is the problem of evil as linked to a generally human disposition. In a second move he focuses on evil and its relation to the law's influence, i.e. the relation between the "bad" will (drives) and the "good" will (conscience) (Lacan, 1992, pp. 97, 104, 101) – the relation between the absence of the father principle (in the imaginary order) and its affirmation (the law as *Non-du-Père*). So, Lacan does recognize the difference between original and actual sin. The sense of guilt still indicates the conflict or tension between drive and morality, between bad and good. His starting point is not, however, the equation of original sin with a sense of guilt. Moreover, Lacan starts with the issue of disposition – *conditio humana* as a "sick", "evil" nature that results from God's hatred (*causa pathomenon*) – after which he moves on to deal with subsequent mental conflicts between interrelated yet opposed forces, which Freud describes in its sundry variants: love versus hate, the polymorphous perversity of the drives versus reaction formations; Id versus ego and superego; wish versus conscience, the pleasure versus reality principles, and primary versus secondary processes.

Lacan sees Luther as a protagonist in a story reflecting human nature in terms of not only a lack of goodness but also a "pursuit of evil". The filiation between Luther and Freud concerns a problematic that touches on deeper layers of Freudian thought than its psycho-Lamarckism or treatment of religion and pathology as analogous. Freud's focus is not on extraordinary psychic dispositions but he argues that psychopathology shows in an excessive manner ordinary aspects and mechanisms of the human psyche that constitute subjectivity. From the start he depicts this subjectivity in terms of a human constitution in which the good is lacking, e.g. a natural inclination towards sympathy and altruism. Furthermore, Freud's characterization is one in which clearly amoral and immoral traits and mechanisms largely dominate the ego and death drives, hate (aggression), the sexual drive's sadistic components, the pursuit of selfish needs and incestuous wishes, the pleasure principle, etc. For Lacan the consequences of this characterization are clear: at the heart of man's destiny lies the problem of evil. Like Luther Freud also emphasizes the importance of truth – recognition of the (psychological) truth of human nature (Freud, 1915, p. 284). In a sense then Freud echoes Luther's position (against the scholastics): "We lay a stronger emphasis on what is evil in men only because other people disavow it and thereby make the human mind, not better, but incomprehensible" (Freud, 1916–1917, p. 147).

It takes Freud a number of years to recognize this evil nature – this "truth". As early as 1880 he characterizes the "psychology of the common man" as not only lacking refinement but also acting out the drives in a brutal manner (Freud, 1960, pp. 50–51). But this world of the common man is the world of others, and in proceeding years Freud remains firmly committed to his belief in the refinement – the high moral standards – of himself and his hysteric patients, anchored in the innocent world of childhood. He expresses this in his 1896 seduction theory: hysteria originates from sexual trauma (sexual abuse) inflicted by a perverted parental figure (mostly the father), a trauma that is experienced passively (Freud, 1896a). Evil is thus located outside the patient; the inner conflicts of Freud's patients could be traced back to guilty deeds of others. His analyses of obsessional neurotics, however, point in a different direction. There the infant's sexual experience is actively and aggressively pursued with fervour. Only a year later Freud denounces his faith in the seduction stories of his hysteric patients. This is the beginning of a period marked by Freud's self-analysis that eventually culminates in *The Interpretation of Dreams*, and a gradual shift in attention from hysteria to obsessional neurosis. Having rejected his own seduction theory, Freud is now free to expand on obsessional neurotic traits – the sexual drive's sadistic component, the severity of conscience – and typical dreams that fascinate Freud the most, those that express the wish to kill a loved parent (the father). In *Three Essays* Freud radically denies the innocence of either child or man, and the popular "fable" regarding normal sexual drives and aims, turning pathology – generally considered abnormal, a moral aberration – into a paradigm for normal psychic constitution (Freud, 1905, p. 136). Normality is the result of the risky and fragile restraint of the drives' perversity; it describes the outcome of a process of socialization of various pathological dispositions.

A fuller elucidation of these issues in Freud's later writings is unnecessary. The main point is clear: neither is abnormality a lack of refinement nor is pathology the effect of someone else's sins. The problem is not that man lacks the good – a lack that might then be compensated for through techniques, virtues, merits, personal growth, insight, integration, maturation, healing, or adaptation to shared norms and values. Not only are such compensations often expressions of an illusionary belief in human goodness that sustain narcissistic perceptions of one's integrity, says Freud, but they can also be regarded as reaction formations against repressed drives, wishes and desires, hence, neurotic symptom formations. Man, in short, is a sick animal with naturally "evil" impulses.

Moral responsibility and the ethics of honesty

There is good reason to speak of these impulses of human nature as "evil" since, as we saw in the previous chapter, Freud uses this word at times to describe destructive inclinations present in the very constitution of human beings.[8] Freud employs the adjective "evil" in an interesting text on moral responsibility as well (Freud, 1925). The question he asks in this text is should a person hold himself responsible for the immoral character and content of his dreams. If dreams are nothing but a "meaningless product of disordered mental activity" then there is no reason to assume responsibility, since the disorder is not only beyond human control but also reflects a state in which the person is – as it were – dissolved. Yet Freud's interpretation of dreams shows that dreams are not the product of disorder but expressions of egoistic, "immoral, incestuous and perverse impulses or of murderous and sadistic lusts". When censorship fails these impulses surface disguised as dream content. The fact that censorship fails to function here, i.e. that pre-consciousness fails to do its duty, might lead us to believe that a person – as rationally conscious moral being – cannot be held responsible. And yet Freud argues to the contrary:

> Obviously one must hold oneself responsible for the evil impulses of one's dreams. What else is one to do with them? Unless the content of the dream (rightly understood) is inspired by alien spirits, it is a part of my own being. If I seek to classify the impulses that are present in me according to social standards into good and bad, I must assume responsibility for both sorts; and if, in defence, I say that what is unknown, unconscious and repressed in me is not my 'ego', then I shall not be basing my position upon psycho-analysis, I shall not have accepted its conclusions (...) It is true that in the metapsychological sense this bad repressed content does not belong to my 'ego' – that is, assuming that I am a morally blameless individual – but to an 'id' upon which my ego is seated. But this ego developed out of the id, it forms with it a single biological unit, it is only a specially modified peripheral portion of it, and it is subject to the influences and obeys the suggestions that arise from the id.
>
> (Idem, p. 133)

In this passage we see that meta-psychological distinctions such as those between Id, ego, and superego can be misleading, notably when the ego is associated with good and the Id with either bad or evil. In that case the fact that Id and ego (and superego) form a biological unity and that the ego is nothing other than a modified portion of the Id is lost to sight.[9] The consequences should not be overlooked: psychoanalysis is unconcerned with applying the distinction between a good, healthy ego and an evil, unhealthy Id, consisting in a psychology that would aim at strengthening the ego against the Id. As used in the above quotation, the term "defence" makes clear the problem with such an approach. Associating good with the ego and evil with the Id only serves defence mechanisms that on the one hand consist of projections (It is not I who am responsible for the dream but an alien force) and on the other sustains illusionary narcissistic wishful thinking (I am good). For "the ethical narcissism of humanity" should be content with evidence of both its "moral nature" as censor and "evil nature". Whoever wants to become "better than he was created" will probably attain nothing other than "hypocrisy and inhibition" (Idem, p. 134). Freud's motto that "Where Id was, there ego shall be" (Freud, 1933, p. 80) could be best be interpreted according to the above quotation as the ego taking responsibility for the Id, thereby acknowledging the biological unity that exists between them: where the dream is at night should the ego accept as its own during the day – not insofar as the mature ego should feel a sense of responsibility and then work up the requisite moral strength to work against and control the Id's instincts, but insofar as a person is responsible for his dreams because they are his own.

Although this text is relatively underappreciated in the secondary literature, I believe it lies at the heart of a Freudian ethics, what Philip Rieff rightly calls an "ethics of honesty", which consists in the replacement of inefficient moral commitments. The ineffective method whereby certain instinctual impulses are suppressed by means of a too-severe repression should be replaced with another procedure. This is Freud's aim in working through layers of hypocrisy, secrecy, and fantasy to reach a different assessment of oneself and one's relation with reality – a method that presupposes the absolute honesty of his patient as the fundamental rule of therapy (Rieff, 1961, p. 346). The sense of guilt in neurosis shows two poles involved in this diagnosis. Normal man is "not only far more immoral than he believes but also far more moral than he knows" (Freud, 1923a, p. 52). In other words, Freud aims at a more truthful assessment of both one's moral and immoral nature. The problem of the neurotic's sense of guilt is a result of not only the strength of their evil impulses but also the severity of a moral function's (conscience, superego) repression, i.e. the firm belief in a moral ideal. Admitting one's nature, working through one's wishes, desires and impulses, and taking responsibility for these is psychoanalysis' formal creed. Yet psychoanalysis presents neither criteria and descriptions concerning the precise content of this standard nor an ideal for the development of one's personality and moral conduct. It is committed to a freedom of speech that results in self-knowledge through the expression of one's desires. However, in Freudian thought such a procedure does not imply that this process of healing, development, and maturation ever reaches its zenith as a victory of Eros over Thanatos, love over hate, intellect over drive, or ego over Id. Nor does it imply an individual will become capable of living a balanced and harmonized life. As a procedure that consists in the analysis of affective motives, desires, and unconscious representations and attachments, Freud's ethics of honesty never merges with a message of salvation. Quite to the contrary, its final conclusion is an acceptance of many thoughts and beliefs as mere illusions.

Freud already writes the following in his early reflections on the therapy of his hysteric patients: "But you will be able to convince yourself that much will be gained if we succeed in transforming your hysterical misery into common unhappiness" (Breuer & Freud, 1895, p. 305). His writings on psychoanalytic therapy are not the only evidence of Freud's attempts to uncover the defences and illusions. In *Thoughts for the Times on War and Death* he reflects on the sudden loss of civilized morality in times of war, and the raw, brutal forms of hatred and disgust that arise towards enemies and strangers. Times of war show several things: first, man's primitive nature is hidden under the façade of civilization; second, that the "good" is not innate; third, people are not inclined to act according to utilitarian principles. The fact that all of these are denied by European culture that firmly believed in the illusion of its untouchable superiority, which made enthusiasm for war greater and, thus, threatened society itself. War cannot be abolished, says Freud, and yet a different attitude towards life might be taken that makes war appear as a less plausible option. The ingredients of this attitude are the unmasking of illusions regarding heroism, invincibility, and immortality, and the acceptance of death as part of life. Tolerating the fragility of life "remains the first duty of all living beings" (Freud, 1915, p. 299). This tolerance of life's fragility is not intended to result in a passive submission to the inevitable. On the contrary, it is an activity, an intellectual activity to be more precise. It consists in the quest for the "historical truth" regarding man's "evil" nature and its effects, which not only lie repressed under a façade of rationality and morality but are also the very motor of the "advancement of intellectuality" – i.e. "decisiveness of thought", "strength of will", and "energy of action" (Freud, 1937, p. 269; 1939, pp. 109–110). Freud's account of – and what might even be called identification with – Saint Paul gives us a clear picture of what happens here. According to Freud Paul had the rare pre-psychoanalytical intellectual capacity to deeply penetrate and assess Judaism and Jewish identity. He was capable of analysing his own identity and religiosity, concluding they were the outcome of a sense of guilt originating from Moses' murder. Instead of taking a quasi-ignorant distance to this repressed historical truth or simply submitting to its inevitable nature Paul takes responsibility. He accepts this sense of guilt as his own and actively transforms it via contemporary language and representations. His novel missionary theology is evidence of this, one in which this sense of guilt can be worked through. The restorative and regressive teachings of his successors result in the failure of Paul's intellectual project (Westerink, 2007). In this way Paul is Freud's final example of what Goethe expresses in one Freud's favourite quotations: "Was du ererbt von deinen Vätern hast, erwirb es, um es zu besitzen" (Freud, 1912–1913, p. 158, 1940, p. 207).

Freud regards self-knowledge as good and liberating. The patient can be liberated from defences and attachments that prove too much, and saved from the repetitive return of the repressed that causes excessive mental conflicts. It is at this point though that psychoanalysis' filiation with (Protestant) Christian thought reaches its limit. Freud refuses interpretations of psychoanalysis as a religious philosophy of life contra Pfister, and as a message of salvation and redemption contra Jung. Most importantly, Freud's theories reflect an enlightened belief in the power of intellectual thought and science, and as it concerns religion he undisputedly follows Feuerbach and Nietzsche in their critiques. There is also no doubt a ("godless") Jewish trait in Freud's work. For example, he praises the Jewish advancement of intellectuality and pleads for an acceptance of death as a way of giving meaning to life (Freud, 1915, p. 299) – a plea that resounds the ancient wisdom of Qohelet. Only by admitting to the vanity and shortness of things can one see the meaning of life in work and pleasure (Qoh.3:12-13). At no point however does Freud ever endorse features of Christian thought, which he finds hypocritical (preaching the love for one's fellow man combined with intolerance and anti-Semitism), illusionary (the continuation of narcissistic feelings of omnipotence and faith in immortality), regressive (its low standards for intellectuality), oppressive (religion as a moral doctrine), and suggestive (the church's hierarchy and its manipulation of the masses).

Spinozian ethics

Lacan gives his own twists to Freud's conceptions of moral responsibility, as well as the individual and collective's knowledge of historical truth. In his exegesis of Freud's famous, much discussed sentence "Wo Es war, soll Ich werden", Lacan stresses the meaning of "soll" as an "imperative", "a duty in the moral sense" (Lacan, 2006, pp. 417, 801, 865). As it concerns Freud, this sentence and duty are often construed as meaning the ego should be strong enough – at some point in the future, or as the aim of therapy – to mediate between the Id and superego without being a powerless spectator in the conflict between their opposing forces. Reflecting on the meaning of this sentence in terms of a critique of ego psychology that overemphasizes the ego's strengthening to dislodge the Id, for Lacan this duty is "to assume my own causality", which is to say, recognizing and assuming the symbolic causes and determinations of one's being as one's own (Idem, p. 865).[10] Without denying the fundamental distinction between the subject of the unconscious (Id) and the ego, says Lacan, "I" (ego) must admit that I am "born of this very locus insofar as it is a locus of my being" (Idem, p. 417; Neill, 2005). The way in which he translates Freud's sentence is indicative of this interpretation: "Where Id was, there must I come to be a subject" (Lacan, 2006, p. 864). The subject should recognize itself as determined by the Other's discourse and desire, in the sense that it is the desire of the Other in the subject that determines its being rather than the subject's conscious, supposedly free actions.[11] The fact that Lacan immediately associates this causality with "the Spinozian self-cause" that "takes on the name of God", makes clear that he interprets Freud's sentence in terms of his comments regarding the Cartesian *cogito* (Idem, p. 865). The ego is caused by the Id, but the Id appears as cause and effect at the moment of its appearance as an effect: by articulating desire and, thus, bringing desire into existence. The subject does not simply express a pre-existing desire already there to be uncovered, but its very expression is also a creative act. A person has the "duty" to assume the Other's discourse as his own, and as the cause of his own subjectivity – failure to assume this causality makes the subject "fundamentally dishonest" (Idem, p. 524).[12] This assumption is nothing but that of responsibility, holding oneself responsible for this articulated desire that results from the unconscious, the discourse of the Other. In other words, the Other's discourse is the locus of one's inscription, thus becoming a responsible subject.

Whereas Freud's critique of both cultural and religious illusions is usually associated with Feuerbach's anti-dogmatic interpretation of religion as the outcome of imagination, needs, and wishes, Lacan's Freudian disavowal of illusion and dishonesty has a clearly Spinozistic flavour.[13] His own thought is in line with Spinoza's on several points, for example, the denial of free will and human autonomy, of teleology in (human) nature and of a God-given soul, a notion of immanent causality, the absence of moral precepts, the denial of the objectivity of notions such as good and evil, and the idea that insight into and the articulation of one's affects is in some way liberating.[14] Spinoza presents a practical philosophy in which illusions are done away with in favour of something else, notably, growth in wisdom, accepting the truth that one's existence is determined by blind desire and the natural-divine forces of necessity, accepting one's being as a particular mode in and of nature. The natural world is an expression of a radically impersonal and indifferent God, understood as a single substance expressing itself in an infinite, endless, purposeless process of production. According to Spinoza, human beings have faith in the illusion that their actions are free and conscious, and aim at specific higher goals willed by God (Lloyd, 1996; De Dijn, 2009).[15] Not only is this to mistake the nature of God but also – as we have seen – to deny the unconscious "causes whereby those actions are determined". Freedom from illusions is possible when an obsessive fixation on single causes, objects, and purposes is given up in exchange for insight into the general causal patterns of which the person is a part (Spinoza, 1677, V prop. 2). When experienced in a particular way knowledge of the world as the expression of one substance is what Spinoza calls love of God (*amor intellectualis Dei*). This results in the individual's suffering less from emotions and fear of death – hence, happiness and relative freedom in comparison with ordinary man's enslavement to illusions (Idem, V prop. 38, 42; Schneewind, 1998, pp. 216–223). Lacan largely devotes the final chapter of his seminar on the ethics of psychoanalysis to the unconscious cause of subjectivity, the value of self-knowledge as it concerns immanent causes, discrediting egocentric illusions, responsibility as the assumption of this cause as one's own, an acceptance of life as a being-for-death, and the particularity of personhood in terms of the expression of one's desire by means of the symbolic order.

Were one to confine this insight to human nature, both Spinozistic and Freudian conceptions of self-knowledge are nothing other than variants of Plato's *γνῶθι σεαυτόν*, which Lacan says amounts to the insight that a deeper meaning guides lived experience. Psychoanalysis goes beyond this "catharsis", asking, "Will there be nothing but goodness?" when one excavates desire's deeper layers (Lacan, 1992, p. 312). At bottom for Lacan this question concerns the possibility and effect of linking the dialectic of demand, need, and desire "to that well-founded and legitimate function we might call the service of goods" (*service des biens*), that is to say, "private goods, family goods, domestic goods, other goods that solicit us", etc (Idem, p. 303). If so then psychoanalysis is a utilitarian theory and practice that accommodates social demands, shifting the demands of the subject for happiness into the arena of shared norms and common welfare. The instincts then encompass the natural inclination towards the realization of harmony However, Lacan denies the ethics of psychoanalysis consists in making "ourselves the guarantors of the bourgeois dream" by prescribing and regulating human conduct (Idem, pp. 303, 312–314). He relates the aim of such an ethics – an ethics belonging to ego psychology and the like – to Aristotle's traditional morality, choosing the middle path of modesty and temperateness as an ideal, characterized by a utilitarian logic regarding the exchange and substitution of goods, a socializing process in which everyone contributes to the welfare of the other (Idem, ppp. 314ff). The effect of such prescriptions and regulations is the avoidance of a real "confrontation with the human condition", and for this reason such procedures and aims can only have a very limited result in psychoanalysis' field of inquiry (Idem, pp. 303, 315). We have already seen what is at stake here: By providing access to *Ersatzobjekte* that offer some form of satisfaction the law of the father – the symbolic order – organizes desire within the limits of certain socially-acceptable goals and ideals. And yet, a person is more than the effects of socialization and adaptation. Desire for the Thing shows us that man's adaptation to the arena of cultural norms and obligations, conventions and customs, and useful social rules is far from self-evident. As a desiring being man moves between two poles, namely, desire of the ultimate object of enjoyment on the one hand, and desire's satisfaction in the symbolic order through signification on the other (see also Chapter 4).

At this point Spinoza enters the stage once again. We recall that Lacan quotes Spinoza's statement that "desire is the essence of man". Desire structured within the symbolic through signification circles around its ultimate object – the Thing. According to Lacan, the final "ethical judgment" with which psychoanalysis confronts a person is the following: "Have you acted in conformity with the desire that is in you?" This question is not to be read as an imperative. Psychoanalysis does not demand from a patient that he or she act in conformity with his or her desire. Rather, the question is ultimately one of honesty, with the aim of finding a freer, more flexible and personal way of making moral choices for oneself and of discovering "the value of prudence" (Idem, p. 323), which is to say, a mild yet personal and adequate conception and (self-)understanding of good and bad, relative to one's nature and mode of existence, which serves as a fragile inner limitation of excessive desires and attachments (Moyaert, 1994, pp. 86–90). It calls for assessment, whether one lives according to Aristotle's morality, choosing the path of compromise and socially-acceptable living, or is there more, another desire, namely, desire of an ultimate object that cannot be exchanged for another object, i.e. an object desired for its own qualities without being in the service of other means and purposes. Such a pure desire does not have as its touchstone either one's own happiness or pleasure (the good in a social context), but transgresses this towards an object for which one is prepared to suffer. Lacan's exegesis of Sophocles' *Antigone* concerns precisely this point. According to Lacan this play shows us the essence of tragedy, namely, the dialectical relation between Creon, who represents a law that promotes the happiness and good of all people belonging to the polis, and Antigone, who represents desire for an object – her dead brother, Polynices – for whom she is prepared to suffer and die (Van Haute, 1998). Following Aristotle's account of tragedy as the evocation of a catharsis of feelings by the spectator, and Freud's view on tragedy as the staging of psychological conflict, Lacan refers to self-knowledge of one's desire as catharsis (purification) (Lacan, 1992, pp. 312, 315).[16] Like psychoanalysis, tragedy does not present ideals or imperatives but insight regarding the nature of human desire. The question "Have you acted in conformity with the desire that is in you?" concerns a confrontation with the tragic character of the human condition, which is avoided when psychoanalysis becomes a moralizing practice.

In this way then the shortcomings of ego psychology's limited focus on the relation of inner motivations to moral behaviour becomes apparent when one inquires into the nature of desire. In other words, the focus of an ethics of psychoanalysis does not consist in supporting sundry adaptive styles. In fact, behaviour is only a secondary issue. This relates, once again to Spinoza. His ethics do not offer rules of moral behaviour and action. Spinoza argues that acts are neither good nor bad in themselves, since actions consist in merely physical motions that are sometimes regarded as good and at other times as bad, depending on the way of thinking and relating one thing to something else (Spinoza, 1677, IV preface def. 1–2). However, he does employ good and evil to determine the extent to which a person lives according to his ideal, that is to say, according to his desire as it is conditioned by his nature. Because of this focus on desire rather than behaviour, the Freudo–Lacanian ethic with its focus on the deployment of desire can indeed be called a Spinozian ethic rather than as an integration or modification of the subject for the sake of socially-acceptable interests (Roudinesco, 1997, p. 312). At the same time, however, there is a limit to Lacan's Spinozism.

According to Lacan only a few people are capable of *amōr intellectualis Dei*.[17] Only a few are able to envision the hidden God, i.e. Moses' Thing hidden behind revelation as its real cause (Lacan, 1992, p. 180). At first glance Lacan's reference to *amor intellectualis Dei* seems to express the following: Spinoza shows that, in a sense, the intellectual contemplation of Luther's abyss, *Deus absconditus*, is only possible if one is prepared to give up all illusion and every attachment to traditional religious thought. But Lacan writes that Spinoza's transcendental love "is not tenable for us", since Spinoza is incapable of accounting for the evil and monstrosities of which man is capable. Spinoza regards living according to the laws of desire as a sovereign right of the individual (whether reasonable and sane, or not), a right "to exist and act according to its natural conditions", that is, to live according to the rules of nature and his own powers – just as fish enjoy and desire water since they are conditioned for swimming. Spinoza's blind spot, says Lacan, consists in the fact that desire in its pure state culminates in sacrifice and murder (Spinoza, 1670, pp. 200f; Lacan, 1998b, p. 275). Spinoza acutely envisions the unconscious as the immanent cause of man's subjectivity, and desire as the essence of man, but fails to see that at the heart of the unconscious lay the problem of evil.[18]

It is interesting to note that Spinoza defended his philosophical ideas against criticisms by religiously motivated writers, mostly Calvinists, who point towards the same problem Lacan mentions here.[19] Willem van Blyenbergh, a grain broker from Dordrecht with a keen interest in theological matters, for example, accuses Spinoza as early as 1664 of defending a conception of God as the cause of both mind and each and every endeavour and motion of the mind. From this it necessarily follows "either that there is no evil in the movement or will of the Soul, or that God himself is the immediate cause of evil" (Spinoza, 1966, letter XVIII). Consequently, he argues that Adam's sin is either not evil or is caused by God when God provokes Adam's transgression of his own commands. Blyenbergh is here reasoning in terms of a strictly Calvinist train of thought, quasi-speculating on God's motives and yet also trying to avoid imputing to God the role as either the cause or author of evil. Spinoza's reply is telling. He writes that neither sin nor evil have a positive existence. Adam's decision is imperfect, but is neither evil nor against God's will since human beings cannot desire contrary to God's will or intellect. Evil can only be perceived as something that inhibits the pursuit of the ideal of knowledge, not as a pursuit of evil (Idem, letter XIX). Blyenbergh's response is as follows: If evil is only a term relative to our imperfect knowledge, how then can one describe the state of man as sinful? If evil is nothing other than a negation or privation, in what then does the sinner's pursuit of evil consist? Speaking of evil in terms of imperfect knowledge nullifies any and all distinctions between the good and the wicked (Idem, letter XX). Spinoza reacts, arguing that Blyenbergh ascribes personal and anthropomorphic qualities to God, with the result that God is described as a judge punishing the wicked, letting them live and die like animals. Adam's sin is only evil from a human point of view, not from the divine perspective. From a divine perspective sin is merely a lack of something in comparison to something else, as blindness is a lack of sight compared to those who can see, but not in comparison with stones (Idem, letter XXI).[20]

It is precisely this denial of evil's positive reality in human nature that Lacan calls "not tenable". In a sense he connects up with Blyenbergh's Calvinist critique of Spinoza, and from this perspective we can understand why an intellectual, Spinozistic contemplation of Luther's *Deus absconditus* and Calvin's abyss is impossible. Such an intellectual ideal can never be captured in terms of a serene beatitude or intellectual love. What one would be confronted with here, rather, is the problem of evil as an inner bodily reality. A "true confrontation with {the} human condition" – one avoided by the ego psychologists who focus on goodness as the source of moral behaviour – is a confrontation with the problem of evil as a problem of desire (pathos, concupiscence) that radically separates us from the good (or God).

Chapter 4

Conscience

In previous chapters the main focus was Lacan's seminar on the ethics of psychoanalysis and the components of his claim regarding a filiation between psychoanalysis and Reformation thought. In this chapter I will sketch the most important currents within medieval thought concerning conscience and natural law, after which I will explore an important point of convergence between Freudian and Lacanian psychoanalytic theory and the theologies of Luther and Calvin, more specifically, the formation and internalization of conscience, as well as the two ways in which the imperatives of conscience function: a review of inner life and the regulation of outer duties. Although Lacan does not explicitly mention this issue as part of the filiation between psychoanalysis and Reformation thought, the subject is highly relevant from the perspective of the dialectic between law and desire as conceived in Reformation theologies.

Synderesis and conscience: a sketch

In the work of Thomas Aquinas *synderesis* refers to a natural and innate habit or disposition of the human mind by which man apprehends both general and basic moral principles of natural law, i.e. divine law insofar as it is inscribed in human nature. Conscience (*conscientia*) is the application and regulation of this intuitive moral knowledge in the conscious judgments and actions one makes everyday. Since basic moral principles are formulated generally rather than specifically – for example, "do good and avoid evil" – moral dilemmas are at times difficult to assess. Since individuals can be mistaken in specific judgments and deceived by sinful passions, scholastic scholars such as Aquinas stress one's obligation to avoid moral risks and the need of moral authority, which is provided by the church as an institution that codifies moral norms. The moral judgments and actions of individuals are thus embedded in an order that is both natural and divine, a general human disposition, and an authoritative institution (Schüssler, 2009).

Whereas Aquinas formulates his conceptions of *synderesis* and conscience in terms of rational and cognitive qualities of the soul, his contemporary

Bonaventure (1221–1274) conceives of *synderesis* as an inclination of the natural will towards the divine Supreme Good (Baylor, 1977, p. 28; Langston, 2001, ch. 2). Neither is this movement deliberate nor directed by the free will. It is a natural instinct that makes persons desire the good and avoid evil. From this perspective it can be described as a weight (*pondus*); it is "a sort of natural weight towards the good" (Greene, 1997, p. 189).[1] Conscience then depends on *synderesis* and is conceived in terms of one's knowledge of moral principles based on revelation, natural law and church authority, and the application of these principles in actions. Exercises in virtues improve this application, and it is only here that a believer has any kind of control over his spiritual advancement. Later medieval thinkers attempt to harmonize Aquinas and Bonaventure's views on *synderesis*, and in these cases the concept is comprised by both intellectual cognition and a natural weight towards the good.

Church authority plays an important role in the thought of both Aquinas and Bonaventure. An important factor in the steady decay of church authority as a guide for moral life was the Great Schism (1378–1417), which split the unified church and undermined its guarantee as the foundation of moral truth. The schism evoked uncertainty and moral pluralism, as well as the need for new criteria to guide moral judgments and actions. This contributed to an atmosphere in which people could elect new models of moral reason and new spiritual practices flourished, for example, the *devotio moderna* with its heavy emphasis on education and the daily self-examination of one's conscience.[2] Many have recognized the influences on the Reformation of the subjective piety of this (initially lay) movement (McGrath, 1987, pp. 9–12).[3] In the background of, for example, the thought of Jean Gerson (1363–1429) and his attempts at reforming and revitalizing church practices (confession) with a clear pastoral aim (assurance of conscience), stands the general uncertainty that results from this disintegration of moral authority (Burrows, 1991; McGuire, 2005). On occasions Luther refers to Gerson and praises him as a critic of papal and church authority, as well as a rare expert on conscience, its confusions, and admonitions (Grosse, 1994).

It wasn't only political circumstances that contributed to the downfall of the Aristotelian universal order, one in which both divine and natural order, human nature and authority are attuned. At least as important as the shock of the schism was the rise of nominalism. We have already discussed the general contours of William of Ockham's thought on *potentia absoluta*, *potentia ordinata*, and its potential consequences, notably, the breach between one's apprehension of moral order as ordained by God and the omnipotence and freedom of God's will (Freppert, 1988; McCord Adams, 1999; McGrade, 1999). Despite the fact Ockham stresses the congruence of reason and revelation, he does not employ a conception of *synderesis*, since this would imply a logically untenable connection between God's free, omnipotent will and man's knowledge of universal moral principles. The ordained order is contingent and God's will supersedes the moral order as understood by human reason. God creates the world and continues to act in it, unbound in principal to earlier decrees and universal laws. Whereas *synderesis* plays no role in his writings, as a conception of reason that is in agreement with God's will conscience gains increasing importance in his writings (Baylor, 1977, pp. 70–91). The highest moral principle is to obey the will of God. We should not overlook a potential consequence of this view, namely, that obedience to God makes the rejection of general moral consensus logically plausible, even resulting in an act that is neither reasonable nor beneficial from the perspective of an existing moral order (McCord Adams, 1999, pp.265–266). Although unintended, Ockham here introduces a framework that his followers further reflect on that eventually gains currency in the Reformation era.

Later nominalists such as Gabriel Biel also emphasize the conformity of God's will (*potentia absoluta*) and natural law (*potentia ordinata*). Biel therefore reintroduces *synderesis*, defending it as man's naturally innate and immutable intellective potency by which general and basic moral principles are apprehended, conscience as the application of this moral knowledge in everyday judgments and actions, and salvation as its reward (Oberman, 1963; Baylor, 1977, pp. 81–118). Hence, Biel followed Aquinas in relating *synderesis* to the intellect, and even raises it from an inclination or habit to a potency of the soul, thus anticipating an understanding of conscience as a faculty.

In Luther's earliest writings we find clear traces of medieval thought regarding *synderesis* and conscience. In a sermon entitled *On the Proper Wisdom and Will* (1514), for example, Luther argues that the will of God and that of humans has one and the same goal: the individual's salvation. This desire is attributed to *synderesis*, which Luther describes as follows: "A preservation, a remainder or a left-over portion of our nature in the corruption and faultiness of perdition. It is like a tinder, a seed, and the material of our future revival and the restoration of our nature through grace" (cited in Baylor, 1977, p. 158). This natural, uncorrupted desire aims towards the good and away from evil. It desires that man be saved and, thus, hates to condemn. *Synderesis* includes a knowledge of God that cannot be obscured by corruption: the idea that God exists with certain qualities (immortality, justice, etc.). As in other late medieval literature, Luther regards *synderesis* as an aspect of both reason and will. However, whereas most medieval thought conceives of *synderesis* as both the ontological and intellectual basis of the morally good, virtuous actions of man, Luther's sermon evidences only a shadow of this optimistic view regarding human reason, will, and moral attitude. He stresses that desire for salvation is only a "left-over portion": "In speaking about the whole will in the same way, it itself is deficient in loving the good, just as the reason is in knowing the right and the true" (Idem, p. 159). In other words, sin so fundamentally corrupts man that neither reason nor will either know or desire salvation. No longer here is there any correspondence between the pale remains of *synderesis* and conscience as the application of knowledge in moral acts. In fact, when considering the whole of man's sinfulness, *synderesis* plays no role in the obstruction of one's inclination to evil. According to Luther, the scholastic scholars overestimate *synderesis* and neglect the importance of corruption.

In his lectures on Saint Paul's *Epistle to the Romans*, Luther continues to employ *synderesis*, although this concept takes on marginalized status in his adaptation of a radical Augustinian view, one that soon leads to the disappearance of *synderesis* from his writings altogether (Idem, pp. 173–208). The revealed law teaches us sin, says Luther, and shows us God's will, the sole guidance for human action. But if this is so then what about gentiles who will certainly perish, although without knowing either divine law or sin? Luther argues that gentiles perish because – despite the fact that knowledge of certain laws, basic moral principles, and spiritual matters (such as the existence of God) is inextinguishably inscribed in their hearts – they lack faith and thus sin even when they act rightly (Idem, pp. 134ff). Even if a person acts in accordance with that which is "permissible and good", this act is still a sin if it "does not proceed from faith" (Luther, 1515–1516, p. 118).

We see here the limited importance of *synderesis* and new meaning of natural law (not a naturally innate desire for the good but a God-given knowledge of basic moral laws): even though the gentiles can act in accordance with a law written in their hearts, they are sinners and will consequently be damned and perish. Since the nature of both original and actual sin is known through the divine law in its written and oral variants, *synderesis* is no longer important. As soon as the law reveals the corruption and fundamental deprivation of human nature, it is clear that a supposed knowledge of divine, universal moral principles is insufficient for either salvation or justification. Instead the principles of predestination and grace determine who knows the law, will have faith, will act without sinning, and will be saved and justified. In short, *synderesis* points at a "tiny motion toward God, which man is naturally capable of" – a tiny motion towards the good that loses significance when a person discovers through the revealed law his inclination towards evil and that his entire being is corrupt (Baylor, 1977, p. 175). *Coram deo*, *synderesis* means nothing.[4] When one considers that fundamental human passions are caused by God's hatred – unlike in the hedonist tradition that Lacan identifies with Aristotle and Aquinas, a convergence between pleasure and the good, a natural inclination toward the good, looks highly untenable.

In his *Judgment on Monastic Vows* (1521) Luther distances himself from a medieval conception of conscience as the power to do works, saying that conscience should be understood as the power to judge works. Regarding the nature of these works, he points out that scholastic theologians incorrectly focus on general principles and norms of moral behaviour and neglect to "apply this conscience to those great and deep sins of the heart" (Luther, 1521, iii-277; Zachman, 1993, pp. 20–24). Following Aristotelian ethics these theologians have a limited scope. They can only conceive of *synderesis* and conscience as the actualization of moral principles, ones traveled on rules of conduct established by moral authorities for the benefit of society. Luther has the entire person in mind when he mentions judgment of works, i.e. that human nature is fundamentally corrupt because of original since, not only external actions or internal actions and virtues. This is one of Luther's major theological innovations, making conscience the inner judge of the person (Baylor, 1977, p. 234). No longer can *synderesis* account for the self-knowledge one receives through divine law necessary in faith, nor can it be a decisive factor in salvation. At the heart of man's moral sensibility conscience take the place of *synderesis*. It judges and subsequently redirects the whole person:

> The proper work of conscience (as Paul says in Romans 2[:15]), is to accuse or excuse, to make guilty or guiltless, uncertain or certain. Its purpose is not to do, but to pass judgment on what has been done and what should be done, and this judgment makes us stand accused or saved in God's sight. Christ has freed this conscience from works through the gospel and teaches this conscience not to trust in works, but to rely only on his mercy.
>
> (Luther, 1521, iii-299)[5]

We are already familiar with the step Luther makes from here. Through the words of God's law man "is warned and instructed as to what he ought to do, not what he is able to do" (Luther, 1525a, III-127). Conscience thus judges the "works" a person ought to do but is incapable of doing because he is a sinner.

Now that conscience is no longer understood as the deployment of knowledge of moral principles (*pondus* towards the good) but instead as judge of the entire person *coram deo*, the way is paved to conceive of conscience as a faculty of the soul. Although neither Luther nor Calvin does so explicitly both the Puritans and Reformed orthodox, such as William Perkins (1558–1602) and Willem Teellinck do. Perkins defines conscience as a faculty "from whence knowledge and judgment proceede as effects", located between man and God, ideally guided by God's will that accuses of sin and excuses for doing well (Perkins, 1966, p. 5, 99). Teellinck conceives of conscience as a faculty that knows and judges the inner, spiritual state of man before God. In this way then conscience rules the soul like a "little God", "another person in a person" that echoes the will of God (Westerink, 2002, pp. 186–194). The crucial point here is that conscience is not conceived as a faculty concerned with applying knowledge to action. It knows and judges the person's entire state before God, according to the will of God as it is inscribed in or engraved on the human heart. Needless to say this inscription should not simply be understood in terms of obedience to either worldly authorities or natural law. Original sin fundamentally corrupts the human soul, including the soul's capacity to know and judge one's inner state. *Synderesis* is certainly absent here.[6] Only through an act of grace is knowledge of God's will revealed.

Conscience can subsequently perform its function by redirecting a person through accusation and excuse.

In Calvinism this gives rise to an activism based primarily on the conscience of the individual, as well as decisions to oppose and reorganize social structures, "to clean up the human mess or at least to mitigate the tremendous continuing insult done to God" (Taylor, 1989, p. 228).[7] The employment of conscience against an established political and moral order begins with Luther – it comes to light in his 1521 confrontation with the German emperor at the Diet of Worms where Luther refuses to renounce his faith. In his writings Luther expresses this deployment of conscience as follows:

> But surely it is preferable to lose the world rather than God the creator of the world, who is able to create innumerable worlds again, and who is better than infinite worlds! For what comparison is there between things temporal and things eternal? This leprosy of temporal evils ought therefore to be endured rather than that all souls should be slaughtered and eternally damned while the world is kept in peace and preserved from these tumults by their blood and perdition, seeing that the whole world cannot pay the price of redemption for a single soul.
>
> (Luther, 1525a, III-53)

The writings of both Luther and Calvin are crucial to transformations in the conception of conscience, from will or applied practical reason to a faculty of self-knowledge guided by God's revealed will. This transformation concerns not only conscience's redefinition in terms of a faculty of judgment regarding thoughts and works, but also a shift in emphasis from the general to individual. Since medieval conceptions of conscience concern the application of a moral knowledge or will with which all people are endowed equally they refer to the synchronization of outer behaviour with moral convention. According to Aquinas, people who are rational and obedient to the church's moral authority freely choose the good and, therefore, also apply this knowledge in their everyday actions. But this model changes when Luther adopts a radical Augustinian theology. From that point on the focus of his analyses are principles such as *sola gratia* and *sola fide*. Not only does the latter concept express the means by which an individual receives salvation but also brings the inner life of the individual to the forefront. General human traits and inclinations of conscience fall short (Luther, 1521, iii-299).

Luther's two kingdoms

When Luther places original sin at the heart of human nature he simultaneously discards the scholastic tradition of compensating for or battling actual sin through good works and virtues. This does not mean, however, that Luther rejects natural law – he does however give the concept a new meaning.

Luther continues to ascribe to the view that regardless of their beliefs human beings know the law as a principle that commands the good and forbids evil for society's common good, despite the fact that human beings – naturally inclined to sin – generally understand the good in terms of selfish personal interests. Hence, in his *Lectures on Romans* Luther writes that "the Gentiles have not received the rites and orders of the law of Moses", yet "they have received a spiritual law which the rites and ceremonies indicated in the moral sense", a law that is natural insofar as it is "impressed upon all people, Jews and Gentiles, and to this law all people are bound" (Luther, 1515–1516, p. 180). Written during the same period as *The Bondage of the Will*, Luther declares the following in his 1525 *How Christians Should regard Moses*: "For to have a God is not alone a Mosaic law, but also a natural law, as St. Paul says, that the heathen know of the deity, that there is a God" (Luther, 1525b, iii–98). Natural law is thus not limited to an awareness of God's existence that leads to subsequent belief in evident in worship. Luther argues in fact that both the Mosaic law and its Paulinian recapitulation should also be understood in terms of natural law: "Thus, 'Thou shalt not kill, commit adultery, steal, etc.,' are not Mosaic laws only, but also the natural law written in each man's heart". The same goes for Paul when "he sums up all the commandments of Moses in the love which also the natural law teaches in the words, 'Love your neighbor as yourself'". Luther makes an important remark regarding this point: were these laws "not naturally written in the heart, one would have to teach and preach the law for a long time before it became the concern of conscience". There must be a natural point of connection between the human heart and divine commandments "otherwise it would become a matter of conscience for no one" (Idem). It must then be assumed that in a sense the law of God somehow resonates with human nature, since otherwise people could easily disavow the law.

The fact that the natural law is inscribed in the human heart means that both gentiles and ignorant sinners can still do good works. These works cannot, however, be understood as the effects of faith but only in terms of the sinful, selfish pursuit of interest. At this point we should not be surprised to find Luther praising Aristotle's knowledge of law and civil righteousness. He writes that unjust, uneducated people should read Aristotle's ethics for the sake of moral training. But *coram deo* this civil righteousness means nothing since original sin lies at the heart of man (Lazareth, 2001, p. 145).[8] For Luther this point comprises an important aspect of his thought regarding the so-called two kingdoms or governments (Whitford, 2004; Pesch, 2004). Since a selfish pursuit of interest lies at the heart of human inclinations and actions, Luther pleads for a strong, secular political authority that demands obedience to civil laws for the sake of regulating social affairs (Pearson, 2010). Authority should wield a repressive sword to defend the common good, to restrain transgressions by the wicked that cause social chaos. Luther is unreserved in his support of such a view in pamphlets and letters against revolting peasants

(Luther, 1525c). In more general terms he writes the following: "If there were a better way to rule over a mob, God would have established some other form of government for them than the sword and tyrants" (Luther, 1526, iii-112).

Secular (positive) law and political authority are understood by Luther as God's gifts to man, gifts included in God's plan of creation for the sake of restraining sin and protecting the common good. In this way then there are limits to political authority.

> The temporal government has laws which extend no further than to life and property and external affairs on earth, for God cannot and will not permit anyone but himself to rule over the soul. Therefore, where the temporal authority presumes to prescribe laws for the soul, it encroaches upon God's government and only misleads souls and destroys them.
>
> (Luther, 1523, III-105)

The purview of worldly government and its authority are those of worldly affairs, external dealings, and regulations. It should not interfere in matters of faith and conscience. Luther thus boasts that "not since the time of the apostles have the temporal sword and temporal government been so clearly described or so highly praised as by me" (Luther, 1526, iii-95), while at the same time resisting the Emperor at Worms, the highest authority, because of the government's attempts to constrain faith by force (Luther, 1523, III-108).

An interesting example of this model's application of can be found in *Trade and Usury* from 1524. Luther argues that since Christians are rare, "the world needs a strict, harsh temporal government which will compel and constrain the wicked to refrain from theft and robbery". This is particularly true of trade. Trade falls within the public domain and for this reason sinful human nature easily corrupts social life – unhindered man's "wicked, wily, self-seeking nature" submerges society in avarice, such as the time preceding Noah's flood Because of this the government "must keep the roads safe, preserve peace in the towns, enforce law in the land, and let the sword hew briskly and boldly against transgressors" (Luther, 1524, III-256ff). So that the faithful can engage in trade and commerce without severe conflicts of conscience such regulation is important: "It is enough that with a good conscience you make the effort to arrive at what is right, though the very nature of trade makes it impossible to determine this exactly" (Idem, III-250).

Calvin's double government

The distinction between these kingdoms refers to two particular realms: one worldly and ruled by the devil, and another ruled by God. Both faith and conscience belong to the second – conscience is the power to judge the entire person *coram deo*. As it concerns the worldly kingdom, if one transgresses the natural law inscribed in the heart of each and every individual then civil authorities should deal with this transgression or civil violation (Whitford, 2004, p. 58). Recent studies rightly point out that Calvin's views regarding spiritual and civil government also imply a two kingdoms doctrine, albeit with different nuances than Luther's (Walhof, 2003; VanDrunen 2004, 2010). Calvin distinguishes between Christ's spiritual, inward kingdom, which "resides in the soul or inner man and pertains to eternal life", and civil jurisdiction or government, "which pertains only to the establishment of civil justice and outward morality" (Calvin, 1559a, 4.20.1). As it concerns the duties of civil government, Calvin is in full agreement with Luther regarding the role of the state. Calvin writes that the state should "adjust our life to the society of men, to form our social behaviour to civil righteousness, to reconcile us with one another, and to promote general peace and tranquillity". Yet his views regarding the tasks of the civil government diverge from Luther's when he adds that the government is appointed "to cherish and protect the outward worship of God, to defend sound doctrine of piety and the position of the church" (Idem, 4.20.2). In other words, not only should the civil government defend the common good (property, peace, etc.) by restraining the insolence and wickedness of evil men, but also provide "that a public manifestation of religion may exist among Christians" (Idem, 4.20.3). Although Calvin demands obedience to authority, since "there are no powers except those ordained by God", on the one hand he also criticizes the tendency of the king towards tyranny, as well as dangers of popular rule such as sedition and anarchy on the other. His ideal is "a system compounded of aristocracy and democracy" to exercise the kind of authority equal to its tasks (Idem, 4.20.8). Whereas Luther simply leaves the world to the rule of secular authority, Calvin argues that God deserves more obedience than human authority, and consequently people should not simply submit to those in positions of authority: "If they command anything against him [God, H.W.], let it go unesteemed" (Idem, 4.20.32). Criticizing government is possible precisely because civil government has a duty to be guided by and implement God's commands – not a critique aimed at overthrowing the government but one that consists in reminding the government of its duties and virtues.[9] This is the source of later Calvinist activism, a drive to reorganize both the church and state, controlling and redirecting the lives of the godly and ungodly alike.[10]

Calvin's thought regarding the two kingdoms is closely related to his views on natural law and conscience. This is clear when he defines the two kingdoms in terms of two worlds "in man" over which different laws have authority rather than church and state:

> Therefore, in order that none of us may stumble on that stone, let us first consider that there is a twofold government in man: one aspect is spiritual, whereby the conscience is instructed in piety and in reverencing God;

> the second is political, whereby man is educated for the duties of humanity and citizenship that must be maintained among men. These are usually called the "spiritual" and the "temporal" jurisdiction (not improper terms) by which is meant that the former sort of government pertains to the life of the soul, while the latter has to do with the concerns of the present life—not only with food and clothing but with laying down laws whereby a man may live his life among other men holily, honorably, and temperately. For the former resides in the inner mind, while the latter regulates only outward behaviour. The one we may call the spiritual kingdom, the other, the political kingdom.
>
> (Idem, 3.19.15)

As it concerns duties of humanity and citizenship, like Luther Calvin argues that God creates all men with knowledge of his existence, knowledge "naturally inborn in all, and is fixed deep within, as it were in the very marrow", and that this innate awareness constitutes the "seed of religion" (Idem, 1.3.1).[11] More precisely, awareness of God's existence compels human beings to worship God, as well as giving to God those things that are owed to him. The Mosaic law expresses this point, which Calvin relates to natural law: the "inward law in a sense asserts the very same things that are to be learned from the two Tables" (Idem, 2.8.1; Pryor, 2006). In short, natural law is the innate version (engraved in the heart) of that which is elsewhere engraved in stone. Calvin says the purpose of natural law is the "apprehension of the conscience which distinguishes sufficiently between just and unjust, and which deprives men of the excuse of ignorance, while it proves them guilty by their own testimony" (Calvin, 1559a, 2.2.22). In *Commentary on the Epistle to the Romans* Calvin further elucidates his claim that natural law is the seed of religion. Since both Jews and gentiles receive the law in either writing or the heart, they cannot claim ignorance of "their inward depravity by the veil of outward holiness". They have a conscience that binds them to this law, and because they have transgressed this law "they could not free themselves from the charge of iniquity" (Calvin, 1540, p. 21). In this way then conscience and natural law are the seeds of religion. The desire for salvation springs from an awareness of sin that results, in turn, from the fact that human beings become aware of their sinful inclinations through conscience. Given that men have knowledge of justice and injustice, virtue and vice, honesty and dishonesty through the natural law inscribed in their hearts, "we are not however so blind, that we can plead our ignorance as an excuse for our perverseness" (Idem, p. 52).[12] Engraved in the heart of humanity, Calvin stresses that natural law mitigates ignorance of correct social conduct. Here his focus is on natural law insofar as it is an innate version of the second table of Mosaic law – the moral law insofar as it functions to structure social affairs. Depraved by original sin, most of humanity learns the same thing from natural law as one does from the Mosaic law. However, "man is so shrouded in the darkness of errors" that not only is he ignorant of the type of worship acceptable to God, but also "so puffed up with haughtiness and ambition, and so blinded by self-love, that he is as yet unable to look upon himself and, as it were, to descend within himself". God thus gives the written law as "a clearer witness of what was too obscure in the natural law, shake off our listlessness, and strike more vigorously our mind and memory" (Calvin, 1559a, 2.8.1). For gentiles, however, the natural law is never anything more than a set of innate moral principles that guide social conduct, in the very least through its ability to restrain sinful desires. In short, since natural law is engraved in the heart, man is a social animal.

We can deduce from this last point that natural law and conscience are inseparable. Calvin emphasizes the role of the individual's conscience even more than Luther. Hence, no human being is "utterly blind as to the conduct of life". And as a result even gentiles are punished and perish despite not having a written record of the law. The law is inscribed in their hearts, which is to say, in their conscience: "for them conscience stands in place of [the Mosaic or moral, H.W.] law" (Idem, 2.2.22). Conscience is in the first place an innate sense or knowledge of natural law. It is important to recognize here that Calvin stresses that the distinction between the two kingdoms should also be applied to conscience. There is a difference between knowledge of earthly and heavenly things. Earthly things concern only the present life, as it is directed by either household management or government, whereas heavenly things pertain to a pure knowledge of God, mysteries of his Kingdom, the nature of true justice (or righteousness), and the blessedness of eternal life. As it concerns the management and governance of the present life, Calvin says the following:

> Since man is by nature a social animal, he tends through natural instinct to foster and preserve society. Consequently, we observe that there exist in all men's minds universal impressions of a certain civic fair dealing and order. Hence no man is to be found who does not understand that every sort of human organization must be regulated by laws, and who does not comprehend the principles of those laws. Hence arises that unvarying consent of all nations and of individual mortals with regard to laws. For their seeds have, without teacher or lawgiver, been implanted in all men.
>
> (Idem, 2.2.13)

Conscience's first function is to give man an apprehension and knowledge of the innate natural law that results in the arrangement of social life: "some seed of political order has been implanted in all men" (Idem; Conditt, 1973, pp. 126–148; Walhof, 2003; Fuchs, 2009). We can thereby understand why Calvin refers to the political part of the two kingdoms – the twofold nature of government – as "in man" regulating "only outward behaviour".

Civil government should not simply be equated with an external authority. Calvin focuses on the individual's inner life and its governance, arguing that conscience's primary function is shared by the whole of humanity. It is an innate sense of natural law and consequent judgments regarding the justice or injustice, honesty or dishonesty, virtuousness and iniquity of outward behaviors. The fact that just, well-educated people perform good works is a sign of this. On this score Calvin writes the following regarding virtuous yet ungodly men: God may curb "the perverseness of nature, preventing it from breaking forth into action, yet without rendering it inwardly pure" (Calvin, 1559a, 2.3.3). God thus sets limits to the sinfulness of some men to maintain basic social structures. Society is unimaginable if everyone simply acted out on his or her sinful nature.[13] On this level then conscience serves the common good. It facilitates acceptance of shared norms and rules of conduct, as well as civil duties. I would call this conscience's civil or common welfare function – this function indicates a point of natural continuity between animals and humanity on the one hand, and point of connection with spiritual governance on the other (Zachman, 1993, p. 149).

When discussing the various functions of the Mosaic law and spiritual conscience, Calvin makes clear that both political government and civil conscience have a limited function: "the consciences of believers, in seeking assurance of their justification before God, should rise above and advance beyond the law, forgetting all law righteousness", since works are not taken into account concerning justification. After all, justification results from neither merit nor is it obtained by following the moral law, but only the mercy of God. Hence, "if consciences wish to attain any certainty in this matter, they ought to give no place to the law" (Calvin, 1559a, 3.19.2). Salvation results from a free act of grace by God. It does not result from obedience to innate, guiding principles that concern outward behaviour alone. Since both salvation and justification are thus independent of obedience to the political law, Calvin argues that spiritual conscience sets the believer free. Whereas common conscience demands obedience to civil laws, not even tyrants or civil government can make claims on spiritual conscience (Idem, 3.19.16).

In the writings of Luther and Calvin, conscience becomes the locus of one's personal relationship with God – the "forum of conscience".[14] Calvin's distinction between political and spiritual government draws attention to spiritual conscience as *con-scire*, as a knowing-together, as a communication between man and God that should not be confused with civil conscience, one that guides human conduct in social life. Insofar as it is concerned with actions and outward behaviour, the conscience is useful for society, although nobody should place their trust in this as a means to salvation and justification. Civil conscience can be deceiving: It might suggest a person be regarded as righteous because of merit. Hence, the emphasis in spiritual conscience on its role as an accuser and excuser – two functions Luther identifies as bad and good conscience.

The most cruel of all executioners

Not only does the Mosaic law restrain the wicked and convince people what they should do – this is the law's function insofar as it educates and regulates social duties – but also shows what people cannot do. The law exposes man's self-love and impurity, thus making him guilty before God. Calvin says the moment conscience is struck with an awareness of original sin iniquity grows. Added to the law's transgression is a stubborn, persistent disobedience and the increase of guilt. The more the law reveals God's righteousness, the more is iniquity exposed, provided it meets with suitable hearers. The latter remark is important as many sinners persist in ignorance, and iniquity's exposure only has a positive effect among the elect. For the faithful the law is a dailyan instrument in learning the nature of God's will and an education in obedience to his will. But "even for a spiritual man not yet free of the weight of the flesh the law remains a constant sting that will not let him stand still" (Idem, 2.7.12) Despite the sting that arises because of man's corrupted nature, serious, constant meditation on the law to live according to its dictates comes close to what might be called moral integrity – assuming moral integrity consists in an inner sensibility regarding one's "evil" inclinations and the motivations guiding one's thoughts and actions as opposed to an adjustment to shared norms and rules of conduct.

Closely related to the use of law is conscience's function. Calvin says conscience is "a sense of divine judgment, as a witness joined to them, which does not allow them to hide their sins from being accused before the Judge's tribunal" (Idem, 3.19.15).[15] Conscience is an innate power to both discern and judge between good and evil actions and motivations, and also ultimately to understand one's sinful disposition (Idem, 2.2.22). For this reason then it leads to moral self-evaluation, as a response to God's judgment. Hence, Calvin describes conscience as a "witness", "attorney", or "forum": people can only rightly and entirely examine themselves from the perspective of God's judgment. Central to this self-examination authored is the relationship between man and God; only a judgment of this type reveals the whole of one's evil acts and motivations, as well as the totally perverse nature of human existence (Bosco, 1986). Somewhere within me stands a strange witness, one who makes me aware of my estrangement, my dislocation.

Calvin follows Luther in his formulation of conscience as a scrutinizing tyrant that judges the entire person *coram deo*. Conscience anticipates God's judgment, and because iniquity increases in view of the law, conscience can be "the most agonizing of all torments and the most cruel of all executioners", for, "everyone is agonized and driven to madness by his own guilt; they are terrified by their own evil thoughts and by the pangs of conscience" (Calvin, 1559b, pp. 475–476; Bouwsma, 1988, pp. 41ff). With respect to the nature of this terror, Luther describes guilty conscience in terms similar to those of Calvin. Luther writes the following: "Since the law is the power of sin in that it serves only to reveal and not to remove sin (...) it makes the conscience guilty before God, and threatens it with wrath" (Luther, 1525a, III-272). Elsewhere he writes that conscience's proper work is "to pass judgment on what has been done and what should be done, and this judgment makes us stand accused or saved in God's sight" (Luther, 1521, iii-298; Baylor, 1977, ch. 6).

In his *Lectures on Galatians* Luther describes the proper task of law at length, which undermines self-confidence since it reveals sin, death, damnation, hell, and God's wrath at human depravity. The role of conscience is crucial here. It "senses that it has not satisfied the Law; it cannot satisfy the Law or bear the wrath of God, which the Law reveals". The law thus "terrifies us, accuses us, and shows us our sins. Thoroughly frightened, we run away and exclaim with Israel: 'We are going to die, we are going to die!'" (Luther, 1535, vii-150). A problem here is easily recognizable. One need only think of Luther's distinction between adoration and despair. As soon as conscience's terror threatens despair, "the Law has reached the prescribed manner, time, and purpose when it must stop exercising its tyranny". Law's function is fulfilled at precisely the point adoration and despair depart:

> Then let the Law withdraw; for it was indeed added for the sake of disclosing and increasing transgressions, but only until the point when the Offspring would come. Once He is present, let the Law stop disclosing transgressions and terrifying. Let it surrender its realm to another, that is, to the Blessed Offspring, Christ; He has gracious lips, with which He does not accuse and terrify but speaks better things than the Law, namely, grace, peace, forgiveness of sins, and victory over sin and death.
>
> (Idem, vii-317)

If a person is to avoid despair, conscience's struggle with God's judgment and sense of wrath must come to an end – and it does with Christ's call of merciful grace and liberation of conscience. One finds in Calvin a similar line of thought. The law displays to people their estrangement from God, miserable and ruinous condition, and God's wrath, "destined for a dreadful destruction". It is at this very point that "Christ interceded as his advocate", and in so doing Christ appeases God's wrath, thus providing a foundation for peace between man and God (Calvin, 1559a, 2.16.2). In other words, Christ lifts people from despair (Idem, 3.3.3).

According to Calvin then a real danger exists that law evoke an overwhelming fear of God, a tormenting sense of guilt, submerging a person in a "deep whirlpool of sorrow" from which one might not again rise (Idem, 3.3.15). As we have already seen, a philosophical enquiry into God's hidden will and doctrine of predestination can precipitate such a whirlpool; an insistent, compelling confession of one's sins can also cause this despair. Furthermore, a "natural feeling of sorrow" – a melancholic nature – increases this risk of despair

(Idem, 3.8.10).[16] However, not only does law confront people with their depravity and cause despair but also causes people to flee from sin and desire salvation. Not only does conscience repeatedly accuse but also excuses – in so doing the law's task is to keep faith's inner dynamic as a movement between recognition of sin and assurance of salvation in motion.

Conscience and the sense of guilt

In light of the previous analyses there is good reason to reconsider Freud's interest in a religious sense of guilt.[17] His preoccupation with this sense of guilt and morality – including Freud's views regarding religion as morality – is often considered in terms of his relation to Victorian morality in general and the Viennese cultural morality in particular. This is undoubtedly true, and Freud's depictions of his female patients make this abundantly clear. They are described mostly as well educated, intelligent women of high moral integrity and an awareness of their duties; they represent Vienna's middle-upper class bourgeoisie, and thus a culture focused on moral restraint, a pressure cooker of repressed passions underlying refinement and religious conformism (Schorske, 1981; Oosterhuis, 2000). Besides this, Freud's interest in morality and a religious sense of guilt is related to his Jewish background. His fascination for Moses is evident in two studies on Moses as the founding father of Judaism and Jewish identity, his admiration of Moses' moral character, and Freud's analyses of Jewish guilt as a hidden source of advancement in intellectuality, cannot be overlooked (Freud, 1914a, 1939).

Among others, Lacan opens up a new perspective on Freud's engagements with religion: Freud as an analyst of (early) modern culture and religion. *Totem and Taboo* is crucial here – a text in which Freud seems to carefully avoid an interpretation of Jewish religion and focuses solely on Christianity as the final stage of – what is essentially – a primitive reaction formation to primal parricide. It is in this text, the first of his major writings on religion, that Freud reveals himself as an archaeologist of Christian guilt and morality. In addition to minor texts and passages from works written before, *Totem and Taboo* makes a reduction of Freud's interest in religion to his Jewish background problematic: Freud's engagements with religion begin with Christianity.[18] In short, Freud recognizes defining aspects of Christianity, as well as the significance of a religious tradition that consists in cultivating and experiencing a sense of guilt, which is an important aspect of the general, neurotic malaise characteristic of his time and cultural environment. What Freud does not recognize, however, is that the Christian preoccupation with guilt and its reflection in a guilt culture emerges in the late medieval period, finding its zenith in Reformation and Counter-Reformation doctrines, faith models, and practices.

In Chapter 1 I showed that a sense of guilt becomes important to Freud's thought at the moment he begins reflecting on the relation between the drives and morality, in terms of the obsessional neurotic's infantile sexual aggression.

The "essence" of obsessional neuroses is the "invariably transformed self-reproaches which have re-emerged from repression and which always relate to some sexual act that was performed with pleasure in childhood" (Freud, 1896b, p. 169). The obsessional neurotic's infantile aggression and sadism form the nucleus of what Freud later describes as polymorphous perversity, hate, immoral, incestuous and perverse impulses, murderous and sadistic lusts. These comprise a person's "evil" nature, what Christianity describes as original sin.

One of the problems Freud addresses in his early writings concerns the origin of morality and a sense of guilt. As already mentioned, like his contemporaries Freud begins with the assumption that children are innocent and ignorant – tabula rasa, unspoiled by adult perversions and unacquainted with moral codes. It is only in puberty when the child adopts cultural norms concerning sexual morality that it begins reproaching itself for childhood memories. But Freud's analyses of his compulsive neurotic patients lead to a series of innovative thoughts. If obsessional neurosis can be traced back to an aggressive sexual act that the child experiences as pleasurable, then the child is most likely not the innocent victim of adult seduction. If sexual pleasure exists in childhood then it is already repressed in childhood. Furthermore, if pleasure is already repressed in childhood then this repression must not result from the internalization of cultural morality, since experience shows that when powerful enough the libido easily overrides morality (Freud, 1896c, p. 222). If external morality does not cause repression in childhood then it must result from elsewhere, an "independent source for the release of unpleasure" expressed mainly in self-reproaches (Idem). The central complex of obessional neurosis is self-reproaches that reemerge from repression and relate to a sexual act experienced with pleasure in childhood (Freud, 1896b, p. 169). These self-reproaches connect with cultural morality, giving morality the strength it has to repress. In the absence of this unpleasure morality is not internalized, which results in the appearance of a later perversion – perversion is therefore the relatively unhindered expression of a normal human disposition. What most people consider normal is the inhibition of perversion (Freud, 1905, p. 165).

The sense of guilt has, therefore, an independent source. For Freud this source remains somewhat of a riddle. In the case of the Rat Man Freud argues that the origin of the Rat Man's obsessional neurosis should be sought in a strongly developed, constitutionally-basic dynamic of love and hate, a sadistic component of the libido – a libido whose essence remains "completely obscure" (Freud, 1909, p. 240). What he seems to mean by this is a constitutional disposition, one with the potential to trigger this sense of guilt, although Freud is reluctant to explore this option. Instead he turns his attention to what, according to Freud, is far less obscure, namely, the Oedipus complex and its components: identification with a beloved father, hatred for a frustrating father, conscience formation, and this sense of guilt. Throughout his work, especially in the 1920s and 1930s, the Oedipus complex becomes the dominant paradigm in Freud's theories.

Freud's earliest theories rest on the following assumptions: the child is innocent and ignorant; there is no reason to assume an innate, "evil" nature that resists moral education. One might in fact assume the child plays a cooperative role in its development and, hence, accepts and adjusts to the cultural norms and codes in which it is brought up. Moral authorities (parents, teachers, priests, even doctors) have a duty of to instruct children with respect to their duties and civil conduct. The emphasis in this paradigm is on discipline and external behavior insofar as it is desirable for social stability and progress. However, this model malfunctions in the pressure cooker of Viennese society, as well as on Freud's sofa: neurotics suffer from memories of "evil" representations and wishes. When Freud uncovers the inner conflicts and thus discovers the "evil" nature of his patients, their repressed feelings of hate and sadistic impulses, the source of this morality arises as a question. This question poses a serious problem when Freud's thought regarding the pleasure principle and polymorphous perversity leads him to assume a primary, inner resistance to cultural norms and authority.

We see here how Freud rediscovers the same problem that confronts Luther and Calvin once they adopt a radical view regarding man's perversity and original sin. How can people become moral agents when their nature is perverse, and when, perhaps, no innate point of connection exists between this inner nature and external moral authority? Luther makes this problem explicit when arguing that a natural point of connection between the human heart and divine commandment must exists, as "otherwise it would become a matter of conscience for no one". His answer lies in assuming a minimal degree of natural law that – even in the worst cases of ignorance and stubbornness – takes the form of conscience and a sense of guilt that gnaws like a worm in the back of people's minds. Calvin expressed this as follows: "Although Diagoras and his like may jest at whatever has been believed in every age concerning religion, and Dionysius may mock the heavenly judgment, this is sardonic laughter, for the worm of conscience, sharper than any cauterizing iron, gnaws away within" (Calvin, 1559a, 1.3.3).[19] Despite a resistance to and repression of knowledge of God and his judgment, as natural law conscience and subsequent feelings of guilt cannot be erased. It is a law "which nature itself permits no one to forget, although many strive with every nerve to this end" (Idem, 1.3.3). According to Calvin repression of conscience and feelings of guilt is thus foolish: some hardened sinners "furiously repel all remembrance of God, although this is freely suggested to them inwardly from the feeling of nature" (Idem, 1.4.2).[20] The same goes for those who believe themselves righteous, capable of earning salvation through merit: unconsciously there exists the voice of conscience accusing man's perverse nature. Hence, as a gnawing feeling of guilt this repressed voice of conscience bridges the gap between corrupt human nature and divine judgment/command. Only because of conscience and this feeling of guilt is a sinner capable of opening his heart to knowledge of God, his judgment and law, and only through this route is the restraint of sin possible.

This relation between "evil" human nature, law, and an unconscious or even repressed sense of guilt and conscience appears in Freud's writings at the moment he loses faith in the moral innocence of childhood. For this reason he must reconsider the relation between human nature and morality. It is in this context, in terms of this connection that an unconscious superego/conscience and sense of guilt gain their importance.

We can go a step further. In scholasticism conscience is situated between conscious knowledge of moral principles and virtues and moral behavior. This model is changed dramatically in the thought of both Luther and Calvin. Conscience is now an inner forum guided by God's judgment and law, knowing and judging even the depths of the human soul. In short, conscience is internalized and situated between conscious knowledge and hidden depths. For most people it resembles a gnawing worm within, an oft-neglected inner voice whispering, "What are you doing? What are you thinking?" "What are you desiring?" No longer are either virtue or merit crucial but one's inner spiritual state, one's inclinations and disposition from which actions arise. No longer is moral sensibility defined by the correct application of an authorized moral principle for practical purposes *coram hominibus* – what Luther and Calvin generally refer to as "hypocrisy"[21] – but the correct evaluation of one's inner self *coram deo*.

According to Calvin conscience knows more of the sinner's inner life than the person's "ignorant" conscious thought. Any "Dionysius" can mock heavenly judgment on a conscious level, but gnawing from within conscience knows better. Calvin thus assumes conscience can pass judgment causing one to feel guilty without a person being consciously aware of this. It is on this point then that his conceptions of conscience and guilt anticipate Freudian discoveries: "not only" is a person "far more immoral than he believes but also far more moral than he knows". For this reason then one should jettison a "scale of values" that associates high moral values with consciousness and immoral drives with the unconscious (Freud, 1923a, p. 26, 52). Formulated explicitly in the 1920s, this principle appears as early as Freud's work on obsessional neurosis. He first expresses it in his interpretation of Shakespeare's *Hamlet*. In a letter to Wilhelm Fliess from 1897 Freud says that Hamlet's conscience "is his unconscious sense of guilt" (Freud, 1985, p. 273). In his reading of this play Freud comes close to discovering the importance of the early modern period's novel conception of conscience as an inner forum. This is evident in *The Interpretation of Dreams* when Freud discusses the differences between Oedipus' ignorance (unaware of killing his father and marrying his mother) and the guilt associated with Hamlet's conscience (because of wishing his father's death). He then writes that the "cultural epochs of civilization" reveal "a secular advance of repression in the emotional life of mankind", an advance that comes to light in Hamlet's unconscious conscience, which brings with it an awareness of one's most deeply repressed wishes (Freud, 1900, p. 264). It is precisely this advance that Freud later considers "the most important problem in the development of civilization" (Freud, 1930, p. 134). The restraint and renunciation of drives, an internalization of aggression as demanded by culture, and, hence, the nourishment of an unconscious sense of guilt produce unhappiness, dissatisfaction, and discontent. Not only the individual with a normal predisposition towards obsessionally neurotic thoughts and behaviours, but also entire cultures, are more moral than people previously thought. Not only does this excessive, unconscious morality spur on intellectuality (such as in Judaism) and motivate the development of moral law (such as is expressed in Kant's categorical imperative), but also gives rise to the *malaise* Freud discovers in Paul's Mediterranean world and – of course – modern civilization.

Calvin makes it clear that, as an innate sense of natural law, this unconscious conscience knows man's inner disposition. For this reason it secretly whispers, "What are you thinking?" "What are you desiring?" It is always aware of the law's two central elements: 1) God's existence and the necessity of worship (the seed of religion); 2) laws regulating social life (the seed of political order). In this way then Calvin supposes a general, human predisposition to religion and social life. Freud denies both: neither is there a natural religious feeling – as he makes clear in his exchange with Romain Roland (Idem, ch. 1) – nor an innate social instinct. The necessity of social relations begins with an experience of helplessness, and is then further organized in terms of object choice and mechanisms of identification. This position diverges fundamentally from Calvin's. Consequently, this makes a claim of cultural paternity on this point seem impossible. However, we should not overlook the increasing secular nature of Freud's thought over Calvin's. In part the rise of secularism takes place within religious thought itself. On the one hand, Puritans such as Perkins deny a human predisposition to religion and political order, arguing that – in principle – human beings are atheists and murders. Humanity is fundamentally estranged from God, a God who chooses some for election, calling them to faith, and restrains the sins of others to prevent a state of all-out war. Hobbes picks up this line of thought, turning it into a secular political theory. On the other hand we find the idea of an innate social instinct and conscience in, for example, the thought of Darwin. He argues that, "moral sense is fundamentally identical with the social instincts" serving the general good or welfare of the community. Feelings of sympathy (and even love) are only more highly developed forms of those also found in animal life – for example, obedient, conscientious dogs (Darwin, 1871, pp. 97–98; Westerink, 2009b, pp. 124–126). In Freud one finds is a radically secular reflection on human nature and its relation to a moral sense. Conscience does not express a social instinct or innate moral law, and it is certainly not the echo of God's judgment as Calvin conceives it. In Freud's second, topographical model of mind, conscience's whisper, the unconscious superego, is an internalized moral authority that denies one's desire both to take the other's place and possess his or her object choices. As such it cherishes the father. Besides the inner representative of an external authority, the superego is also the "residue of the earliest object-choices of the id", casting desire in a concrete form, that of the ego ideal. The question "What are you thinking?" or "What are you desiring?" thus has a double meaning: not only is it a prohibition – you should not think/desire this or that – but also a concrete expression of the id's drives and wishes – this is what you think/desire, since this is what you really want. The superego is familiar with one's deepest wishes and desires, not because it is capable as an external authority (God) of penetrating the heart, but because the superego is the id's advocate.

This modern radically secular model is the eventual outcome of a process that begins in the Reformation era, notably, in Calvin's thought: an understanding of conscience that consists in an internalized moral authority representing prohibitions and commandments, and a "power" that brings one's deepest desires to light, insofar as conscience relates sin (as lack, as desire) to what one actually needs and wants (grace, salvation). In the thought of Calvin and Freud conscience is primarily an inner constellation in relation to which one's external acts and behaviors are a matter of only secondary concern. They are merely situated at the level of symptoms.[22]

The obscure, blind, and tyrannical superego

To understand Lacan's thought regarding conscience and the superego we must briefly examine the debate that takes place in the late 1920s between Freud and the London School (Westerink, 2009b, pp. 261–273). During a period when Freud's thought on the oedipal relations, identification with the beloved, frustrating father, conscience formation and sense of guilt have their acme in texts such as *The Ego and the Id*, a new generation of psychoanalysts explore a variety of theoretical perspectives that often have their points of origin in ideas Freud leaves relatively underelaborated. One such issue concerns the question of whether conscience formation and a sense of guilt necessarily originate from frustration, or whether privation – i.e. the absence or denial of the satisfaction of one's needs – can cause a chain reaction, arousing feelings of hate, fear, and guilt. Melanie Klein, Joan Riviere, Susan Isaacs, and Ernest Jones investigate this idea. On the basis of child analysis, Klein argues the child develops feelings of severe aggression against the mother that result from the fact the mother denies the child total satisfaction and refuses to place herself at the child's complete disposal. This increases when the little girl becomes the mother's rival in relation to the father. As a result of this interplay the child fears the loss of the mother's love and develops feelings of guilt. Hence, the superego's initial contours appear during a period preceding the Oedipus complex. Here privation functions in a manner analogous to frustration. For this reason Jones simply equates the two: every privation ("I haven't got what I want") is a frustration ("You deny me"). He adds, however, that the sense of guilt originating in privation should be regarded as a "prenefarious stage of guilt", as the earliest forms of conscience and guilt appear during a time in which moral categories such as good and evil do not yet exist – after all, these are a matter of cultural consensus (Jones, 1929, p. 309). The logic involved in the thought of Klein and Jones amounts to the claim not only that different stages exist in the development of conscience and guilt, but also that these consist in different contents and characteristics. Jones argues this implicitly when he writes that the primitive contours of conscience and guilt are determined by sadistic mechanisms experienced as "intolerable" (pain, suffering), although the Oedipal conscience and sense of guilt are bound to the adjective "wrong" (Idem).

On this line of reasoning guilt results from the inner dynamic of fear and hate rather than as the imposition of something from without, although – as Jones argues – the child explores any and all *moralisches Entgegenkommen* as strategies to be imposed with moral demands and duties in order to avoid a confrontation with such inner dynamics. Lacan latches onto this principle in his seminar on the ethics of psychoanalysis, concluding that "in the end it is easier to accept interdiction than to run the risk of castration" – it is better to avoid something "wrong" than to suffer that which is "intolerable" (Lacan, 1992, p. 307). He goes on to suggest the Freudian superego that appears at the moment of the Oedipus complex's decline is different from the one Melanie Klein argues is born "in reaction to sadistic drives".

Initially Lacan follows Klein. In his earliest writings Lacan proposes a preoedipal superego, stressing sadistic fantasies of dismemberment, castration, and corporeal mutilation, as well as subsequent regressive and nostalgic tendencies towards a primal, imaginary entanglement with the mother (Lacan, 1984, pp. 59–62). Even later when Lacan calls for a return to Freud Klein's influence is still clearly discernible. Her views on the archaic origins of the superego are part of this heritage. On the one hand Lacan argues in an essay from 1950 that an oedipal superego exists that is formed through identification with the father's authority, which might be referred to as "collective" (*surmoi collectif*), organizing desire in the symbolic, demanding its fulfilment in socially acceptable aims and ideals. On the other hand, he says that a more archaic superego (*surmoi individual*) exists, an "obscure", "blind and tyrannical agency, which seems to be the antinomy, at the individual's biological pole, of the ideal of pure Duty that Kant posited" (Lacan, 2006, p. 137; Moyaert, 2012). In his first seminar (1953–1954) Lacan discusses the superego's two sides (Lacan, 1975, pp. 164–165; Evans, 1996, pp. 200–201). Located in the symbolic order and closely related to law, the superego orients the individual within social life. But at the same time the superego resists this procedure, working against the person's insertion within this broader symbolic chain – it is a blind, senseless, and tyrannical imperative, an oppressive and destructive repudiation of the law. Thus, says Lacan, at one and the same time the superego is both the law and its destruction (Lacan, 1975, p. 165). To the "biological individual" the superego's imperative is a fascinating, "ferocious figure" that demands a return to the primitive, traumatic experiences to which this individual was subjected – the Thing as desire's ultimate object. The "biological" – what says Lacan Luther refers to as "waste matter" – cannot be inserted into the symbolic.

Conscience is thus a composition, a multi-layered agency that prevents the person's entire integration in and adaptation to cultural aims and ideals, which results from its biological makeup. When primitive conscience does link up with cultural aims and ideals it can lead to a "complete disintegration of society". This takes the form of eagerness by the masses to sacrifice their lives for "the ideals of nothingness" (Lacan, 2006, p. 137). Lacan expresses the same concern that Freud did earlier in his critique of the misplaced enthusiasm with which Austrians endorsed the First World War – he seems to be referring here to the obscene conscience made collective in Goebbels' total war (Freud, 1915).

The distinction here should not be confused with Freud's between the individual and cultural superego. According to Lacan the latter seems to be merely an extension of that which is initially collective, namely, an oedipal superego that results from one's acceptance and interiorization of the law of the father and entrance into the symbolic order. Lacan's distinction concerns that between what he refers to as "*Pathologisches*", on the one hand, and a traditional morality concerned with "what one was supposed to do 'insofar as it is possible'", on the other. His explicit reference here to the *facientibus*-principle is telling: as presented by Lacan Aristotle's morality is "no doubt a tidied-up, ideal order" providing peace, tranquility, and social welfare, as well as serving the common good, albeit only insofar as it is possible ... In this respect then psychoanalysis unmasks the "impossibility in which we recognize the topology of our desire" (Lacan, 1992, p. 315). In his own way Freud already argues for this when stressing the necessity of restraining aggressive drives. However, this social and cultural necessity does not make us happy. Not only are the majority of ethical commandments excessive and unpsychological (Freud, 1930, pp. 141–144) but aggression's internalization – the return of aggression to its inner source as opposed to its natural, outward direction against strangers – also causes profound discontent and unhappiness. This takes the form of a superego that aggressively admonishes the ego (Idem, ch. 7). It is precisely this unpsychological character of – what Lacan calls – traditional ethics that he uncovers in his analyses of desire and hate.

The superego thus has two layers with two directives expressed in the same imperative, "You must!" (*Tu dois*) (Lacan, 1975, p. 165). The collective superego says "Do the good!" or "Perform your duty!" The individual superego says "Enjoy!" (*Jouïs!*). We can understand the relation between these commands on the basis of our analyses of Luther's thought regarding *Deus absconditus* and

Deus revelatus. Doing the good and performing one's duty are commands expressed by the revealed law. But at the moment one reflects on, questions, or doubts such commands, at the moment one doubts one's duty, its purpose, and one's capacity to fulfill these imperatives – i.e. as soon as one demands certainty with respect to the nature of the good – in the background appears a hidden desire as the motive of these commands, one "below the words and works" – i.e. the arbitrary will of God that elects and condemns, loves and hates, according to his good pleasure. The individual superego steers a person in this direction, *ad fontes*: it commands enjoyment, in this case enjoyment in knowledge of a ferocious God, enjoyment in the knowledge one is nothing but an object of God's pleasure and indifference. Whoever inquires into this, says Luther, despairs and will perish; it is an abyss of suffering. One is protected from this abyss through faith in the revealed God, Christ the savior. In short, the dialectic between law and desire relates to the superego's two movements, its two commands.

This correlation actually points towards a filiation most evident in the relation between Lacan's thought and Calvin's on double government. In Chapters 1 and 3 I showed that Luther and Calvin contribute to the introduction of a new direction in thought. This concerns a critique of the medieval, Aristotelian tradition that conceives of man as naturally participating in a divinely ordered universe, knowing what to do (the good), how to transfer this knowledge into action (conscience), how to act (virtues and duties), and to what purpose (happiness, pleasure). As far as Luther and Calvin are concerned this model no longer functions. At the level of social duty, virtue and merit are deceitful and uncertain since they neither tell us anything about one's underlying motives nor guarantee their purpose. That which makes a person ultimately happy (salvation, justification) is disconnected from public duty and behaviour; no longer is the Supreme Good synonymous with the common good. Calvin introduces his distinction between inner and outer government, spiritual and common conscience in this context. To maintain social structures man is inclined to fulfill social duties and adhere to laws. God sets limits to preserve social cohesion, peace and tranquility. Indeed, on this level Calvin's thought moves in the direction of the typical virtues connected with Calvinism that regulate outer behavior: innocent commerce, honesty, temperance, and modesty (VanDrunen, 2010, p. 79). However, the inner life is neither so peaceful nor so modest. Internally rage inner conflicts between man's sinful disposition and evil inclinations on the one hand, and spiritual conscience – the "most cruel of all executioners" – on the other.

The filiation between Calvin's double conscience and Lacan's double superego can be understood in terms of an unmasking of the "unpsychological" character of what Luther calls simply scholastic *Sautheologie* and what Lacan refers to as Aristotle's traditional ethics. In other words, this filiation concerns the introduction of Luther's and Calvin's movement *ad fontes* as a "descend within himself" (Calvin, 1559a, 2.8.1), a movement into hidden motives and dispositions that cause conscious, moral actions – the problem of evil as the fundamental problem underlying moral law and behaviour. Lacan's psychoanalytic archaeology of morality and law – a more philosophically-oriented elaboration of Freudian questions regarding the origins of morality and its relation to desire – is a secular offspring reflecting on and conceptualizing the same fundamental problem: the problem of the relation between hate as *Pathologisches* related to the Thing on the one hand, and the law insisting on adaptation to pragmatic moral consensus and normal civil conduct on the other.

Final remarks

I have discussed what Lacan considers fundamental problems addressed by Freudian psychoanalytic theories inaugurated at a specific moment in the history of Western thought, namely, the Reformation era. Central to the medieval scholastic tradition is the harmonization of a natural desire for the good, pleasure, and happiness. Evil is conceived as an absence of the good, a freely willed stubbornness to reject the good, not to engage in virtuous, meritorious behaviour. The basic principles of natural law are known to all people and can be conscientiously brought to bear on acts. In short, if a reasonable person wants then he can discipline himself or – better yet – be disciplined in obedient, righteous living. The belief thus exists that, both individually and collectively, human beings are fundamentally good, in spite of original sin. Even in their critique of *via antiqua* the nominalists affirm a belief in human goodness, expressed in the *facientibus*-principle. As a member of the tradition in which Paul and Augustine are authoritative figures, not only does Luther reject certain church practices and authority structures as well as call into question the efficacy of good work, virtue, and merit for salvation, but also fundamentally re-characterizes human nature in terms of evil, as well as saying relations between people have a "fundamentally bad character" (Lacan, 1992, p. 97). He does away with the relation between desire for the good and pleasure. According to Lacan, Freud implicitly endorses Luther's position. This is most evident in Freud's commitment to the pleasure principle as the main regulator of psychic life: The pleasure principle is a-social in nature and serves the organism alone. Furthermore, with his theories of the drives and of the child's helplessness, Freud shows that human relationships are based primarily on self-interest. One's sense of morality is by no means innate, which becomes clear in the child's dispositional, ambivalent feelings of love and hate towards its first significant others – the parents and father in particular. Rather, morality results from internalization; in relation to the father morality gains its strength because of the vicissitudes of these ambivalent feelings. The father is both loved and hated by the child. As an ideal the child identifies with the father in love. At the same time, however, to some extent the father always remains an evil *Fremde*, a tyrant against whom the original crime is committed that lead to the introduction of law. Orienting this analysis in terms of a wider context, Lacan introduces *das Ding*. As the ultimate object of desire the Thing is the supreme good while at the same time strangely evil, causing one to defy the pleasure principle and a search for happiness, to suffer from *jouissance* – the subject's relation with *das Ding* is thus "marked as bad". One is incapable of withstanding the extreme good the Thing promises; at the same time the individual superego commands enjoyment (Idem, p. 74).

Both psychoanalysis and Reformation thought address what Lacan calls the fundamental problem at the heart of man's destiny, the problem of evil, a fundamental hatred created even before the world's foundation, before its cultural, moral, and religious teachings and institutions. At the beginning of modernity Luther thus gives voice to man's fundamental dislocation, desolation, and exile from a universe based on the good and good relations with one's self, one's fellow man, and God. Among other Reformers such as Calvin, Luther raises questions regarding the moral law's foundation, as well as where and how people find moral orientation after a break with the medieval, Aristotelian-scholastic unity of moral and natural law, as well as a break with the intrinsic relation between one's knowledge of moral principles, natural desire, and the good as the object of this desire. Various Reformation theologies propose answers and solutions to these problems and questions – divine messages and acts of grace, mercy and salvation. Lacan does not follow this tact. In his final chapter on the ethics of psychoanalysis, he does not offer a solution but rather proposes a series of questions: "Will there be nothing but goodness" once one excavates the deepest layers of desire? "Have you acted in conformity with the desire that is in you?", a question that – in its demand of honesty – has the force of a Last (private) Judgment (Idem, p. 314). "What will transpire once the book has been eaten?", by which Lacan means what will happen when, as a secular "science of desire in the form of an enormous question mark", psychoanalysis is added to the canon of sciences – the one science with knowledge of man's nature and its transgressive desire (Lacan, 1992, p. 325). The Judaeo–Christian tradition functions as an archive here to the intellectual problems this science addresses. Unlike this tradition, however, psychoanalysis offers no message of salvation, reestablishes no universal moral foundation, introduces neither transcendent signifiers and values nor objective standards of good and evil – God is dead (or God is unconscious) and, thus, transcendence is lost. Lacan is primarily interested in an honest diagnosis of the problem of evil and the modern crisis in ethics. And yet, he does more than simply highlight historical problems and questions when identifying their re-articulation within Freudian psychoanalysis. He refers to a "value of prudence" that gains in importance once a crisis in ethics is fully recognized, which concerns an ability of the intellect to make decisions appropriate to the individual regarding matters of good and bad. This is a move towards Spinoza, as well as the development of conceptions of good and bad relative to one's own nature and mode of existence, one that is mild but adequate, that serves to establish a fragile inner limit to excessive desires and attachments (Idem, p. 323; Moyaert, 1994, pp. 86–90; De Kesel, 2009, ch. 9). What becomes clear after reading Luther's views regarding evil, sin, the enslaved will, law and desire, is the value of practical wisdom and practical philosophy, which theologies such as Luther's lack.

This study has delved into largely unexplored terrain. A filiation or cultural paternity between psychoanalysis and early Reformation thought is not, after all, self-evident. In my opinion, however, this has been highly fruitful, not only for its interpretation of central aspects of early Reformation thought – one that opens pathways for research beyond the obvious ones undertaken to date such as those dealing with Lacan and Catholic mysticism and Freud and Judaism – but also for the sake of understanding Lacan's complex thought. I presented the basic strands of thought Lacan distinguishes in the history of philosophy, ethics, and theology, as well as showing why he calls on authors such as Luther. Since Kant and Hegel play such important roles in debates between psychoanalysis and philosophy, the Lutheran characteristics of their philosophies and their importance to psychoanalysis seem like particularly promising lines of future inquiry. Kant's views regarding radical evil as a propensity towards the pursuit of selfish interests for the sake of happiness – a naturally sinful perversity against the moral law – undoubtedly resonates with Lutheran thought regarding the soul of man as torn between heaven and hell, God and satan. Kant expresses this in his 1793 *Religion within the Boundaries of Mere Reason* (Lilla, 2007, pp. 139–157).

There are good reasons to stress Lacan's questions as I have in the final pages of this study. Examining psychoanalysis' reception in theology one generally finds either a critical disavowal of Freudian thought or the deployment of psychoanalysis as an auxiliary science. One might paraphrase Lacan by asking, "Auxiliary for the good of what?" Is it simply another enlightened method for domesticating desire? When pointing towards the fundamental problems both Luther and Calvin raise Lacan confronts theologians with questions and problems at the heart of theology and religiosity: What is the nature of religion's singularity, strength, message, and function, if it is not to be reduced to or equated with a form of morality that pushes for the adaptation of individuals to shared norms and values, insisting on duties and obligations that support the common welfare and obedience to moral authorities? What is religiosity if it cannot simply be captured in optimistic, progressive models concerning faith's maturation and personal development, spiritual growth and ego integration? What is the nature of theology and theological thought if underneath intellectual speculation lies a disturbing, hidden desire that Luther, for example, associates with philosophical inquiry into God's hidden will? What is the nature of love and what can it mean to say, "God is love" when, according to Freud, love includes a sadistic component or can be conceived as a reaction formation against repressed hate? Since it raises these questions psychoanalysis can hardly be called an auxiliary science. It does not really resolve anything. It raises questions, pointing towards the heart of human destiny, desire, and its vicissitudes – whether good or bad. Psychoanalysis thus reminds theologians of the dynamics of Luther's and Calvin's thought and their views regarding man's tragic nature: He is alienated from the good, incapable of self-salvation, and uncertain of a destiny that depends on God's inscrutable will.

When pointing towards the filiation between Reformation thought and psychoanalysis Lacan questions both psychoanalysis' heteronomy and destiny: What is psychoanalysis' destiny if it is linked to a specific current within Christian thought that – as Lacan seems to argue – is the only one capable of these deep, momentous insights into repressed desires that are otherwise veiled? What if psychoanalysis' future is linked to the process of secularization, which is to say, the gradual process of guilt's vaporization, as well as the structures of conscience and an awareness of (specific forms of) sin based on their constitution in early modernity? When Lacan links psychoanalysis to inaugural moments in history, authoritative traditions, and new directions in thought – rooted in certain religious and philosophical modes of thought that address specific problems – then psychoanalysis is also related to the "exits" in history (De Certeau, 1986, p. 59). These include the failure of Paul's project in Christianity (according to Freud), the end of the "new direction of thought" in Enlightenment's transformation of religion into practical, socially useful morality, and even the (temporary?) end of Freudian psychoanalysis in post-Freudian psychologies. Might this have been apparent to Lacan? Was this the reason for his dissolution of the École freudienne de Paris in 1980? But this very interplay between beginning and end – a movement comparable to the one between repression and the return of the repressed – also paradoxically establishes its lasting significance. Avoiding definitive institutionalization and dogma psychoanalysis – or even more precisely, psychoanalysis-inspired perspectives – can and will continue to be a critical instrument regarding ethical issues such as autonomy, responsibility, moral development and processes of integrative psychic maturation, adaptation to norms and values, the integration of minorities, and use of human resources in production processes. Not least of all psychoanalysis can and should critique both religious and scientific worldviews that either negate or neglect "the heart of human destiny", which are nonetheless themselves "animated by some mysterious desire" for certainty and knowledge (Lacan, 1992, p. 97, 325).

Notes

Introduction

1. An important study exploring the implications of Lacanian theory for the understanding of theological discourse and his importance for the philosophy and psychology of religion is Wyschogrod, E., Crownfield, D., and Raschke, C.A. (eds) (1989), *Lacan and Theological Discourse*, Albany: SUNY Press.
2. The father, the law, and the symbolic are central themes in the work of Antoine Vergote, a Belgian psychologist of religion. He applies the concept of the symbolic order to Catholic religion as a recognizable cultural entity that structures a person's religious desire (Westerink, 2009a).
3. Lacan first broke with the *Société Psychoanalytique de Paris* in the mid 1950s, then established a new society with other psychoanalysts, the *Association Française de Psychanalyse*, which was not recognized by the IPA. Lacan eventually established his own society in 1964, the *École Freudienne de Paris* (Roudinesco, 1997).
4. Regarding choice of material, I might also have included Kant and Hegel whose philosophies are both deeply influenced by Lutheran theology. However, I abstain from so doing because explications of these philosophies and engagements with debates in the literature would require considerable attention thereby obscuring the balance and transparency of the present study. As soon as Kant and Hegel enter the stage other actors have a tendency to become figurants. This is what I want to avoid.

1 Cultural paternity: mapping the terrain

1. Lacan has strongly emphasized this aspect of psychoanalytic therapy. Therapy is basically a confrontation with the fact that there is no ultimate meaning or fixation of existence. It thus confronts with the ultimate object of desire – the 'Thing' – that is not-there (see also Van Haute, 1993).
2. One should not underestimate the extent of Freud's resentment. Even after his initial critique of Jung, Freud continues throughout the rest of his life and work to elaborate on themes first dealt with by former protégés such as Jung. As much as 20 years after Jung's engagement with the matter, Freud finds it necessary to comment on an issue first analysed by Jung (and Karl Abraham): the Prometheus myth (Freud, 1932).

3. For example, Frazer's *Golden Bough* and Robertson-Smith's *Lectures on the Religion of the Semites*, or Robert Kleinpaul's *Die Lebendigen und die Toten in Volksglauben, Religion und Sage.*
4. For example, William Trotter's *Instincts of the Herd in Peace and War* or William McDougall's *The Group Mind.*
5. For example, James Mark Baldwin's *Mental Development in Child and the Race*, Eduard Westermarck's *Ursprung und Entwicklung der Moralbegriffe* [Origin and Development of Moral Concepts] and Henry Breasted's *The Dawn of Conscience.*
6. Freud's interests in the origins of morality predate his psychoanalytic practice. His teacher Theodor Meynert was – like Darwin – highly interested in the evolutionary development of conscience and morality. He describes civilization's progress in terms of what he calls the "parasitical ego's" further repression by the "secondary ego". Freud integrates these notions into his own conceptions of primary and secondary egos in *The Interpretation of Dreams* when he describes the child's amorality and egoism, as well as in his conceptions of primary and secondary processes, which are later transcribed in terms of the pleasure and reality principles (Meynert, 1889; Freud, 1900, p. 250).
7. In Augustine's earlier writings such as *De Libero Arbitrio*, free choice is a means to turn to God, to have faith and thus be saved (Creswell, 1997, pp. 27–60).
8. As early as his 1955–1956 seminar on psychoses Lacan associates Descartes' philosophical project with Judaeo-Christian voluntarism, as opposed to classical Aristotelian rationalism (Lacan, 1993, pp. 64–66).
9. Throughout his seminars Lacan regularly refers to Saint Augustine, for example, in the first seminar, *Les écrits techniques de Freud*, the seminar on the ethics of psychoanalysis, and the twentieth seminar, *Encore.*
10. In his explanation of the formula Spinoza adds: "I understand by the name 'desire' all human endeavours, impulses, appetites, and volitions, which vary in accordance with the disposition of the same man, and which are often so opposed to each other that a man is dragged in different directions and does not know where to turn". In this formulation we find two elements that appeal to Lacan: 1. man is ruled by desire; 2. desires can oppose each other and evoke conflict.
11. The term "social psychology" is a reference to Wilhelm Wundt, one Freud's main intellectual opponents in *Totem and Taboo*, and particularly well known for his major study *Völkerpsychologie* [Folk Psychology].
12. According to Freud, obsessional neurosis is an exaggeration of the general human entanglement of love and hate, one in which its mutual stimulations and compensations are developed in a particularly pronounced fashion. This entanglement is constitutional and, therefore, precedes and determines later object relations, i.e. relations with significant persons (Freud, 1909).
13. For a general introduction to Lacan see Fink, B. (1995). *The Lacanian Subject. Between Language and Jouissance.* Princeton: Princeton University Press; Fink, B. (1997). *A Clinical Introduction to Lacanian Psychoanalysis: Theory and Technique.* Cambridge (MA): Harvard University Press; Van Haute, Ph. (2002). *Against Adaptation. Lacan's subversion of the subject.* New York: Other Press.
14. Lacan points out that alienation is to be thought of in terms of a distinction between *je* and *moi*. "Il [le moi, H.W.] est autre chose – un objet particulier à l'intérieur de l'expérience du sujet. Littéralement, le moi est un objet – un objet

qui remplit une certaine fonction que nous appelons ici fonction imaginaire" (Lacan, 1978, p. 67).

15. A difference between Freud's and Lacan's versions of the Oedipus complex is the fact that the latter not only begins with the needs or desires of the child, but also the mother's absorbing desire. Thus, the law of the father is not only a prohibition but certainly also a liberation from the absorption and fear-evoking desire of the mother. We should not here overlook Melanie Klein's influence. Beginning in the 1920s she claims the origins of the superego, anxiety, and a sense of guilt can be traced to the relation between the little child and the mother. Since the mother is an exclusive source of the satisfaction of the child's needs and the denial thereof, the mother can also be an object of severe hatred and anxiety.
16. Lacan's version of the Oedipus complex and entrance into the symbolic order are first described in his seminar on the formation of the unconscious (Lacan, 1998, pp. 143–248).
17. In his later case study of Little Hans Freud argues that children respond in the same way to the arrival of brothers and sisters, who are also understood as strangers and thereby automatically evoke aggression. Compare this with the following: "Considering too, the fundamental kinship of the concepts of 'stranger' and 'enemy', the paranoiac is not so far wrong in regarding this indifference as hate" (Freud, 1922, p. 226).
18. As early as his 1932 thesis entitled *De la psychose paranoïaque dans ses rapports avec la personnalité*, Lacan expresses this idea, quoting Spinoza's claim that the desire of every individual differs insofar as the essence of each and every individual differs, the idea that the uniqueness of each person is essential and attached to desire.
19. Alain Juranville shows that Saint Augustine – one of Lacan's favourite authors – already made the distinction between *jouissance* as "s'attacher à une chose par amour pour elle-même" and pleasure (utility) as "ramener l'objet dont on fait usage à l'object qu'on aime" (Juranville, 1984, p. 223).
20. One of these references concerns the commandments to love one's neighbour and one's enemy. In Christian teaching the commandment seems to impose a moral ideal that is reasonable in terms of giving up one's purely selfish interests and advancing in altruism. Freud criticizes the impossibility of this commandment for two reasons. First, one cannot love a stranger who has no significance in one's emotional life. Second, it would be unjust to love a stranger in the same way as one's friend or family member. Lacan devotes a chapter to this commandment in which Freud's *Nebenmensch* as *Fremde* plays a decisive role. Lacan agrees with Freud: the commandment is "cruel". It asks me to love my enemy, that is to say, one who hates me. What Freud neglects, according to Lacan, is the fact that the enemy is a stranger to whom we naturally respond with aggression. Lacan thereby emphasizes the problem of how or why to love one's neighbour (Freud, 1930, pp. 109f; Lacan, 1992, ch. 14; DiCenso, 1999, p. 35).
21. For a Lacanian interpretation of the Epistle to the Romans, Chapter 7, see Antoine Vergote's article on the apostle Paul's letter (Vergote, 1973).
22. The function of the law as increasing sin "proves" why merits are worthless: "The divine law – which ought to assist toward righteousness, if anything can – has not only not helped, but has even increased sin. For the more the law forbids,

the more our evil nature hates the law, and the more it wants to give reign to its own lust" (Luther, 1523/1546, III-375).

23. "So the law reveals a twofold evil, [one] inward and [the other] outward. The first, which we inflict on ourselves, is sin and the corruption of nature; the second, which God inflicts, is wrath, death, and being accursed" (Luther, 1521, III-224; Zachman, 1993, pp. 43–49).
24. In his 'Introduction to the Names-of-the-Father Seminar', Lacan writes regarding the God of Moses: "God is something one encounters in the real, inaccessible" (Lacan, 1987, p. 90).
25. In the Late Middle Ages, discussions between various theological schools were limited to the religious elite of a few universities and monastic congregations. The major importance of Luther is that these ideas come to have a profound influence on the thoughts and ways of life of ordinary people. In Luther we thus find the important translation of an academic-monastic debate into a practical-theological psychology.
26. Luther is neither the first nor only theologian of his time to reject scholastic views concerning *synderesis*. Adrian of Utrecht, a Leuven professor who later became pope Adrian VI (1522–1523) and Luther's opponent, also denies *synderesis* as an innate knowledge of basic moral principles (Hein, 1999).
27. J. Calvin, 1559a, 2.3.3. On Calvin's ethics see Conditt, M.W. (1973). *More Acceptable than Sacrifice. Ethics and Election as Obedience to God's Will in the Theology of Calvin*. Basel: Friedrich Reinhardt Kommissionsverlag; Hoitenga, D.J. (1997). *John Calvin and the Will. A Critique and Corrective*. Grand Rapids: Baker Books; Fuchs, E. (2009). Calvins Ethik. In M.E. Hirzel & M. Sallmann (Eds.), *1509 – Johannes Calvin – 2009. Sein Wirken in Kirche und Gesellschaft. Essays zum 500. Geburtstag*. Zurich: Theologischer Verlag, 183–200.
28. Bruce Fink's English translation of the Écrits follows the original, 1966 French pagination – I follow this pagination as well.
29. Lacan understands Luther to be defending a supralapsarian doctrine of predestination, a doctrine in which even before the foundation of the world God decides who to save and condemn. This reading is in no way self-evident since it is not clear in Luther's text whether reprobation should be considered in the context of supralapsarianism or infralapsarianism. The fact is that in later theological debates on predestination Luther's text was used to defend opposite positions (Brosché, 1978, pp. 100–102).

2 The will and the hidden God

1. Bradwardine's writings were not widely disseminated and, therefore, barely known to later scholars. He, however, indirectly influenced the Reformation via his student John Wyclif (?1320–1384), a major precursor to Reformation thought, in large part because of his criticisms of the church's hierarchy and secular authority. Wyclif ultimately concludes that Bradwardine's thought is too deterministic, and for this reason his own thought develops by carefully avoiding both modern Pelagianism and Bradwardine's fatalism (Lacey, 2009).
2. Rimini's doctrine of double predestination was rejected by most members of the Augustinian order to which he belonged, mainly because it implies that God causes sin. But he also had supporters, for example, Marsilius of Inghen

(?1340–1396) in Heidelberg and Pierre d'Ailly (1351–1420) in Paris, both of whom kept his ideas alive (Halverson, 1998, pp. 164–166).

3. Luther opens his *Disputation against Scholastic Theology* with the following statements: "1. To say that Augustine exaggerates in speaking against heretics is to say that Augustine tells lies almost everywhere. This is contrary to common knowledge. 2. This is the same as permitting Pelagians<p><p><p> and all heretics to triumph, indeed, the same as conceding victory to them" (Luther, 1517a, IV-9).
4. Compare, "We say that philosophy knows nothing at all about man. Aristotle assumes a *primum mobile* or mover. Hence he concludes that all things are done by the prime mover with inner cooperation, and so he dreams that the prime mover acts like a nursemaid who rocks the cradle of a child, yet admires herself. Thus Aristotle condemns us. In short, philosophers know nothing about God the creator and man made of a lump of earth" (Luther, 1536a, III-143).
5. In his *Disputation against Scholastic Theology*, for example, many of Luther's theses are directed against nominalist scholars such as Ockham and Biel. Sometimes Luther simply refers to a nominalist thesis as a "scholastic" one.
6. Compare the following theses: "26. Therefore those who say that natural things have remained untainted after the fall philosophize impiously in opposition to theology. 27. The same is true of those who say that a man 'in doing what is in him' is able to merit the grace of God and life; 28. So also, of those who introduce Aristotle (who knows nothing of theological man) to witness that reason aspires to the best things; 29. Also, those who say that the light of God's countenance is in man, as an imprint on us, that is, free will which forms the precept right and the will good; 30. In like manner, that it rests with man to choose good and evil, or life and death, etc. 31. All such neither understand what man is nor do they know what they are talking about" (Luther, 1536a, III-139).
7. There is discussion among scholars of whether the fact that in 1508 – the year of Luther's appointment as professor in moral philosophy – the faculty of arts at the University of Wittenberg allowed the teaching of *via Gregorii* indicates 1) the introduction of *schola Augustiniana moderna* or 2) merely *via moderna*. I follow the latter interpretation (Oberman, 1977, pp. 90–91; McGrath, 1987, pp. 108–121).
8. One example of this intellectual discernment is scholarly speculation regarding whether God can lie and deceive. Luther's response is sharp and short: Scripture teaches us that God does not lie. Hence, God does not lie. "For it is an irrefutable and self-evident proposition that God does not lie and is not deceived. There are no obscure or ambiguous words here, even if all the most learned men of all the centuries are so blind as to think and speak otherwise" (Luther, 1525a, III-185).
9. Antoine Vergote calls Freud's conception of the psychic apparatus "libidinal body", as well as "psychic body". He thereby indicates that Freud's notion of this apparatus is broader than his positivism and attempts to develop a scientific psychology modeled on the standards of the natural sciences. His conception of the "libidinal body" allows one to situate Freud's thought in the broader contexts of theological and philosophical thought regarding the relation between body and mind (Vergote, 1997). Concerning Freud's views on mental functioning in relation to body and mind see Lear, *Love and its Place in Nature* (1990) as well.

10. "We must not ask the reason for the divine will, but simply adore it, giving God glory that, since he alone is just and wise, he does no wrong to anyone and can do nothing foolishly or rashly, though it may seem far otherwise to us" (Luther, 1525a, III-61).
11. Gerrish suggests that faith be understood as a flight from the hidden God towards Christ (*ad deum contra deum*) (Gerrish, 1973, pp. 290–291).
12. This is nothing more than the application of Luther's thesis that he formulates in *Disputation against Scholastic Theology*: "The best and infallible preparation for grace and the sole disposition toward grace is the eternal election and predestination of God" (Luther, 1517a, IV-11).
13. This splitting is later elaborated by Melanie Klein as characteristic of what she calls the paranoid-schizoid position, one in which the image of the mother is split into a good and evil one, a position later corrected in the depressive position of mourning and acceptance of the loss of the mother as good object through symbolization. These two 'positions' anticipate Lacan's distinction between the imaginary and the symbolic (Segal, 1964).
14. We find the same associations in Calvin's use of the word "abyss". He refers to God's will, his judgments, and governance as "abyss", as well as chaos, wickedness, and confusion. Bouwsma draws the following conclusion regarding this point: "The abyss was thus a symbol of Calvin's horror of the unlimited. It signified the absence of boundaries and the unintelligibility of things, the void, nothingness, disintegration of the self". At times Calvin also links this horror of nothingness with "dung": not only does excrement point at dislocation, but also formlessness, chaos, and nonbeing (Bouwsma, 1988, p. 46).
15. Lacan describes Luther as "ce fou furieux excité de Wittenberg". This remark regarding Luther's "furious" character conforms to descriptions given by his contemporaries: Luther was often furious in debates with both his opponents and sympathizers.
16. The bible expresses this accurately says Lacan: one first has to "eat the book" in order to be able to preach or prophesize what the Other wants (Lacan, 1992, p. 332).
17. Lacan makes a connection between the emptiness of the vase and the religious fear of the Thing that is essentially evil (*méchanceté fondamentalle*) (Lacan, 2005, p. 54).
18. Based primarily on the earlier versions of Melanchthon's *Loci communes*, Kusukawa rightfully argues that Melanchthon's views on *synderesis* and human will are quite similar to those of Luther's views (Kusukawa, 1995).
19. In history of *The Bondage of the Will*'s reception it is a remarkable fact that "the late sixteenth and seventeenth century Calvinists cited it more prominently and favorably than Lutherans" (Kolb, 2005, p. 9).
20. "So far as the fall of Adam was the subversion of equity, and of well-constituted order, so far as it was contumacy against the Divine Law-giver, and the transgression of righteousness, certainly it was against the will of God; yet none of these things render it impossible that, for a certain cause, although to us unknown, he might will the fall of man. It offends the ears of some, when it is said God *willed* this fall; but what else, I pray, is the *permission* of Him, who has the power of preventing, and in whose hand the whole matter is placed, but his will?" (Calvin, 1554, p. 81).

21. Compare: "Aquinas had almost civilized Jahweh into an Aristotelian; Luther turns him into Nobodaddy for good. And at this point the resemblances between Luther and Calvin are more important than the differences. For, (...) Calvin too presents a God whose goodness we cannot judge and whose commandments we cannot interpret as designed to bring us to the τέλος to which our own desires point" (MacIntyre, 2010, p. 199).
22. Scatological imagery is clearly present in Luther's writings, but also Calvin sometimes uses terms like "filth" or "stinking excrement" to indicate sin (Bouwsma, 1988, pp. 36–37).
23. The fact that the fall does not result in a complete loss of the image of God in man, but that some traces of this image remain, means means that the human race can still be distinguished from animals (Calvin, 1559a, 2.2.17). On this point Calvin follows Luther when he writes: "Thus even if this image has been almost completely lost, there is still a great difference between the human being and the rest of the animals" (Luther, 1535–1545, p. 67).
24. Compare: "There is nothing in which man excels the lower animals, unless it be his spiritual communion with God in the hope of a blessed eternity" (Calvin, 1539, p. 99).
25. A line of continuity connects Freud's thought regarding primary and secondary processes to his ideas concerning the pleasure principle and its relation to the reality principle.
26. Puritans such as William Perkins use terms such as "Atheist" and "murderer" to refer to naturally worldly and sinful men as opposed to the godly "Antipodes to all the world", a difference he feels is far greater than that between man and brute beast. (Luttmer, 2000).
27. Hobbes says the fundamental law of nature, man should be "contented with so much liberty against other men, as he would allow other men against himselfe", is also expressed in the biblical law that "whatever you require that others should do to you, that do ye to others" (Hobbes, 1651, p. 92).
28. Compare: "Hobbes preserves a version of familiar Christian belief, but with its spiritual vitality drained away. His God is a *Deus absconditus* with a vengeance: Reformation voluntarism stressed God's ever-present power, Hobbes his omnipotent remoteness" (Damrosch, 1979, p. 346).
29. Jerome Neu argues that Spinoza can be understood as the "philosopher of psychoanalysis" (the expression stems from Lou Andreas-Salomé) for several reasons. First, Spinoza and Freud are in agreement with respect to the importance of thoughts and reflexive knowledge to analysing human nature and coping with emotions. Second, the psychologies of both Spinoza and Freud are dynamic. Third, both Spinoza and Freud basically consider emotions in terms of discharge (Neu, 1977).
30. An example can be found in the case of the Rat Man. On the one hand the Rat Man's compulsive denial in his prayers ("God protect me ...not") is the effect of unconscious and ambivalent feelings and doubts that surface, on the other his conscious expressions of love for his father cause the severe repression of feelings of hate in the unconscious (Freud, 1909, pp. 193, 239).
31. Perkins describes reprobation as "that part of predestination whereby God according to the most free and just purpose of his will hath determined to reject certain men unto eternal destruction and misery, and that to the praise of

his justice". This decree is hidden and ordained by God out of "good pleasure" before creation. Only after the fall is the execution of this will known to man: "Whom God rejecteth to condemnation, those he hateth. This hatred of God is whereby he detesteth and abhorreth the reprobate when he is fallen into sin, for the same sin. And this hatred which God hath to man comes by the fall of Adam and is neither an antecedent nor a cause of God's decree". There is thus hatred in God that becomes visible in the execution of this decree (Perkins, 1591, pp. 250–251; Muller, 2008, pp. 160–171).

32. We might think here of the debates between Domingo Bañez and Luis de Molina, and later those between the Augustinianism of Michel Baius and Cornelius Jansenius on the one hand, and the Jesuits on the other (Lamberigts, 1994).
33. Richard Muller argues that the Puritans and Reformed orthodox develop christocentric doctrines that could make speculation on *deus absconditus* redundant. If the decree by which God determines all things from eternity is understood as the decree of the triune God rather than *deus absconditus* then there is no predestination *extra Christum*. Consequently, "there can be no *deus nudus absconditus* because the Christ who redeems is, according to his divinity, the God who decrees" (Muller, 2008, p. 170).

3 Original sin and moral responsibility

1. Luther makes an interesting remark on this issue showing that he held high esteem of *devotia moderna*: "I have not found so clear a discussion of the subject of original sin as in Gerard Groote's treatise *Blessed Is the Man*, in which he speaks not as an arrogant philosopher but as a sound theologian" (Luther, 1515–1516, 299).
2. Luther argues that Adam's disobedience is a transgression of law ("do not eat the fruits from the tree of knowledge of good and evil"), which he interprets as synonymous with the Mosaic law. The first is given to the righteous to provide direction without either judgment or political use, whereas the second is given to the unrighteous to reveal their sins (Lazareth, 2001, pp. 71–84; Whitford, 2004, pp. 47–48).
3. Compare also: "'Through the Law is knowledge of sin'. For the Law does nothing else than reveal sin or make it alive; before the Law was known, this sin lay there as though dead or sleeping, just as is stated below to Cain (Gen. 4:7): "If you do evil, your sin will lie still until it is revealed.' It lies still while it is active; but when the Law comes, then the eyes are opened, and man becomes aware of what God has commanded and what punishment He has established for the transgressors. When the Law thus gains control in the conscience, then there is the true knowledge of sin, knowledge which human hearts cannot bear unless comfort comes from God" (Luther, 1535–1545, 164).
4. Compare: "Again: 'The law was given for this purpose: to make you, being great, little; to show that you do not have in yourself the strength to attain righteousness, and for you, thus helpless, unworthy, and destitute, to flee to grace'" (Calvin, 1559a, 2.7.9).
5. Freud's psycho-Lamarckism is the subject of considerable debate. Reacting to Yosef Yerushalmi's landmark study of Freud's *Moses and Monotheism*, Richard Bernstein and Jan Assmann, among others, attempt to assuage difficulties associated with Freud's Lamarckism by reformulating the idea of inherited psychic

dispositions in terms of "tradition" or "cultural memory". In these reformulations the transmission of unconscious memory traces can be upheld via the transmission of cultural artefacts, thoughts, texts, etc. in the place of inherited dispositions. These reformulations come strikingly close to what Lacan calls the symbolic order, as both the order of culture and of language – including the language of the unconscious. Lacan argues that the forgotten drama (of primal parricide) comes down through the ages in the unconscious as an expression in language received from and shared with the outside rather than as an expression of archetypes or dispositions: "The fact that the symbolic is located outside of man is the very notion of the unconscious". Language lies both in the heart of man's self-awareness as a means to experience and express oneself and outside as the language in which we communicate with others and understand reality (Lacan, 2006, p. 469; Westerink, 2009a, pp. 197–205).

6. In the case of the Wolf Man Freud introduces "inherited schemata" – strikingly similar to Jung's conception of archetypes – to make sense of features of the Wolf Man's otherwise inexplicable complexes (Freud, 1918, p. 119).
7. Hartmut Raguse argues that original sin should be interpreted neither as incestuous sexual desire nor murderous impulse, but as the "anti-oedipal creation of a fatherless undifferentiated world" (my translation). Sin can thus be interpreted in terms of perversion, i.e. the disavowal of the father principle (Raguse, 1994, pp. 255–262).
8. The quotation marks Freud employs at times when describing evil instincts and impulses indicate that concepts such as good and evil are inadequate to describe the whole of the human character (in isolation) as either good or evil, since such concepts also derive their meanings from social context and consensus.
9. Freud indicates this in *The Ego and the Id* when he makes clear that the superego is (the unconscious) part of the ego that represents the id, that casts the id's wishes in a concrete form (Freud, 1923a). In the passage on moral responsibility Freud expresses this again.
10. Simon O'Sullivan rightfully points out the affiliation between Spinoza and Lacan as it concerns causation. He writes: "For Spinoza, as for Lacan, the relentless pursuit of causation will necessarily go beyond the mere 'knowledge' of the causation. Indeed, the avowed goal of analysis, 'to become a cause of oneself', is the same as the goal of Spinoza's *Ethics*, namely to 'arrive' at a state of being when one is no longer subject to the world (and to those within it), but authors oneself" (O'Sullivan, 2010, p. 55).
11. Lacan expresses this as the goal of psychoanalysis as early as his first seminar: man should move beyond the level of speech he shares with others in his daily life, and aim at an "existential recognition" that "You are that", which is to say, that one is determined by the unconscious discourse of the other (Lacan, 1975, ouverture). Van Haute compares this ordinary level of speech with Heidegger's conception of *Gerede*, indicating a non-personal speech that reproduces general opinions (Van Haute, 2002, pp. 52–53).
12. In the final pages of his seminar on the ethics of psychoanalysis Lacan's reference to Oppenheimer – the inventor of the nuclear bomb – makes perfectly clear that one's inability to restrain desire makes the world a dangerous place. Oppenheimer's remorse can neither undo the science behind nuclear warfare nor change the fact

that the bombs have been dropped. Moral reflection always comes after desire and action, and for precisely this reason one needs a science "in the form of an enormous question mark" reflecting the motives that obstruct a free, rational decision between good and evil – this science is psychoanalysis. Lacan's plea for a "science of desire" that might contribute to a safer future (since it enables a certain consciousness of – and thus also responsibility for – one's desire before desire is pushed to its limit) echoes Freud's final pages of *Thoughts for the Times on War and Death*.

13. Although Freud's critique of religious illusions is usually associated with Feuerbach, Freud's implicit Spinozistic commitments have also been recognized, notably, in his correspondence with Romain Rolland and *The Future of an Illusion* (Yovel, 1989, pp. 162–163; Vermorel, 2009).
14. Spinoza does not reason in favour of a form of repression or the affects' control by the superego but – in a remarkably "psycho-therapeutic" way – says that one ceases to suffer from affects by forming clear perceptions of them (Spinoza, 1677, V prop. 3). Yovel convincingly maps similarities and differences between Spinoza and Freud on the subject of self-knowledge and its liberating effects. He concludes: "With all their naturalistic determinism, both Freud and Spinoza are motivated, perhaps paradoxically, by the pathos of human liberation – liberation not only from illusions and inhibitions, but from what Freud called 'neuroses' and Spinoza 'bondage' to the passions. This liberation is hard-won and painful, forcing as it does a new understanding and self-image of man, free from illusions and metaphysical self-flattery" (Yovel, 1989, ch. 6).
15. Compare also: "Given that in God and nature is neither will nor end, Spinoza's project of a scientific ethics could be understood as an attempt to 'enlighten' humans with regard to this absolute absence of a final cause and to accept the purposeless or meaningless character of life" (Kiarina Kordela, 2007, p. 6).
16. Catharsis stands at the centre of early psychoanalytic therapy: Josef Breuer describes his therapeutic method as "cathartic", indicating the abreaction of affects that results in a reduction of mental tension. Breuer was certainly inspired by Jakob Bernays' study of Aristotle and tragedy – Bernays was an uncle of Freud's fiancée Martha. In this study Bernays stresses the fact that Greek tragedy consists in the staging of catharsis, a release of emotions resulting in relief (Westerink, 2009b, pp. 4ff). For Lacan catharsis has nothing to do with abreaction, but consists in a purifying knowledge of immanent causality (De Kesel, 2009, pp. 238–241).
17. In the final chapter of Lacan's seminar these few are called "heroes" to distinguish them from ordinary men. This distinction in Lacan has its parallel in Spinoza's distinction between the religiosity of the intellectual few and the ordinary masses. Compare: "All are able to obey, whereas there are but very few, compared with the aggregate of humanity, who can acquire the habit of virtue under the unaided guidance of reason. Thus if we had not the testimony of Scripture, we should doubt of the salvation of nearly all men" (Spinoza, 1670, p. 199). Connecting obedience with a certainty of one's salvation Spinoza presents a way of thinking in opposition to a Calvinist culture in which doubt and despair can be regarded as signs of faith in the few elected.
18. Lacan echoes in his own words here what Freud already suggests in his study of Leonardo da Vinci whose intellectual advancement, his "insatiable and indefatigable

thirst for knowledge", can be compared with Spinoza's conception of beatitude. Freud indeed describes Leonardo in terms of Spinozistic enlightenment: his knowledge as intellectuality is beyond love and hate; detachment from the fundamental passions as the prime movers of human activities; "indifference" towards good and evil; his reflections on and insight into the determining causes of all that exists; the religious pathos with which he praises God's creative majesty (Freud, 1910, pp. 74–76; Yovel, 1989, pp. 140–143).

19. Graeme Hunter argues that Spinoza's thought should not be regarded as in complete opposition to radical Calvinist religiosity (Further Reformation) as the dominant piety in the Netherlands in Spinoza's era. Since Spinoza was highly concerned with the question of how to reconcile Christian thought and the modern age, several important traits of Calvinist thought find their way into his writings, such as a belief in providence, determinism, one's need for salvation, and obedience (Hunter, 2005). However, it is also clear that Spinoza sought an alternative to a Calvinist worldview in which humans suffer from despair regarding election, punishment, damnation or salvation by a God actively participating in human lives and worldly affairs. Spinoza reverses this picture, proposing that the highest form of religiosity consists in an intellectual participation in an indifferent God.
20. In his major writings Spinoza repeats his critique of the notion of a God-Judge, views on the relative nature of good and evil, and conception of sin as one without a positive nature. In the *Ethics* and *A Theologico-Political Treatise* Spinoza argues that the state of nature must be conceived as free of both religion and law; good and evil are defined relative to individual's self-centred desires. This natural state is without sin, injustice, or wrong. Compare: "The state of nature must by no means be confounded with a state of religion, but must be conceived as without either religion or law, and consequently without sin or wrong: this is how we have described it, and we are confirmed by the authority of Paul". The latter remark points to Paul's having said that we only know sin through the law (Spinoza, 1670, p. 210; Verbeek, 2003).

4 Conscience

1. *Pondus* is interesting because Lacan uses the same word (*poids*) to refer to the importance or weight given to the Thing in the presence of a moral agency, the law. As we saw, the weight given to the Thing is different from an instinct towards the good. It is interpreted, rather, in terms of evil (Lacan, 1992, p. 20).
2. Interestingly, the spiritual program of the modern devotees is marked by a high appraisal of both Augustine's theology and Cassian's spiritual instructions, as examples of self-examination, fraternal admonition and spiritual guidance, and the battle against vices and progress in virtues (Van Engen, 2008, pp. 266–304).
3. Luther knew of and praised the writings of Geert Groote, the founding father of *devotia moderna*.
4. Michael Baylor and Douglas Langston both show that while *synderesis* loses relevance to Luther's theology, conscience gains in importance (Baylor, 1977, ch. 5–6; Langston, 2001, 74ff).
5. Erasmus of Rotterdam, Luther's opponent on the issue of free will, comes remarkably close to the Paulinian view regarding conscience that Luther himself promotes.

Erasmus describes conscience as a conscious self-judgement *coram deo* (Hein, 1999, pp. 335–342).

6. Although Teellinck follows Calvin in affirming minor vestiges of God's image in man after the fall, these are described less in terms of "partly weakened and partly corrupted" bits of reason seeking "truth" and more as an "indefinite desire", one that fails to find satisfaction in temporary objects thus making people aware of a fundamental inner "lack" or "loss". Only through an act of grace does this desire meet its proper object (Christ) (Westerink, 2002, p. 196, 266, 302).
7. Anna Maria van Schurman's *Eucleria* is an example of this deployment in its most radical outcome. Because of her faith and obedience to God, no longer can she remain a part of a church in ruins and the sinful world. It may sound unreasonable, but she acts with a proud dignity, in conformity with her conscience. For her compromise was out of the question – she is prepared to give up everything for her unrequited love of God (De Certeau, 1992, p. 285).
8. Compare: "Thus the first understanding and use of the Law is to restrain the wicked. For, the devil reigns in the whole world and drives men to all sorts of shameful deeds. This is why God has ordained magistrates, parents, teachers, laws, shackles, and all civic ordinances, so that, if they cannot do any more, they will at least bind the hands of the devil and keep him from raging at will. (...) The other use of the Law is the theological or spiritual one, which serves to increase transgressions. This is the primary purpose of the Law of Moses, that through it sin might grow and be multiplied, especially in the conscience" (Luther, 1535, vii-309).
9. The difference between Luther and Calvin's respective conceptions of the two kingdoms consists in the fact that Calvin does not consider this distinction in terms of a separation between the kingdom of God and the world: both kingdoms are – or should be – governed by God, albeit in distinctive ways (VanDrunen, 2010, p. 71).
10. It is often argued that one of the main differences between Calvin and Luther is Calvinist political activism versus Luther's passive obedience to worldly government. David Whitford argues that this assessment needs correction: in the Lutheran tradition one also finds resistance to tyranny, although Calvinism follows a more militant tradition (Whitford, 2001).
11. Calvin adds: "If once religion is absent from their life, men are in no wise superior to brute beasts, but are in many respects far more miserable". Here, we see that Calvin again compares men with animals (Calvin, 1559a, 1.3.3).
12. Compare: "He indeed shows that ignorance is in vain pretended as an excuse by the Gentiles, since they prove by their own deeds that they have some rule of righteousness: for there is no nation so lost to every thing human, that it does not keep within the limits of some laws. Since then all nations, of themselves and without a monitor, are disposed to make laws for themselves, it is beyond all question evident that they have some notions of justice and rectitude, which (...) which are implanted by nature in the hearts of men. They have then a law, though they are without law: for though they have not a written law, they are yet by no means wholly destitute of the knowledge of what is right and just; as they could not otherwise distinguish between vice and virtue" (Calvin, 1540, pp. 72–73).
13. We find the same line of thought in the writings of Puritans such as Perkins. However, they stress the asocial aspect of human nature. Every man is by nature

a murdering atheist governed by the flesh. Yet if all men were sinners, murderers, and atheists, then coexistence would be impossible. Everyday life and experience shows, however, that such coexistence is possible, and so the Puritans have to assume God bestows a common grace for the good of human society. God sets limits to restrain man's wickedness (Luttmer, 2000).

14. Calvin refers to a "forum of conscience" in contradistinction to an "outer forum" in his discussion of the two governments. This distinction does not appear in Luther's work, although it is anticipated in the writings of Pope Adrian VI, one of Luther's opponents. Former professor from Leuven University, in his academic writings Adrian makes a distinction between a forum of the soul (*forum animae*) or forum of conscience – referring to the subject's inner moral imperatives – and an outer forum (*in foro exteriori*) – indicating duties imposed by external authorities (Hein, 1999, pp. 228–232).
15. Given the way in which conscience mediates between man and God, Perkins and Teellinck call conscience the "highest" faculty of the soul. Perkins states that conscience is placed in the middle between man and God, so it is under God, and yet above man. According to Teellinck, God creates conscience so that man knows all his powers and capacities should be oriented toward God. Conscience is a sense of man's spiritual state before God, an "echo" of God's judgment (Westerink, 2002, pp. 186–192).
16. The use of despair is discussed at length later with respect to Puritan and Reformed orthodox devotional literature. In spite of Calvin's warnings not to enquire into God's will and the doctrine of predestination, the decree becomes a central issue to theological debates and religious life. God's wrath at man's corruption has the potential to excite profound doubt and despair regarding one's spiritual state. The solution to this problem proposed by various Puritans and, later, by Gisbertus Voetius is the idea that God can withdraw his grace temporally. "Temporal despair" consists in a feeling of damnation that should be understood as "a preparative to the child of God to keepe him from sinne in time to come" or as "purgatorie in this present life". In short, temporal despair is a sign of faith, and true doubt regarding election is a sign of assurance. This temporal despair remains, nonetheless, difficult to make sense of: in the first place because it can only be interpreted as temporal retrospectively and, therefore, distinguished from other forms of despair and doubt (God's punishment; in the second place because despair is often difficult to distinguish from what in that time is generally recognized as melancholia, especially when the believer has a natural inclination to this pathology (Frijhoff, 2002; Bruhn, 2008).
17. In an earlier study I show this sense of guilt is central not only to Freud's psychoanalytic texts but also his writings on applied psychoanalysis, notably, his texts on religion (Westerink, 2009b).
18. Not only is *Moses and Monotheism* a reflection on Freud's own Jewish background, but also a reaction to studies by his students on Judaism. Theodore Reik analysed Judaism, applying Freud's reasoning in *Totem and Taboo* to the one religion Freud had not yet analysed – his own. Reik argues that, like Christianity, Judaism emerges from primitive pre-monotheistic Semitic religions, of which traits are still visible, especially in the figure of Moses. According to Reik Moses was originally a deity. Freud's *Moses and Monotheism* reconstructs Judaism in such a way that it cannot be traced back to primitive religion directly but comes from

another source, namely, the pre-existing monotheism of Akhenaton. Judaism's primitive elements are secondary. Reasoning in this way Freud secures for Judaism a unique development and place amongst other religions (Westerink, 2008).

19. Calvin adds: "I do not say, as Cicero did, that errors disappear with the lapse of time, and that religion grows and becomes better each day. (...) I only say that though the stupid hardness in their minds, which the impious eagerly conjure up to reject God, wastes away, yet the sense of divinity, which they greatly wished to have extinguished, thrives and presently burgeons" (Calvin, 1559a, 1.3.3; also Bosco, 1986, pp. 349–351; Zachman, 1993, pp. 117–118).
20. Compare also: "In this passage [Jes.44:11, H.W.], therefore, Isaiah appeals to the consciences of wicked men; because, although they are actuated by the most inveterate obstinacy and rebellion, yet sometimes they are constrained to tremble, when they ask themselves, 'What are we doing?' and inquire into the reason of their actions; for they have nothing that is firm or solid, on which they can safely rest. They are bold so long as they are hurried on by their rage, but when they come to themselves, and take some leisure for reflection, they are terrified and dismayed" (Calvin, 1559b, pp. 190–191).
21. For example, Calvin criticizes a full confession of one's sins: "while wholly occupied with the cataloguing of sins, they in the meantime forget that hidden slough of vices, their own secret transgressions and inner filth, the knowledge of which ought particularly to have brought home to them their own misery". In short: "depriving sinners of a true awareness of their sins, it makes them hypocrites, ignorant of God and of themselves" (Calvin, 1559a, 3.4.18). We recall that Freud uses the term "hypocrisy" to refer to the difference between what results from moral self-evaluation (ethical narcissism) and a correct assessment of one's "evil" nature (Freud, 1525, p. 134).
22. There is good reason to invoke the term "symptom" in relation to Calvin's thought: He regularly refers to sin as a sickness of the soul (f.e. Calvin, 1559a, 2.7.6, 4.17.42). Compare also: "There is also another special confession when suppliants ask release from punishments. It is that at the same time they may pray for the pardon of their sins. For it would be absurd to wish the effect to be removed while the cause remained. We must guard against imitating foolish sick folk, who, concerned solely with the treatment of symptoms, neglect the very root of the disease. We must make it our first concern that God be favourable toward us, rather than that he attest his favor by outward signs, because he wills to maintain this order, and it would have been of small profit to us to have him do us good unless our conscience, feeling him wholly appeased, rendered him altogether lovely" (Idem, 3.20.9).

References

Aquinas, T. (1984). *The Summa Theologica of Saint Thomas Aquinas*. In: R. Maynard (ed.), *Great Books of the Western World, Vol. 19*, Chicago: Encyclopedia Brittanica.

Augustine, A. (1998). *The City of God against the Pagans*. R.W. Dyson (ed.), Cambridge: Cambridge University Press.

Basse, M. (2001). *Die dogmengeschichtlichen Konzeptionen Adolf von Harnacks und Reinhold Seebergs* Göttingen: Vandenhoeck & Ruprecht.

Baylor, M.G. (1977). *Action and Person. Conscience in Late Scholasticism and the Young Luther*. Leiden: Brill.

Bermon, P. (2007). *L'assentiment et son objet chez Grégoire de Rimini*. Paris: Vrin.

Boothby, R. (2001). *Freud as Philosopher. Metapsychology after Lacan*. London: Routledge.

Bordo, S. (1987). *The Flight to Objectivity. Essays on Cartesianism and Culture*. Abany: SUNY Press.

Bosco, D. (1986). Conscience as Court and Worm: Calvin and the Three Elements of Conscience. *Journal of Religious Ethics* 14(2), 333–355.

Bouwsma, W.J. (1988). *John Calvin. A Sixteenth Century Portrait*. Oxford: Oxford University Press.

Bradley, D.J.M. (1997). *Aquinas on the Twofold Human Good. Reason and Human Happiness in Aquinas's Moral Science*. Washington: The Catholic University of America Press.

Bray, J.S. (1975). *Theodore Beza's Doctrine of Predestination*. Nieuwkoop: De Graaf.

Brennan, T. (1993). *History after Lacan*. London: Routledge.

Brown, P. (1969). *Augustine of Hippo. A Biography*. Berkeley: University of California Press.

Brosché, F. (1978). *Luther on Predestination. The Antinomy and the Unity between Love and Wrath in Luther's Concept of God*. Stockholm: Almqvist & Wiksell.

Bruhn, K. (2008). 'Sinne Unfoulded': Time, Election, and Disbelief among the Godly in Late Sixteenth- and Early Seventeenth-Century England. *Church History* 77(3), 574–595.

Burrows, M.S. (1991). *Jean Gerson and* De Consolatione Theologiae. *The Consolation of a Biblical and Reforming Theology for a Disordered Age*. Tübingen: Mohr Siebeck.

Calvin, J. (1539). *Reply by Calvin to Cardinal Sadolet's Letter*. In: H. Beveridge & J. Bonnet, (eds.) *Selected Works of John Calvin. Tracts and Letters, Vol. 1. The Comprehensive John Calvin Collection*, Rio (WI): Ages Software, 2000–2004.

Calvin, J. (1540). *Commentary on the Epistle to the Romans* (J. Owen, transl., ed.). *The Comprehensive John Calvin Collection*. Rio (WI): Ages Software, 2000–2004.

Calvin, J. (1544). *Letter to Bullinger, Letter 122*. In H. Beveridge & J. Bonnet, (eds.) *Selected Works of John Calvin. Tracts and Letters, Vol. 4*, Letters 1528–1545 (*The Comprehensive John Calvin Collection*). Rio (WI): Ages Software, 2000–2004.

Calvin, J. (1551). *Sermons on Election and Reprobation* (J. Fielde, transl.). *The Comprehensive John Calvin Collection*. Rio (WI): Ages Software, 2000–2004.

Calvin, J. (1552). *A Treatise on the Eternal Predestination of God*. In *Calvin's Calvinism. A Treatise on the Eternal Predestination of God. A Defence of the Secret Providence of God* (H.P. Cole, transl.). Grand Rapids: Eerdmans, 1950.

Calvin, J. (1554). *Commentary on Genesis* (J. King, transl., ed.). *The Comprehensive John Calvin Collection*. Rio (WI): Ages Software, 2000–2004.

Calvin, J. (1558). *A Defence of the Secret Providence of God*. In *Calvin's Calvinism. A Treatise on the Eternal Predestination of God. A Defence of the Secret Providence of God* (H.P. Cole, transl.). Grand Rapids: Eerdmans, 1950.

Calvin, J. (1559a). *Institutes of the Christian Religion* (F.L. Battles, transl.). *The Comprehensive John Calvin Collection*. Rio (WI): Ages Software, 2000-2004.

Calvin, J. (1559b). *Commentary on the Prophet Isaiah, Vol. 2* (W. Pringle, transl.). *The Comprehensive John Calvin Collection*. Rio (WI): Ages Software, 2000–2004.

Cassian, J. (1958). *Conférences, Sources chrétiennes 54* (E. Pichery, ed.). Paris: Éditions du Cerf.

Causse, J.-D. (1999). *La haine et l'amour de Dieu*. Geneva: Labor et Fides.

De Certeau, M. (1986). *Heterologies. Discourse on the Other*. Minneapolis: University of Minnesota Press.

De Certeau, M. (1988). *The Writing of History* (T. Conley, transl.). New York: Columbia University Press.

De Certeau, M. (1992). *The Mystic Fable. Volume One. The Sixteenth and Seventeenth Centuries*. Chicago: Chicago University Press.

Chadwick, O. (1968). *John Cassian*. Cambridge: Cambridge University Press.

Conditt, M.W. (1973). *More Acceptable than Sacrifice. Ethics and Election as Obedience to God's Will in the Theology of Calvin*. Basel: Friedrich Reinhardt Kommissionsverlag.

Creswell, D.R. (1997). *St. Augustine's Dilemma. Grace and Eternal Law in the Major Works of Augustine of Hippo*. New York: Peter Lang.

Damrosch, L. (1979). Hobbes as Reformation Theologian: Implications of the Free-Will Controversy. *Journal of the History of Ideas* 30(3), 339–352.

Darwin, C. (1871). *The Descent of Man, and Selection in Relation to Sex* (J. Tyler Bonner & R. May, eds). Princeton: Princeton University Press, 1981.

David-Ménard, M. (1990). *La folie dans la raison pure. Kant lecteur de Swedenborg*. Paris: Vrin.

Dawes, G.W. (2001). *The Historical Jesus Question. The Challenge of History and Religious Authority*. Louisville: Westminster John Knox Press.

Delumeau, J. (1990). *Sin and Fear. The Emergence of a Western Guilt Culture 13th–18th Centuries*. New York: St Martin's Press.

Denzinger, H. (1991). *Kompendium der Glaubensbekenntnisse und kirchlichen Lehrentscheidungen* (P. Hünermann, ed.). Freiburg: Herder.

Descartes, R. (1637). *A Discourse on the Method of Correctly Conducting One's Reason and Seeking Truth in the Sciences* (I. Maclean, ed.). Oxford: Oxford University Press, 2006.

DiCenso, J.J. (1999). *The Other Freud. Religion, Culture and Psychoanalysis*. London: Routledge.

De Dijn, H. (2009). *Spinoza. De doornen en de roos*. Kapellen: Pelckmans & Klement.

Van Engen, J. (2008). *Sisters and Brothers of the Common Life. The Devotio Moderna and the World of the Later Middle Ages*. Philadelphia: University of Pennsylvania Press.

Erasmus, D. and Luther, M. (2006). *Discourse on Free Will* (E.F. Winter, ed.), London: Continuum.

Evans, D. (1996). *An Introductory Dictionary of Lacanian Psychoanalysis*. London: Routledge.

Febvre, L. (1928). *Martin Luther, un destin*. Paris: Presses Universitaires de France.

Fink, B. (1995). *The Lacanian Subject. Between Language and Jouissance*. Princeton: Princeton University Press.

Fink, B. (1997). *A Clinical Introduction to Lacanian Psychoanalysis: Theory and Technique*. Cambridge (MA): Harvard University Press.

Forde, G. (2005). *The Captivation of the Will. Luther vs. Erasmus on Freedom and Bondage* (S. Paulsen, ed.). Grand Rapids: Eerdmans.

Foucault, M. (1980). The Confession of the Flesh. In C. Gordon, (ed.) *Power/Knowledge: Selected Interviews and Other Writings 1972–1977*. New York: Pantheon Books.

Foucault, M. (1985). The Battle for Chastity. In Ph. Ariès & A. Béjin (eds), *Western Sexuality. Practice and Precept in Past and Present Times*. London: Blackwell, pp. 14–25.

Foucault, M. (1976). *The History of Sexuality, Vol. 1: The Will to Knowledge*, London: Penguin, 1998.

Freppert, L. (1988). *The Basis of Morality according to William Ockham*. Chicago: Franciscan Herald Press.

Freud, S. (1895). *Project for a Scientific Psychology*. In *The Standard Edition of the Complete Psychological Works of Sigmund Freud (SE), Vol. 1* (J. Strachey, ed.). London: Hogarth Press and The Institute of Psycho-Analysis, 1953–1966.

Freud, S. (1896a). *The Aetiology of Hysteria, SE, Vol. 3*.

Freud, S. (1896b). *Further Remarks on the Neuro-Psychoses of Defence, SE, Vol. 3*.

Freud, S. (1896c). *Draft K, SE, Vol. 1*.

Freud, S. (1900). *The Interpretation of Dreams, SE, Vols. 4–5*.

Freud, S. (1905). *Three Essays on the Theory of Sexuality, SE, Vol. 7*.

Freud, S. (1908). *Character and Anal Erotism, SE, Vol. 9*.

Freud, S. (1909). *Notes upon a Case of Obsessional Neurosis, SE, Vol. 10*.

Freud, S. (1910). *Leonardo da Vinci and a Memory of his Childhood, SE, Vol. 11*.

Freud, S. (1911). *Formulations on the Two Principles of Mental Functioning, SE, Vol. 12*.

Freud, S. (1912–1913). *Totem and Taboo, SE, Vol. 13*.

Freud, S. (1914a). *The Moses of Michelangelo, SE, Vol. 13*.

Freud, S. (1914b). *On the History of the Psychoanalytic Movement, SE, Vol. 14*.

Freud, S. (1915). *Thoughts for the Times on War and Death, SE, Vol. 14*.

Freud, S. (1916–1917). *Introductory Lectures on Psycho-Analysis, SE, Vol. 15*.

Freud, S. (1917). *Mourning and Melancholia, SE, Vol. 14*.

Freud, S. (1918). *From the History of an Infantile Neurosis, SE, Vol. 17*.

Freud, S. (1920). *Beyond the Pleasure Principle, SE, Vol. 18*.

Freud, S. (1921). *Group Psychology and the Analysis of the Ego, SE, Vol. 18*.

Freud, S. (1922). *Some Neurotic Mechanisms in Jealousy, Paranoia and Homosexuality, SE, Vol. 18.*

Freud, S. (1923a), *The Ego and the Id, SE, Vol. 19.*

Freud, S. (1923b). *A Seventeenth-Century Demonological Neurosis, SE, Vol. 19.*

Freud, S. (1924). *A short Account of Psychoanalysis, SE, Vol. 19.*

Freud, S. (1925). *Some Additional Notes on Dream-Interpretation as a Whole, SE, Vol. 20.*

Freud, S. (1927). *The Future of an Illusion, SE, Vol. 21.*

Freud, S. (1930). *Civilization and Its Discontents, SE, Vol. 21.*

Freud, S. (1932). *The Acquisition and Control of Fire, SE, Vol. 22.*

Freud, S. (1933). *New Introductory Lectures on Psychoanalysis, SE, Vol. 32.*

Freud, S. (1937). *Constructions in Analysis, SE, Vol. 33.*

Freud, S. (1938). *Some Elementary Lessons in Psycho-Analysis, SE, Vol. 23.*

Freud, S. (1939). *Moses and Monotheism, SE, Vol. 23.*

Freud, S. (1940). *An Outline of Psychoanalysis, SE, Vol. 23.*

Freud, S. (1960). *Letters of Sigmund Freud* (E.L. Freud, ed.). New York: Basic Books.

Freud, S. (1985). *The Complete Letters of Sigmund Freud to Wilhelm Fliess 1887–1904* (J.M. Masson, ed.). Cambridge (MA): Harvard University Press.

Freud, S. and Breuer, J. (1895). *Studies on Hysteria, SE, Vol. 2.*

Freud, S. and Pfister, O. (1963). *Psychoanalysis and Faith. The Letters of Sigmund Freud and Oskar Pfister* (H. Meng & E. Freud, eds). New York: Basic Books.

Frijhoff, W. (1995). *Wegen van Evert Willemsz. Een Hollands weeskind op zoek naar zichzelf, 1607–1647*. Nijmegen: SUN.

Frijhoff, W. (2002). Predestination and the Farmer: An Incident of Life and Faith in Early Seventeenth-Century Holland. In W. Frijhoff (ed.), *Embodied Belief. Ten Essays on Religious Culture in Dutch History*. Hilversum: Verloren, pp. 93–110.

Fuchs, E. (2009). Calvins Ethik. In M.E. Hirzel & M. Sallmann (eds.), *1509 – Johannes Calvin – 2009. Sein Wirken in Kirche und Gesellschaft. Essays zum 500. Geburtstag*. Zurich: Theologischer Verlag, pp. 183–200.

Gauchet, M. (1997). *The Disenchantment of the World. A Political History of Religion*. Princeton: Princeton University Press.

Gerrish, B.A. (1973). 'To the Unknown God': Luther and Calvin on the Hiddenness of God. *The Journal of Religion* 53(3), 263–292.

Gillespie, M.A. (2008). *The Theological Origins of Modernity*. Chicago: Chicago University Press.

Gilson, E. (1930). *Le role de la pensée médiévale dans la formation du système cartésien*. Paris: Vrin.

Gilson, E. (1994). *The Christian Philosophy of St. Thomas Aquinas*. Notre Dame: University of Notre Dame Press.

Greene, R.A. (1997). Instinct of Nature: Natural Law, Synderesis, and the Moral Sense. *Journal of the History of Ideas* 58(2), 173–198.

Grosse, S. (1994). *Heilsgewißheit und Scrupulositas im späten Mittelalter. Studien zu Johannes Gerson und Gattungen der Frömmigkeitstheologie seiner Zeit*. Tübingen: Mohr.

Halverson, J.L. (1998). *Peter Aureol on Predestination. A Challenge to Late Medieval Thought*. Leiden: Brill.

Hamm, B. (2004). *The Reformation of Faith in the Context f Late Medieval Theology and Piety* (R.J. Bast, ed.). Leiden: Brill.

Van Haute, P. (1993). Michel Foucault: de psychoanalyse en de wet. *Tijdschrift voor Filosofie* 55(3), 449–471.

Van Haute, P. (1998). Death and Sublimation in Lacan's reading of *Antigone*. In S. Harasym (ed.), *Levinas and Lacan. The Missed Encounter*. Albany: SUNY Press, pp. 102–120.

Van Haute, P. (2002). *Against Adaptation. Lacan's subversion of the subject*. New York: Other Press.

Hein, R.B. (1999).*"Gewissen" bei Adrian von Utrecht (Hadrian VI.), Erasmus von Rotterdam und Thomas More. Ein Beitrag zur systematischenn Analyse des Gewissensbegriffs in der katholischen nordeuropäischen Renaissance*. Munster: Lit.

Hobbes, T. (1651). *Leviathan* (R. Tuck, ed.), Cambridge: Cambridge University Press, 1996.

Hoitenga, D.J. (1997). *John Calvin and the Will. A Critique and Corrective*. Grand Rapids: Baker Books.

Huff, P.A. (1999). Calvin and the Beasts: Animals in John Calvin's Theological Discourse. *Journal of the Evangelical Theological Society* 42(1), 67–75.

Hunter, G. (2005). *Radical Protestantism in Spinoza's Thought*. Aldershot: Ashgate.

Jones, E. (1929). Fear, Guilt and Hate. In: *Papers on Psycho-Analysis*. London: Baillière, Tindall and Cox, 1950, 304–319.

Jung, C. G. (1912). Psychology of the Unconscious: A Study of the Transformations and Symbolisms of the Libido (B. Hinkle, transl.). London: Kegan Paul, Trench, Trubner, 1921.

Juranville, A. (1984). *Lacan et la philosophie*. Paris: Presses Universitaires de France.

De Kesel, M. (2009). *Eros & Ethics. Reading Jacques Lacan's Seminar VII*. Albany: SUNY Press.

Kiarina Kordela, A. (2007). *$urplus. Spinoza, Lacan*. Albany: SUNY Press.

Kolb, R. (2005). *Bound Choice, Election, and Wittenberg Theological Method: From Martin Luther to the Formula of Concord*. Grand Rapids: Eerdmans.

Koyré, A. (1922). *Essai sur l'idée de Dieu et les preuves de son existence chez Descartes*. Paris: Leroux.

Koyré, A. (1957). *From the Closed World to the Infinite Universe*. Baltimore: John Hopkins Press.

Kusukawa, S. (1995). *The Transformation of Natural Philosophy. The Case of Philip Melanchthon*. Cambridge: Cambridge University Press.

Lacan, J. (1975). *Le Séminaire, Livre I, Les écrits techniques de Freud 1953–1954* (J.-A. Miller, ed.). Paris: Seuil.

Lacan, J. (1978). *Le Séminaire, Livre II, Le moi dans la théorie de Freud et dans la technique de la psychanalyse 1954–1955* (J.-A. Miller, ed.). Paris: Seuil.

Lacan, J. (1987). Introduction to the Names-of-the-Father Seminar (J. Mehlman, ed.), *October 40*, 81–95.

Lacan, J. (1984). *Les complexes familiaux dans la formation de l'individu. Essai d'analyse d'une function en psychologie*. Paris: Navarin.

Lacan, J. (1986). *Le Séminaire, Livre VII, L'éthique de la psychanalyse 1959–1960* (J.-A. Miller, ed.). Paris: Seuil.

Lacan, J. (1992). *The Ethics of Psychoanalysis 1959–1960. The Seminar of Jacques Lacan Book VII* (J.-A. Miller, ed., D. Porter, Transl.). London: Routledge.

Lacan, J. (1993). *The Psychoses 1955–1956. The Seminar of Jacques Lacan Book III* (J.-A. Miller, ed.). New York: Norton.
Lacan, J. (1998a). *Le Séminaire, Livre V, Les formations de l'inconscient 1957–1958* (J.-A. Miller, ed.). Paris: Seuil.
Lacan, J. (1998b). *The Four Fundamental Concepts of Psycho-Analysis* (J.-A. Miller, ed., D. Macey, intr.). London: Vintage.
Lacan, J. (1999). *The Seminar of Jacques Lacan, Book XX. On Feminine Sexuality, The Limits of Love and Knowledge, 1972–1973 (Encore)* (J.-A. Miller, ed.). New York: Norton & Company.
Lacan, J. (2000). *Le désir et son interpretation. Séminaire 1958–1959*. Paris: Éditions de l'Association Freudienne Internationale.
Lacan, J. (2005). *Le triomphe de la religion precede de Discours aux Catholiques*. Paris: Seuil.
Lacan, J. (2006). *Écrits* (B. Fink, ed.). New York: Norton.
Lacey, S.E. (2009). *John Wyclif*. Oxford: Oxford University Press.
Lamberigts, M. (ed.) (1994). *L'Augustinisme à l'ancienne faculté de théologie de Louvain*. Leuven: Peeters.
Langston, D.C. (2001). *Conscience and Other Virtues: From Bonaventure to MacIntyre*. University Park (PA): The Pennsylvania State University Press.
Lazareth, W.H. (2001). *Christians in Society. Luther, the Bible, and Social Ethics*. Minneapolis: Fortress Press.
Lear, J. (1990). *Love and its Place in Nature. A Philosophical Interpretation of Freudian Psychoanalysis*. New York: Farrar, Straus & Giroux.
Leff, G. (1957). *Bradwardine and the Pelagians. A Study of his 'De Causa Dei' and Its Opponents*. Cambridge: Cambridge University Press.
Leff, G. (1961a). *Gregory of Rimini. Tradition and Innovation in Fourteenth Century Thought*. Manchester: Manchester University Press.
Leff, G. (1961b). Gregory of Rimini: A Fourteenth-Century Augustinian. *Revue des etudes augustinennes* 7, 153–170.
Levi, A. (2002). *Renaissance and Reformation: The Intellectual Genesis*. New Haven: Yale University Press.
Lilla, M. (2007). *The Stillborn God. Religion, Politics, and the Modern West*. New York: Alfred A. Knopf.
Lloyd, G. (1996). *Spinoza and the Ethics*. London: Routledge.
Lohse, B. (1995). *Luthers Theologie in ihrer historischen Entwicklung und in ihrem systematischen Zusammenhang*. Göttingen: Vandenhoeck & Ruprecht.
Lottin, D.O. (1949). *Psychologie et morale aux XIIe et XIIIe siècles*, Leuven: Abbaye du Mont César.
Luther, M. (1513). *Psalm 60*. In J.J. Pelikan, H.C. Oswald & H.T. Lehmann (eds.), *Luther's Works, Vol. 10: First Lectures on the Psalms I: Psalms 1–75*. Philadelphia: Fortress Press, 1999 (CD-ROM).
Luther, M. (1515–1516). *Lectures on Romans*. In *Luther's Works, Vol. 25: Lectures on Romans*.
Luther, M. (1517a). *Disputation against Scholastic Theology*. In *Luther's Works, Vol. 31: Career of the Reformer 1*.
Luther, M. (1517b). *The Seven Penitential Psalms. Psalm 6*. In *Luther's Works, Vol. 14: Selected Psalms III*.
Luther, M. (1518). *Heidelberg Disputation*. In *Luther's Works, Vol. 31: Career of the Reformer I*.

Luther, M. (1519). *Letter to Spalatin concerning the Leipzig Debate*. In: *Luther's Works, Vol. 31: Career of the Reformer I*.

Luther, M. (1521). *The Judgment of Martin Luther on Monastic Vows*. In: *Luther's Works, Vol. 44: The Christian in Society I*.

Luther, M. (1522/1546). *Preface of the Epistle of St. Paul to the Romans*. In: *Luther's Works, Vol. 35: Word and Sacrament I*.

Luther, M. (1523). *Temporal Authority: To what Extent it should be obeyed*. In: *Luther's Works, Vol. 45: The Christian in Society II*.

Luther, M. (1523/1545). *Preface to the Old Testament*. In: *Luther's Works, Vol. 35: Word and Sacrament I*.

Luther, M. (1524). *Trade and Usury*. In: *Luther's Works, Vol. 45: The Christian in Society II*.

Luther, M. (1525a). *The Bondage of the Will*. In *Luther's Works, Vol. 33: Career of the Reformer III*.

Luther, M. (1525b). *How Christians should regard Moses*. In: *Luther's Works, Vol. 40: Church and Ministry II*.

Luther, M. (1525c). *Against the Robbing and Murdering Hordes of Peasants*. In: *Luther's Works, Vol. 46: The Christian in Society III*.

Luther, M. (1526). *Whether Soldiers, too, can be saved*. In: *Luther's Works, Vol. 46: The Christian in Society III*.

Luther, M. (1530). *Psalm 117*. In: *Luther's Works, Vol. 14: Selected Psalms III*.

Luther, M. (1535). *Lectures on Galatians*. In: *Luther's Works, Vol. 26: Lectures on Galatians, 1535, Chapters 1–4*.

Luther, M. (1535–1545). *Lectures on Genesis*. In: *Luther's Works, Vol. 1: Lectures on Genesis: Chapters 1–5*.

Luther, M. (1536a). *The Disputation Concerning Man*. In: *Luther's Works, Vol. 34: Career of the Reformer IV*.

Luther, M. (1536b). *The Disputation Concerning Justification*. In: *Luther's Works, Vol. 34: Career of the Reformer IV*.

Luttmer, F. (2000). Persecutors, Tempters and Vassals of the Devil: The Unregenerate in Puritan Practical Divinity. *Journal of Ecclesiastical History* 51(1), 37–68.

MacIntyre, A. (2010). *A Short History of Ethics. A History of Moral Philosophy from the Homeric Age to the Twentieth Century*. London: Routledge.

Martinich, A. (1992). *The Two Gods of Leviathan: Thomas Hobbes on Religion and Politics*. Cambridge: Cambridge University Press.

McCord Adams, M. (1999). Ockham on Will, Nature and Morality. In P.V. Spade (ed.), *The Cambridge Companion to Ockham*. Cambridge: Cambridge University Press, pp. 245–272.

McGrade, A.S. (1999). Natural Law and Moral Omnipotence. In P.V. Spade (ed.), *The Cambridge Companion to Ockham*. Cambridge: Cambridge University Press, pp. 273–301.

McGrath, A. (1987). *The Intellectual Origins of the European Reformation*. Oxford: Basil Blackwell.

McGrath, A. (1993). *A Life of John Calvin. A Study in the Shaping of Western Culture*. Oxford: Blackwell.

McGuire, B.P. (2005). *Jean Gerson and the Last Medieval Reformation*. University Park (PA.): The Pennsylvania State University Press.

Meynert, Th. (1889). *Gehirn und Gesittung*. Vienna: Braumüller.

Miethke, J. (1969). *Ockhams Weg zur Sozialphilosophie*. Berlin: De Gruyter.

Mjaaland, M.T. (2009). Does Modernity begin with Luther? *Studia Theologica – Nordic Journal of Theology* 63(1), 42–66.

Moyaert, P. (1994). *Ethiek en sublimatie. Over De ethiek van de psychoanalyse van Jacques Lacan*. Nijmegen: SUN.

Moyaert, P. (2002). *Begeren en vereren. Idealisering en sublimering*. Amsterdam: SUN.

Moyaert, P. (2012). Moral life in times of loneliness. Does the notion of double conscience illuminate Lacan's understanding of moral sensibility? In R. Breeur & U. Melle (eds.), *Life, Subjectivity and Art: Essays in Honor of Rudolf Bernet*. Dordrecht: Springer, pp. 481–511.

Muchembled, R. (2003). *A History of the Devil. From the Middle Ages to the Present*. Cambridge: Polity Press.

Muller, R.A. (2000). *The Unaccommodated Calvin. Studies in the Foundation of a Theological Tradition*. Oxford: Oxford University Press.

Muller, R.A. (2008). *Christ and the Decree. Christology and Predestination in Reformed Theology from Calvin to Perkins*. Grand Rapids: Baker Academic.

Nase, E. (1993). *Oskar Pfister's analytische Seelsorge*. Berlin: De Gruyter.

Needleman Armintor, M. (2004). *Lacan and the Ghosts of Modernity: Masculinity, Tradition, and the Anxiety of Influence*. New York: Peter Lang.

Neill, C. (2005). The Locus of Judgement in Lacan's Ethics. *The Journal for Lacanian Studies* 3(1), 85–100.

Neu, J. (1977). *Emotion, Thought and Therapy. A Study of Hume and Spinoza and the Relationship of Philosophical Theories of the Emotions to Psychological Theories of Therapy*. Berkeley: University of California Press.

Oberman, H.A. (1957). *Archbishop Thomas Bradwardine. A Fourteenth Century Augustinian. A Study of his Theology in Its Historical Context*. Utrecht: Kemink.

Oberman, H.A. (1963). *The Harvest of Medieval Theology: Gabriel Biel and Late Medieval Nominalism*. Cambridge (MA): Harvard University Press.

Oberman, H.A. (1977). *Werden und Wertung der Reformation. Vom Wegestreit zum Glaubenskampf*. Tübingen: Mohr Siebeck.

Oberman, H.A. (1986). *Die Reformation. Von Wittenberg nach Genf*. Göttingen: Vandenhoeck & Ruprecht.

Oberman, H.A. (1989). *Luther. Man between God and the Devil*. New Haven: Yale University Press.

Oberman, H.A. (1990). Luther Against the Devil. *The Christian Century* 107(1), 75–79.

Oberman, H.A. (1992). *The Dawn of the Reformation,. Essays on Late Medieval and Early Reformation Thought*. Edinburgh: T. & T. Clark.

Oberman, H.A. (1994). *The Impact of the Reformation: Essays*. Grand Rapids: Eerdmans.

Ockham, W. (1983). *Predestination, God's Foreknowledge, and Future Contingents* (M. McCord Adams & N. Kretzmann, eds.). Indianapolis: Hackett Publishing.

Oosterhuis, H. (2000). *Stepchildren of Nature. Krafft-Ebing, Psychiatry, and the Making of Sexual Identity*. Chicago: University of Chicago Press.

Osmond, R. (1990). *Mutual Accusation. Seventeenth-Century Body and Soul Dialogues in Their Literary and Theological Context*. Toronto: University of Toronto Press.

Paturet, J.-B. (2008). *Incroyables religions. Une lecture psychanalytique du phénoméne religieux*. Paris: Cerf.

Paulsen, S.D. (1999). Luther on the Hidden God. *Word and World* 19(4), 363–371.

Pearson, Th.D. (2010). Martin Luther's Pragmatic Revision of Traditional Natural Law Theory. *Journal of Lutheran Ethics* 10(3), https://www.elca.org/What-We-Believe/Social-Issues/Journal-of-Lutheran-Ethics.aspx (assessed June 2010)

Perkins, W. (1591). *A Golden Chain*. In *The Works of William Perkins* (I. Breward, ed.). Appleford: The Sutton Courtenay Press, 1970.

Perkins, W. (1966). *William Perkins 1558–1602, English Puritanist. His Pioneer Works on Casuistry:* A Discourse of Conscience *and* The Whole Treatise of the Cases of Conscience (Th.F. Merrill, ed.), Nieuwkoop: De Graaf.

Pesch, O. (2004). *Hinführung zu Luther*. Mainz: Mathias-Grünewald-Verlag.

Pope, S.J. (ed.) (2002). *The Ethics of Aquinas*. Washington: Georgetown University Press.

Pryor, C.S. (2006). God's Bridle: John Calvin's Application of natural Law. *Journal of Law and Religion* 22(1), 225–254.

Raguse, H. (1994). *Der Raum des Textes. Elemente einer transdisziplinären theologischen Hermeneutik*. Stuttgart: Kohlhammer.

Rank, O. and Sachs, H. (1912). Entwicklung und Ansprüche der Psychoanalyse. *Imago. Zeitschrift für die Anwendung der Psychoanalyse auf die Geisteswissenschaften* 1, 1–16.

Raunio, A. (2006). Divine and Natural Law in Luther and Melanchton. In V. Mäkinen (ed.), *Lutheran Reformation and the Law*. Leiden: Brill, pp. 21–62.

Reik, T. (1923). *Der eigene und der fremde Gott. Zur Psychoanalyse der religiösen Entwicklung*. Frankfurt: Suhrkamp, 1972.

Reik, T. (1927). *Dogma and Compulsion. Psychoanalytic Studies on Religion and Myths*. New York: International Universities Press, 1951.

Reinhuber, T. (2001). *Kämpfender Glaube. Studien zu Luthers Bekenntnis am Ende von* De servo arbitrio. Berlin: De Gruyter.

Rieff, Ph. (1961). *Freud: The Mind of the Moralist*. New York: Doubleday.

Rorty, R. (1979). *Philosophy and the Mirror of Nature*. Princeton: Princeton University Press.

Roudinesco, E. (1997). *Jacques Lacan*. Cambridge: Polity Press.

Roudinesco, E. (1990). *Lacan & Co. A History of Psychoanalysis in France 1925–1985*. Chicago: Chicago University Press.

Van Ruiten, J. and Vandermeersch, P. (1994). Psychoanalyse en historisch-kritische exegese: de actualiteit van Freud's boek over Mozes. *Tijdschrift voor Theologie* 34(3), 269–291.

Santos Noya, M. (1990). *Die Sünden- und Gnadenlehre des Gregor von Rimini*. Frankfurt: Peter Lang.

Schmidt, W.H. (1989). *Einführung in das Alte Testament*. Berlin: De Gruyter.

Schneewind, J.B. (1998). *The Invention of Autonomy. A History of Modern Moral Philosophy*. Cambridge: Cambridge University Press.

Schorske, C. (1981). *Fin-de-siècle Vienna. Politics and Culture*. New York: Vintage.

Van Schurman, A.M. (1684). *Eucleria, of uitkiezing van Het Beste Deel*. Leeuwarden: De Tille, 1978.

Schürmann, R. (2003). *Broken Hegemonies*. Indianapolis: Indiana University Press.

Schüssler, R. (2009). Jean Gerson, moral certainty and the Renaissance of ancient Scepticism. *Renaissance Studies* 43(4), 445–461.

Segal, H. (1964). *Introduction to the Work of Melanie Klein*. London: The Hogarth Press and the Institute of Psycho-Analysis.

Selderhuis, H.J. (Ed.) (2009). *The Calvin Handbook*. Grand Rapids: Eerdmans.

Shulman, G. (1988). Hobbes, Puritans, and Promethean Politics. *Political Theory* 16(3), 426–443.

Steinmetz, D. (1995). *Calvin in Context*. Oxford: Oxford University Press.

Storfer, A. (1911). *Zur Sonderstellung des Vatermordes. Eine rechtgeschichtliche und völkerpsychologische Studie*. Leipzig: Deuticke.

Spinoza, B. (1670). *A Theologico-Political Treatise and A Political Treatise* (R.H.M. Elwes, ed.). Mineola (NY): Dover Publications, 2004.

Spinoza, B. (1677). *Ethics* (G.H.R. Parkinson, ed.). Oxford: Oxford University Press, 2000.

Spinoza, B. (1966). *Correspondence of Spinoza* (A. Wolf, ed.). London: Frank Cass & Co.

O'Sullivan, S. (2010). Lacan's Ethics and Foucault's "Care of the Self": Two Diagrams of the Production of Subjectivity (and of the Subject's Relation to Truth). *Parrhesia. A Journal of Critical Philosophy*, 51–73, http://www.parrhesiajournal.org/past.html#issue10 (assessed December 2010).

Taubes, J. (1957). Religion and the Future of Psychoanalysis. *The Psychoanalytic Review*, 136–142.

Tausk, V. (1914). Psychoanalyse der Philosophie und psychoanalytische Philosophie. In H. Metzger, (ed.) *Gesammelte psychoanalytische und literarische Schriften*. Vienna: Medusa, 1983, 124–133.

Taylor, C. (1989). *Sources of the Self. The Making of Modern Identity*. Cambridge (MA): Harvard University Press.

Taylor, M. (2007). *After God*. Chicago: University of Chicago Press.

Teellinck, W. (1624). *Wraeck-Sweert, Bepleytende het recht van Gods Verbondt door bloedighe oorloghe, diere tijdt, bleecke pestilentie*. Middelburg: Maarten Jansz. Brandt.

Teellinck, W. (1627). *Noodtwendigh Vertoogh, aengaende den tegenwoordigen bedroefden Staet van Gods volck; waerinne getrouwelijck aengewesen wort, in wat swaricheyt ende vervallinghe wy ghecomen zijn, in wat perijckel wy noch staen met de noodighe remedien om ons verderf te behoeden*. Middelburg: Pieter van Waesberghe, 1647.

Tentler, Th.N. (1977). *Sin and Confession on the Eve of the Reformation*. Princeton: Princeton University Press.

Thurneysen, E. (1946). *Die Lehre der Seelsorge*. Zurich: Theologischer Verlag, 1994.

Thys, M. (2006). *Fascinatie. Een fenomenologisch-psychoanalytische verkenning van het onmenselijke*. Amsterdam: Boom.

Tillich, P. (1967). *Systematic Theology, Vol. II*. Chicago: University of Chicago Press.

Vandermeersch, P. (2000). The Failure of Second Naivety. Some Landmarks in the History of French Psychology of Religion. In J.A. Belzen (ed.), *Aspects in Context. Studies in the History of Psychology of Religion*. Amsterdam: Rodopi, 235–279.

VanDrunen, D.M. (2004). The Context of Natural Law: John Calvin's Doctrine of the Two Kingdoms. *Journal of Church and State* 46(3), 503–525.

VanDrunen, D.M. (2010). *Natural Law and the Two Kingdoms: A Study in the Development of Reformed Social Thought*. Grand Rapids: Eerdmans.

Verbeek, T. (2003). *Spinoza's Theologico-political Treatise. Exploring 'The Will of God'*. Aldershot: Ashgate.

Vergote, A. (1973). Der Beitrag der Psychoanalyse zur Exegese. Leben, Gesetz und Ich-Spaltung im 7, Kapitel des Römerbriefs. In X. Léon-Dufour (ed.), *Exegese im Methodenkonflikt. Zwischen Geschichte und Struktur*. Munich: Kösel, 73–116.

Vergote, A. (1988). *Guilt and Desire. Religious Attitudes and Their Pathological Derivatives*. New Haven: Yale University Press.

Vergote, A. (1997). Husserl et Freud sur le corps psychique de l'action. In J. Petit (ed.), *Problemes et Controverses. Les Neurosciences et la philosophie de l'action*. Paris: Vrin, 1997, 387–396.

Vergote, A. (1998). *Psychoanalysis, Phenomenological Anthropology and Religion* (J. Corveleyn & D. Hutsebaut, eds.). Amsterdam: Leuven University Press.

Vermorel, H. (2009). The Presence of Spinoza in the Exchanges between Sigmund Freud and Romain Rolland. *International Journal of Psychoanalysis* 90(6), 1235–1254.

Vermorel, H. and Vermorel M. (eds.) (1993). *Sigmund Freud et Romain Rolland. Correspondance 1923–1936. De la sensation océanique au Trouble du souvenir sur l'Acropole*. Paris: Presses Universitaires de France.

Walhof, D.R. (2003). The Accusation of Conscience and the Christian Polity in John Calvin's Political Thought. *History of Political Thought* 24(3), 397–414.

Watson, R. (2007). *Cogito, Ergo Sum. The Life of René Descartes*. Boston: David R. Godine.

Weaver, P.S. (1985). *Wallington's World. A Puritan Artisan in seventeenth-century London*. Stanford: Stanford University Press.

Westerink, H. (2002). *Met het oog van de ziel. Een godsdienstpsychologische en mentaliteitshistorische studie naar mensvisie, zelfonderzoek en geloofsbeleving in het werk van Willem Teellinck (1579–1629)*. Zoetermeer: Boekencentrum.

Westerink, H. (2007). The Great Man from Tarsus. Freud on the Apostle Paul. *The Psychoanalytic Quarterly* 76(1) 217–236.

Westerink, H. (2008). Zum Verhältnis von Psychoanalyse und Mythologie. Die Einfluβ Heymann Steinthals Völkerpsychologie auf die angewandte Psychoanalyse. *Psyche. Zeitschrift für Psychoanalyse und ihre Anwendungen* 62(3), 290–311.

Westerink, H. (2009a). *Controversy and Challenge. The Reception of Sigmund Freud's Psychoanalysis in German and Dutch-speaking Theology and Religious Studies*. Vienna: Lit.

Westerink, H. (2009b). *A Dark Trace. Sigmund Freud on the Sense of Guilt*. Leuven: Leuven University Press.

Whitford, D.M. (2001). *Tyranny and Resistance. The Magdeburg Confession and the Lutheran Tradition*. Saint Louis: Concordia.

Whitford, D.M. (2004). *Cura Religionis* or Two Kingdoms: The Late Luther on Religion and the State in the Lectures on Genesis. *Church History* 73(1), 41–62.

Wilks Dolnikowski, E. (1995). *Thomas Bradwardine. A View of Time and a Vision of Eternity in Fourteenth-Century Thought*. Leiden: Brill.

Wyschogrod, E., Crownfield, D. and Raschke, C.A. (eds.) (1989). *Lacan and Theological Discourse*. Albany: SUNY Press.

Yovel, Y. (1989). *Spinoza and Other Heretics. The Adventures of Immanence*. Princeton: Princeton University Press.

Zachman, R.C. (1993). *The Assurance of Faith. Conscience in the Theology of Martin Luther and John Calvin*. Minneapolis: Fortress Press.

Index

For Product Safety Concerns and Information please contact our EU representative GPSR@taylorandfrancis.com
Taylor & Francis Verlag GmbH, Kaufingerstraße 24, 80331 München, Germany

www.ingramcontent.com/pod-product-compliance
Lightning Source LLC
LaVergne TN
LVHW021109300926
849160LV00009B/657

* 9 7 8 1 1 3 8 6 3 1 8 1 6 *